# An Introduction to Theology:
## A Classical Pentecostal Perspective

*Second Edition*

**John R. Higgins**
**Michael L. Dusing**
**Frank D. Tallman**
*Southeastern College of the Assemblies of God*

**KENDALL/HUNT PUBLISHING COMPANY**
4050 Westmark Drive    Dubuque, Iowa 52002

*To our wives*

*Faith*
*Ruth*
*Melinda*

# Contents

# Foreword

In an era when biblical illiteracy is on the increase, a volume that reflects exegetical excellence, doctrinal integrity and practical application indeed is welcomed. The authors of this book have provided serious students with a systematized presentation of doctrinal truth that reflects quality scholarship without compromising a loyalty to Scripture as the infallible Word of God.

Theology is technically defined as rational interpretation of religious faith, practice and experience. As stated in chapter 1 of this work, "Theology is most commonly defined as the study of God." It is, therefore, understood that those who apply themselves to the discipline of theology are essentially striving "to know God."

To be personally acquainted with the authors is to understand that the objective of their labor is not only to expand the mind, but also to impact the life. Sound doctrine may be referred to as healthy doctrine. Healthy doctrine or healthy theology expresses itself through both increased knowledge of God and through motivation to live a consistent Christian lifestyle. Daily interaction with undergraduate ministerial students alerted the authors to the need for theological materials that are presented from a classical Pentecostal perspective and that would both challenge intellectually and impact lifestyle. This volume, with a conscious effort to keep language simple and explanations uncomplicated, adequately addresses this concern. It is the earnest expectation that the students who carefully investigate the materials contained in this book will "grow in grace, and in the knowledge of our Lord and Savior Jesus Christ" (2 Peter 3:18).

The scope of this volume is clearly articulated in its title. This book is to serve as an introduction to basic and significant theological truths. It is not intended as a comprehensive treatise. Twelve chapters outline the material that is presented to the reader. These chapters carefully set forth an overview of the major teachings of the Bible. Many devout followers of the Lord Jesus Christ possess accurate knowledge of biblical truths but their knowledge is incomplete and scattered. This volume presents major theological truths ia a carefully organized, systematized, understandable, and inspirational manner.

Students entering Southeastern College of the Assemblies of God are most fortunate, for they have the privilege of personal interaction with the authors. The students at Southeastern benefit from the spiritual attributes and intellectual qualities of these men. John Higgins, Michael Dusing, and Frank Tallman write from a perspective of quality academic training, a variety of practical ministerial services, and years of classroom instruction in the field of theology.

It is my prayer that each reader will capture the message and the spirit of the messengers as they turn through the pages of this book.

*James L. Hennesy*
President, Southeastern College

# Preface

For several years we have taught introductory and advanced theology courses, spent many morning hours sipping coffee with colleagues and discussing biblical/theological issues, and have continued to have pastoral involvement with persons seeking theological answers to life's difficult and perplexing questions. This has convinced us of the need for an introductory theology which reflects a contemporary Evangelical position and a classical Pentecostal perspective. This work attempts to address both the conceptual and the practical concerns of theology.

It is our desire to present the reader with a text which introduces him or her to the major areas of Christian doctrine as expressed within a Pentecostal-Evangelical context. Ours is an approach which is Evangelical for we hold to the necessity of a set of doctrines whose essence it is to proclaim the reconciling person, purpose, and act of Jesus Christ. Ours is an approach which is Pentecostal in interpretation of and participation in the faith and living the Christian life.

We do not purport to write *the* introduction to theology but *an* introduction to theology. Ours is not a complete bibliographic text of the many fine expositions of theology written by so many competent scholars/theologians, nor is it a comprehensive treatment of the multitude of theological issues inherent to the Christian faith, but it is a survey of the major areas of Christian doctrine as expressed in a classical Pentecostal tradition.

We do not assume the reader has prior in-depth understanding of historical, biblical, or theological content; rather we intend to introduce the reader to a systematic survey of the major doctrines of the Christian faith within a Pentecostal-Evangelical context. It is our intention to provide the reader with a foundation for Christian life and to encourage the reader to pursue further theological study.

We are aware of the debt we owe to the many who have lived and written concerning the Christian faith. As a work of systematic theology the ideas found in this volume are not unique to the volume, but have been shared by many throughout the centuries. Each of us has shared study with mentors in the classroom, in the church, and in the printed word. Not least of all are we grateful to our colleagues and students at Southeastern College of the Assemblies of God who share with us in living and doing theology.

We hope that the experiences we have encountered in pastoring, in missions, in teaching, in our families, and in our living the Christian life have helped to focus the lens of understanding to present an introduction to theology which is both essentially and experientially valuable to the reader.

The primary purpose of writing this text is to provide a needed volume to use in our introductory theology course at Southeastern College. We encourage you, the reader, to adapt this text to other situations. We believe you will find it valuable as a text for use in:
- Lay Bible Studies
- Sunday School and Church Education
- Ministerial Education Courses
- Comparative Theology Courses
- Introduction to Theology Courses
- Continuing Education Courses

The authors of this book have each written in areas of their teaching expertise. The three writers have worked closely together, making valuable suggestions to one another concerning the content and style of their various chapters. While this process has refined and enhanced the material, it should be noted that the finished product of each chapter is still primarily the work of the particular author. Thus, for the reader's benefit the authors and their specific writings are identified.

John R. Higgins—Chapters 2, 3, 5, 8 (the subjects of God, Scripture, Christ, and the baptism in the Holy Spirit).

Michael L. Dusing—Chapters 4, 6, 9, 11 (the subjects of humanity, salvation, the Church, and healing).

Frank D. Tallman—Chapters 1, 7, 10, 12 (an overview of theology, the Holy Spirit, ministry, and last things).

We hope that you will find this volume to be a significant introduction to the articulation of a distinctively Pentecostal-Evangelical theology. We trust you will find it to give contemporary expression to historic doctrines in a manner which gives theological credence to practical Christian living.

*John R. Higgins*
*Michael L. Dusing*
*Frank D. Tallman*
October 1992

# Preface to Second Edition

For the past one and one-half years we have had the opportunity to use this book in the classroom setting. In addition, other colleges have adopted it as a textbook for their institutions. Numerous individuals from both the church and the academic environment have read the book and many have offered supportive and constructive comments to its authors.

From this experience, we believe that this text is providing a valuable resource in helping to train and expand the thinking of inquisitive Christians, young and seasoned alike. Many who wish to develop their theological perception and the ability to communicate their faith more articulately are searching for the tools that will help them in their quest. Some have found vehicles such as this present work to be advantageous in assisting them to achieve and fulfill their spiritual goals. For this, we are extremely grateful.

No work of theology is without its biases and perplexities, and we are aware that this text will sometimes please and other times provoke its readers. Through it all, however, it is our sincere hope that in the final analysis each inquirer will be intellectually and spiritually motivated, stimulated in one's love for Christ and committed to His service. This is indeed the true goal of Christian theology.

*John R. Higgins*
*Michael L. Dusing*
*Frank D. Tallman*
August 1994

# 1

## Watch Your Life and Doctrine Closely
1 Timothy 4:16

## *What is Theology?*

Theology is most commonly defined as the study of God. This definition is derived from the meanings of two Greek words *theos* (God) and *logos* (word). The combination of these two Greek words renders a literal meaning of theology which is "a word about God." This may be more fully understood as "the study of God."

This simple definition carries with it the important concept that theology is essentially the human effort to know God. Theology is the human endeavor to know and understand God as He reveals Himself to humanity (revelation). Therefore, the effort of Christian theology is to know the Living God, both His Being and His Act.[1]

Thomas F. Torrance addresses this critical point in *Reality and Evangelical Theology*.

> It is distinctive of Christian theology that it treats of God in his relation to the world and of God in his relation to himself, not of one without the other. If it did not include the former, we who belong to the world could have no part in it and if it did not include the latter, it could be concerned only with a "Knowledge of God" dragged down and trapped within the world and our relations with it.[2]

Essential to Christian theology is the Living God active in the lives of those to whom He relates. Theology, then, is neither merely a group of abstract ideas about a supreme being nor is it only the "how" of practical Christian living, but theology is at the same time established in the reality of who God is within Himself (His Being) and the reality of who God is in relation to the world (His Act). This brings a second consideration, that is, the beginning point of theology.

## The Beginning Point of Theology

Having defined theology, one now must determine the beginning point of theology. Theologians differ with respect to their response to this question. Some would contend that the proper beginning point is with the person of God while others propose that theology must begin with our knowledge of God.

For the former group it is the intent to consider the doctrine of God (who God is) prior to considering the doctrine of Scripture (our knowledge of God). For the latter group it is the intent to consider the doctrine of Scripture prior to considering the doctrine of God. While it would be possible to construct arguments for each of these positions it is the assumption of the theology contained in this book that a third position is the proper position.

---

[1]God reveals who He is, His Being, through His specific Act(s). It is this theological assumption which prevents the doctrine of God from being framed only in theoretical propositions. The Act(s) of God is the means of His communication with His people. For example in the person of Jesus Christ one knows the love, justice, and mercy of God; as Yahweh one understands the covenental relationship God establishes with His people; in the Exodus is revealed the grace and deliverance of God.

[2]Thomas F. Torrance, *Reality and Evangelical Theology*, 21.

Based on the definition of theology as including both the knowledge of who God is, His Being, and also His involvement with the world, His Act, one can affirm that the proper beginning point for theology is with both the doctrine of God and the doctrine of Scripture. It is not a choice to begin with either the doctrine of God or the doctrine of Scripture but a choice to begin with *both* doctrines taken together. The Christian God is a Living God who through revelation addresses humankind. God is both the subject and the object of revelation. As subject He exists independently of the world (that is within His Being), and as object, He exists in relation to the world (that is through His Act). The Christian God is at once the giver of revelation and the Revealed One.

Having established a definition for theology and a beginning point for understanding theology one can now proceed to examine various aspects of theological study.

## Aspects of Theological Study

Theology has been determined to be the study of the God who exists both within Himself and in relation to the created order. Theological study and work is simultaneously the doctrine of God and the doctrine of Scripture. The "field of theology" and the various aspects of theological study will be considered in the following paragraphs.

In its most general sense "theology" applies to the full spectrum of studies related to the Christian religion. When one chooses to attend a Bible college or seminary, one is choosing to study in a "school of theology." One's studies will include such diverse areas as Old and New Testament, Christian formation, systematic theology, preaching, missions, and church history. This usage of "theology," while correct, is more general than the use of the term in this text.

Theological studies may be subdivided into more specific areas of study. Still at a relatively general level theological studies may be seen to include: 1) exegetical theology (e.g. biblical studies and hermeneutics), 2) historical theology (e.g. church history and history of missions), 3) systematic or dogmatic theology (e.g. doctrinal studies), and 4) practical theology (e.g. preaching, pastoral care, Christian formation). The use of "theology" in this text will primarily refer to systematic theology.

An illustration of the relationships of the various theological studies is presented in Figure 1. Each area of study is very legitimate in its own right but none of the areas should be studied in isolation from the other areas.

Systematic theology is solidly rooted in exegetical theology. Only from focused study of the Old and New Testaments can a legitimate system of Christian theology be developed. The body of knowledge compiled concerning a particular area of systematic theology such as the doctrine of God or the doctrine of the Holy Spirit is built upon the foundation laid in exegetical study. Millard J. Erickson has said that "Biblical [exegetical] theology is the raw material, as it were, with which systematic theology works."[3] The task of systematic theology is to work with the raw materials to develop and fashion a systematic presentation of the truths of the Christian Faith by relating the many isolated texts into an integrated and congruous whole. This task might be likened to the director of a symphony who relates the notes, themes, and instruments in order to provide a musical presentation through which the listener is able to understand and feel the intent and message of the composer.

Historical theology is, according to Bromiley, that component of theological study which "fills the gap between the time of God's Word and the present time of the church's word by studying the church's word in the intervening period."[4] By serving the church in this manner historical theology is able to provide the church with a continuous story, an enduring message of the development of theology through the centuries and a lens through which to view contemporary expression of the Faith.

---

[3] Millard J. Erickson, *Christian Theology*, 25.

[4] Geoffrey W. Bromiley, *Historical Theology: An Introduction*, xxvi.

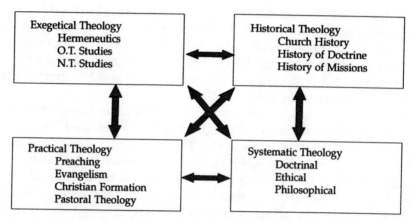

**Figure 1** Relationships within Fields of Theological Study

Practical theology includes the "functioning of the faith-community, pastoral role-fulfillment, and pastoral communication."[5] It is this facet of theological studies which provides the interface of theory and practice. Practical theology is never merely instruction in church skills but is always the engagement of the church with the world through a process of action and reflection. It is the necessary unity of action and reflection into reflective action which constitute *praxis*[6] and is the essential role of practical theology. The reflection is based in the theological areas of exegetical theology, historical theology, and systematic theology thus preserving the necessary interrelationships within the broad area of theological studies.

## The Importance of Theology

Often people express an objection to studying theology because "it complicates the simple faith" necessary for one to be a Christian. It is true that theology is more complex than one's affirmation of faith, but it is also true that theology is an expression of one's affirmation of faith.

Theology is an affirmation of faith because it is essential that the Christian be able to respond to the query of Jesus who, upon engaging

---

[5] Jacob Firet, *Dynamics in Pastoring*, 5.

[6] Thomas H. Groome, *Christian Religious Education: Sharing Our Story and Vision*, 152.

His disciples in a discussion concerning who others believed Him to be, confronted them with their need to respond to the question, "Who do you say that I am?" (Mt 16:13-19). Erickson states that in order to offer a correct response to this question "it is not sufficient to have a warm, positive, affirming feeling towards Jesus. One must have correct understanding and belief."[7]

Christian faith is always and essentially faith in Christ. As faith in Christ, it finds expression through relationship with the Living God whereby the Christian is able to say "I believe" and it finds expression through propositional statements. These propositional statements are valid affirmations which provide a rational expression of the revelation of God. For example, the doctrine of God provides a set of propositions which affirm who God is within Himself and in His interactions with the world. He is merciful through an act of mercy or He is loving through an act of love. Therefore it is clear that the propositions are not merely abstract statements, but rational response to the Being and Act of God.

Thus theology is important for it is a necessary part of the faith response one makes toward Jesus Christ. Inherent in the concept of Christian faith is the idea of understanding. Christian faith is not blind faith but faith in a God who has revealed Himself. To this revelation the person responds, not to the unknown god, but to the God who is known. It is faith and understanding together which comprise proper response. Systematic theology provides a means for enhancing the understanding of the relationship between the believer and God.

Also, theology is important because the Church exists on the basis of the Word of God. Theology is the interpretation, by the Church, of the witness of Holy Scripture. Theology is proclamation by the Church which expresses that it has heard the Word of God and theology expresses the response of the Church to the world. It is through theology that the Church stays integrally related to Scripture. Theology also is the means by which the Church operates by the criterion of Scripture. As the Church receives the Word it exists, and in response to its reception of the Word, it proclaims and acts—hence the integrity of theology as manifested in the Church is substantial.

---

[7] Erickson, 28.

Finally the Church needs theology to be able to maintain its focus on the center of God's revelation. In the post-modern world there is a proliferation of philosophic and scientific challengers to the Christian faith. Through the study of theology the Church and the individual believer are able to recognize these challengers as other than Christian doctrine. It is important at this point to emphasize that it is only through the study of Christian doctrine/theology that the Church can recognize that which is not Christian and not compatible with the Christian Faith. Too often the Church is tempted to devote its efforts toward the study of the false while the ability to recognize the false actually resides only in the truth of revelation.

## Doing Theology—The Method of Theology

As stated above, theology is more than, but not exclusive of, rational statements or propositions. Theology is the response of the Church to the revelation of God through the ordering of Christian doctrine. Therefore theology is something the Church does, it is an active process.

It is important that one begins with the theological assumption that theology as a work of the Church can only be done within the Church. In the secular university one may study what man thinks about God but this is not theology. In the Christian college, and in the church, one may study God's revelation to the world. This is the place for the doing of theology. The difference in the two perspectives may be seen through the issue of relativity. Christian doctrine or theology is relative to the revelation of God while philosophical truth is relative to the human mind. Theology demands a decision concerning the revelation of God, a response composed of both faith and reason.

As depicted in Figure 1, systematic theology is interrelated to the other theological studies. Theology cannot be isolated from exegesis, the history of the church, or the practice of the church and maintain its relevance to both the revelation of God and the life of the church.

Theology emerges from a careful exegesis of Holy Scripture. Never is theology to be placed above the Bible but always beneath it. As one begins the task of doing theology one first begins with careful exegetical attention to the meaning of relevant biblical texts and passages. This includes the use of critical methods such as linguistic, redaction, and historical analyses. At this stage it is also necessary to understand and consider the assumptions made by the commentaries and study tools being utilized. One must be mindful of the importance of church history and history of doctrine to the effort of uncovering the meaning within the passages pertaining to a specific doctrine. One is doing theology by listening to the voice of Holy Scripture and the voices of those who have similarly gained insight into that doctrine.

The next step is to arrange the many passages from the various writers of Scripture into a cohesive and consistent whole. One pays particular attention to allowing the whole Bible to influence the theological decisions being made.

Once the biblical passages are synthesized into a cohesive and consistent whole the task is to determine the doctrinal content. The task is one of distinguishing between a message restricted to a particular culture and a message which applies to all cultures. The efforts of systematic theology are directed toward uncovering the transcultural messages and compiling the messages as a doctrine. For example, the doctrine of the Holy Spirit will be applicable to all cultures in all times. Finally the task of theology is to present its truth in a form that responds to questions being posed by the contemporary world. This means theology is to confront culture with revelation in a form to which culture can respond and make a decision regarding the revelation.

A concluding note on doing theology is needed. This chapter began by discussing the Being and Act of God. The method of theology may be viewed through the paradigm of the Being and Act of God. The definition of theology includes the "human endeavor" to know and understand God as He reveals or discloses Himself to humanity. This brings to focus the methodological question of how God, who is separate from the world, reveals Himself to the world. Matthew 11:27 states:

> All things have been committed to me by my Father. No one knows the Son except the Father, and no one knows the Father except the Son and those to whom the Son chooses to reveal him.

This passage provides us with a lens through which to view the theological task while preserving essentials of the Christian faith.[8] Ray

---

[8] See also 1 Corinthians 2:10-16.

S. Anderson depicts the theological importance of this verse by using the following diagram (Figure 2).[9]

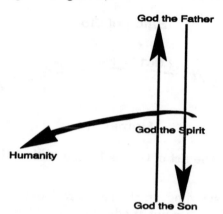

**Figure 2** Paradigm for Theological
Method Based in Trinity

In this paradigm the formulation of the Trinity is affirmed and each person of the Godhead is seen as necessary to the revelatory act. Humanity can only "do theology" because of the Being and Act of God. The doctrine of the Trinity is essential to Christian theology and must be perceived as a central point. In this way God always reveals who He is and is always Himself in revelation (Ex 3:13-14). As no person can know God the Father except God the Son and those to whom the Son reveals the Father through the work of God the Holy Spirit, the unity and diversity of God necessary to a trinitarian theology is established and maintained.

Anderson also notes the necessity of the revelation of God (Being) occurring in concrete events (Act). Anderson terms this place where

---

[9]Ray S. Anderson. Class lecture delivered at Fuller Theological Seminary (Arizona Extension) in Systematic Theology I, 1984. This diagram is a graphic representation developed by Anderson to illustrate the importance of the self-disclosure of God. This provides visual explanation for both the epistemological and pneumatic bases for a theology which begins with the Trinitarian God.

the transcendent God is also the immanent God as the "hermeneutical horizon" (see Figure 3).[10]

**Being of God**

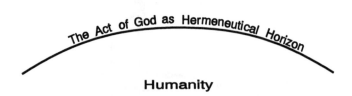

**Humanity**

**Figure 3** The Act of God as Hermeneutical Horizon

If one were standing on the seashore looking out toward the ocean, one would see a point at which one could see no farther. This would be the horizon. The horizon is the point at which the unknown (that beyond the horizon) and the known (that on this side of the horizon) meet. In this same manner, we can understand that the Being of God (beyond the horizon) is known in His Act (this side of the horizon). This method prevents us from reducing God to a set of abstract principles and characteristics and affirms both the Being and Act of God, both the transcendence and immanence of God, and the actuality and possibility of relationship between God and man.

The doing of theology is an active process occurring only within the church and engaging the Christian individual and Christian community in making a decision for God. The decision for God is based on His revelation through His trinitarian Being and through His concrete act. Theology facilitates the Christian's relationship with the Living God by the message of Holy Scripture.

---

[10]This diagram is per Ray Anderson as delivered in a lecture during Systematic Theology III at Fuller Theological Seminary (Arizona Extension) during the 1984-85 academic year. It may not exactly represent Anderson's diagram but does convey the intention.

## For Reflection and Discussion

1.  The literal meaning of theology is a "word about God." Explain what this means in respect to your relationship to God and to the relationship within the Trinity.

2.  What do you consider to be the proper beginning point for theology? Why must the two major options explained in the text be considered together?

3.  Discuss several ways in which theology is important to the life of the Christian and to the life of the Church.

4.  Religion is studied in many different settings. Why is it that theology can only be "done in the Church?"

5.  List and describe several sub-groups which comprise the larger area of theological studies.

6.  Write a one page *credo* (an "I Believe" statement) on "The Place of Theology in the Contemporary Church."

2

# In The Beginning God
## Genesis 1:1

"IN THE BEGINNING GOD . . ." eloquently and forcefully introduces the reader of the Bible to a being beyond one's self, a being through whom man and his universe finds existence and meaning.

Theology proper is the study of this being called God. God is prayed to, is worshipped, is searched for. God is loved, hated, feared, and adored. God is the theme of poems, songs, stories, and dramas. God's presence is invoked at churches, government halls, sports events, weddings, and funerals. God's name is carved in granite monuments, etched in stained glass windows, and printed on T-shirts and bumper stickers.

God is so familiar, yet so unknown. To some God is the "First Cause," the "Cosmic Light," the "Guiding Force," or the "Source of Order." To others God is Brahman, or Allah, or Buddha. Still others see him as the sun, a tree, or an animal. Therefore, it is not enough to believe in some kind of a god. One must seek to know the "one true God" whom to know rightly gives meaning to this life and the promise of life eternal.

## Variety of Belief in God

Rather than attempt to examine every belief in God, it will suffice to briefly consider some of the major categories of concepts about God.[1]

1. *Atheism*—Atheism is actually the absence of belief in a god. The term "theism" combines the Greek word for God (*theos*) with the suffix "ism" (belief) to mean a belief in god. By adding the negative prefix "a," atheism designates one who has no belief in god or is without belief that a god exists. Those who consciously promote the understanding that there is no god are sometimes called dogmatic atheists. Most atheists, however, are practical atheists, in that they simply live their lives as though no god exists. Many anthropologists would deny the reality of true atheism. More likely, the atheist has substituted the worship of science, or philosophy, or technology, or even one's own person for the more traditional object of worship. The one who says "there is no God" is a foolish person, for he denies what is clearly revealed in his world, his history, and in the deep recesses of his own heart (Ps 14:1; Ro 1:2; 3:3). Atheism shuts the door to encounter with God, for the one who comes to God must first believe that He exists and that He diligently rewards those who seek him (Heb 11:6).

2. *Agnosticism*—Agnosticism has been described as the cultured cousin of atheism. The term is derived from the Greek word *gnosis*, meaning knowledge. Combined with the negative prefix "a" and the suffix "ism," the term agnosticism refers to one who is without knowledge of God or who believes that a person

---

[1]For a more thorough treatment on non-Christian views of God, see chapter four, Henry C. Thiessen, *Lectures in Systematic Theology*, revised edition.

cannot have certain knowledge of God. God may or may not exist —one cannot be certain—we have no sure knowledge of his existence. For some, agnosticism becomes a convenient defense for living as though God does not exist and therefore without accountability to Him. For others, agnosticism may be indicative of a personal search for God, who is yet unknown or unacknowledged. However, agnosticism is an untenable position. Continually and consistently God clearly reveals himself, and though man may suppress such truth in unrighteousness it leaves him without excuse (Ro 1:20). God is not far from anyone and will be found when He is diligently sought after (Jer 29:13; Ro 10:6-8).

3. *Pantheism*—Pantheism is the belief that God is all, and all is God. The prefix "pan" denotes "all" or "every." In pantheism, everything is an extension, emanation, or attribute of God. The universe is God, the trees are God, the oceans are God, even man is a part of God. No distinction is made between God and creation—creation is but an expression of God's reality. To allow no distinction between God and creation denies the possibility of personal responsibility for one's actions. God is the one and only reality. Hinduism is perhaps the best known expression of pantheism. The Bible, however, clearly distinguishes a creator God from His creation (Ge 1:2). The distinction is both temporal and qualitative. God exists from eternity; man has a beginning in time (Ge 2:7; Isa 57:15). God is exalted above all that is in heaven or in earth (Ps 97:9). His ways and thoughts are higher than man's and His judgments are unsearchable (Isa 55:8; Ro 11:33). All are not God, but all are merely created for God's pleasure and are responsible to Him.

4. *Panentheism*—Panentheism does not see the world and God being identical as in Pantheism, but sees the world as God's "body." God the Divine mind transcends the world as the human mind transcends the body. God is bipolar, meaning that in a sense He has two natures. There is a potential pole that is beyond the world and an actual pole that is the physical world. Thus God is absolute, eternal, transcendent, and infinite only potentially, while in actuality he is consequent, changing, relative, temporal, and finite. God is not creator and sovereign over the world but

works in cooperation with the world's activity. The world and God are interrelated and interdependent. On the one hand, the world depends on God for its existence, while on the other hand, God depends on the world for His nature and manifestation. All is in a state of change or process including God himself. God is acted upon by the world in process. Panentheism hardly fits with the unchanging creator God presented in the Bible (Mal 3:6).

5. *Dualism*—Dualism is the belief in two opposing gods. They are the god of evil and the god of good, of darkness and light, of right and wrong. Often these gods are understood as impersonal forces which influence man in the course of his life. Zoroastrianism would be a prime example of dualism. Christians have too often unwittingly embraced dualism in a faulty understanding of God and Satan. The reality of Satan and his forces is to be acknowledged. They have wooed man towards evil and wreaked havoc upon humanity. However, Satan is not to be viewed as a second evil god. Nowhere is he assigned the nature of deity. Rather, he is a creation of the one God—a despised, fallen creation at that (Ne 9:6; Isa 14:12-15). Christ came to utterly defeat him and destroy his works (Heb 2:14; 1Jn 3:5).

6. *Polytheism*—Polytheism denotes the belief in many (*poly*) gods. One may remember the variety of gods in Roman and Greek mythology (e.g. Zeus, Venus, Neptune). Often the gods are in conflict; at times they enter the affairs of men; frequently they act with deceit, immorality, and capriciousness. Animism is sometimes viewed as an expression of polytheism, for it may believe in many gods or spirits that abide in such places as trees, or rocks, or rivers. Although philosophical Hinduism is pantheistic, popular Hinduism claims more than 300 million gods, which are popular expressions of the absolute Brahman. The Bible, however, acknowledges the existence of only one God, the true and living God, and forbids the recognition, worship and service of any false gods (Ex 20:3; 1Sa 5:3-4; Isa 44:8-9).

7. *Monotheism*—Monotheism is the belief in only one (*mono*) god. The Bible teaches the existence of only one true God (Dt 6:4; Isa 2:19). Christianity believes that there is only one God, and is therefore a monotheistic religion. Christians, however, are not the only ones who hold to a monotheistic view of God. Monotheism

is also the belief of Judaism (God is Yahweh) and Islam (God is Allah). Also Deism believes in one God who is the transcendent creator who governs his world with set laws, without any personal, immanent relationship to his creation. Therefore, monotheism alone is not sufficient. The Bible teaches a specific monotheism whose one personal God is both transcendent and immanent and exists as three eternal, inseparable persons, namely Father, Son, and Holy Spirit (Mt 28:19).

## The Existence of God

Before examining the nature of God, a brief consideration should be given to the question of God's existence. Over the centuries theologians have presented in varying form what have popularly become known as the rational or traditional arguments for the existence of God.[2] They are listed below with suggested problems within each view.

1. *Cosmological Argument*—Since all things have a cause, the universe must have a First Cause, which cause is God. However, there is no logical reason for denying the possibility of an eternal series of dependent causes.

2. *Teleological Argument*—Since design and order are found throughout the universe, one presumes a Master Designer who is God. However, the value of some design is subjective and may not seem good from another's perspective. Also, against infinite odds it is logically possible for the universe to have turned out as it is by chance.

3. *Ontological Argument*—Since we have the idea of an absolutely perfect being, and existence is an attribute of perfection, therefore such an absolutely perfect being (God) must exist. However, mere ideas or abstract concepts do not necessitate real existence.

4. *Moral (Anthropological) Argument*—Since man is a moral and intellectual being, the being (God) who created him must be of higher intelligence and moral character. However, there is no evidence that supports the idea that cause must always be greater than effect (e.g. evolution).

---

[2]Millard J. Erickson, *Christian Theology*, 156-163.

5. *Ethnological (Historical) Argument*—Since every culture has some concept of a god, such a being must exist. However, universal belief does not guarantee the truth of the belief.

As indicated, the rational arguments all have individual weaknesses. Together they do not identify the god or gods who may exist. If taken cumulatively, however, they lend inductive support to the existence of a god. At the least, they indicate that belief in God is not totally irrational. Two alternative approaches to the belief in God's existence are briefly outlined below.

The first alternative begins by assuming the Scriptures to be a divine revelation. One begins to define its presuppositions, one of which would be the existence of God. Then one proceeds to enumerate evidences for Scripture as an authentic, dependable revelation and for its other presuppositions (for example, the cross, resurrection, apostles, etc.). If Scripture can be demonstrated to be true and reliable in these other areas, then its claim of a God may be expected to be reliable also.

A second alternative is to begin with the hypothesis that the God of the Scriptures exists. One proceeds to show that only on the basis of this postulate are we able to explain the ultimate questions of life (for example, ultimate origins, meaning to life, values, death). God's existence becomes the key to the mysteries of life, the best answer to the world puzzle with which humanity wrestles.

With either alternative, the best one can do is to bring one to an inductive conclusion.

## God is Knowable

It is a great step to move from the idea that a god exists to the understanding of who or what God is.

In trying to determine what God is really like, many mental pictures may flood one's mind. These are conditioned by what one has seen and heard, one's own psychological needs, and one's popular culture. God may be envisioned as a cosmic force, a person, an idea, a life principle, or absolute nothingness. Some may understand Him as a kindly grandfather figure, others as a Santa Claus, still others as a fearsome tyrant threatening people with hell if He does not get His way. Interestingly, as varied as men's concepts of God may be, they are often at least partly correct. However, such partial truth can be as damaging and misleading as it is helpful and instructional. Fortunately we are not left to our own musings and speculations. God has made himself known to us in our world, in our nature, in the Scriptures, and in the incarnation of Christ (God revealed in flesh). God has revealed to us exactly who He is (Jn 1:14; Ro 1:20). This does not mean that we know all there is to know about God, for God transcends His own revelation. However, what He has made known about himself is accurate and sufficient to know Him both cognitively and existenially.

## God as Trinity

Confusion often arises when God is spoken of as one God, yet that one God is designated as Father, Son, and Holy Spirit. The one God is a trinity of persons. Though the term trinity is not found in the Bible, it is used to describe the nature of God's being as revealed in the Scriptures (Dt 6:4; Mt 28:19; Jn 14:16-17; 2Co 13:14).

The idea of a trinitarian God is unique and thus difficult to conceptualize. Theologians through the centuries have tried to explain how God could be both one and three at the same time. Various analogies have been suggested to help one grasp the complexity of the issue. For example, the three persons of Father, Son, and Holy Spirit are likened to the three sides of an equilateral triangle. Together the sides make the triangle; together the three persons comprise the one God. All the persons are distinct but equal and necessary to make up God. Another analogy likens the Trinity to water expressed in three forms—liquid, solid (ice), and gas (steam). All three share the same chemical substances ($H_2O$), but are separate in identity. Yet another analogy uses the parts of an egg—shell, white, and yolk—to express the Trinity. The list seems endless. However, though it is not wrong to use them to help understanding, one should be aware of their inadequacies—analogies are not perfect representations.

It is best simply to stay with what the Bible specifically teaches us about the Trinity, even though one may not understand exactly how it exists or functions. The Bible presents God as one divine being who exists from eternity as three equal persons, namely Father, Son, and Holy Spirit. "Persons" should not be understood as separate beings, but as personal subsistences. In this triune Godhead, the three persons eternally and equally share the same essence or nature. However, each may have primary functions in which the other members of the Trinity share participation. The idea of a Trinity of persons does not destroy the unity of the Godhead. Though the Father, Son, and Holy Spirit are not identical with respect to person, they are not divided with respect to nature, nor in opposition with respect to purpose and cooperation. The three persons are equal with respect to their divine nature, though voluntary subordination of one person to another to fulfill a task has occurred. To illustrate, the Son subordinated himself willingly to the Father in the incarnation in order to provide redemption for fallen mankind (Php 2:6-11). When Jesus spoke of the Father as greater than He, it was in reference to the redemptive role, not His divine person (Jn 8).

As one attempts to maintain a biblical understanding of God as Trinity, it is helpful to avoid two common errors. First, the Trinity does not refer to three separate gods. Tritheism, with its belief in three gods, denies the unity of God and results in an elevated polytheism. The Father is God; the Son is God; the Holy Spirit is God. However, the three are not each *a* God, but *together* are *the* God. Second, one must avoid the error of modalism, usually expressed as Sabellianism (named after the heretic Sabellius who suggested the view in the third century). Sabellius suggested that the one God simply revealed himself in three different modes or manners during different times. In the Old Testament He revealed himself as Father; during the life of Jesus, God revealed himself as the Son; during this age He reveals himself as the Holy Spirit. When the Father was revealed, the Son and Spirit did not exist separately; when the Son was revealed, the Father and Spirit did not exist separately. God was like an actor who changed costumes to play different roles. It was one and the same actor who played each role separately, not simultaneously. Even so, God only revealed himself at different times as Father, Son, and Holy Spirit, but these persons did not exist separately or act concurrently. However, the Bible teaches an ontological trinity (a trinity of being) not just a modalistic trinity (a trinity of revelation).[3]

---

[3]Bruce A. Demarest, "Process Trinitarianism," in *Perspectives on Evangelical Theology.* Demarest deals with a newer and popular challenge to the orthodox doctrine of Trinity.

## The Nature of God

The nature of God refers to the attributes or characteristics which constitute His being. These attributes or characteristics are permanent, intrinsic, essential qualities of His being. They are inherent in His very basic nature. Some theologians distinguish between the essence of God and the attributes of God. However, the attributes of God are not to be understood as qualities added to his essence or nature, but as the expression or outworking of his nature.

When one begins to consider the nature of God, two things need to be kept in focus. First, God is incomprehensible. This does not mean that God is unknowable, but rather one cannot know God fully or completely. One's understanding of God's attributes does not exhaust God's understanding of himself. Second, though one cannot comprehend God, one can know Him truly through what He has revealed to us concerning himself. The attributes of God depicted for us in the Scripture give one an accurate and dependable picture of who God is.

Many different classifications of God's attributes have been suggested by theologians. Some speak of God's absolute and relative attributes (those God has only in himself, and those He has in relation to others). Reformed theologians often use the designations communicable and incommunicable attributes (those God communicates in part to His creation, and those reserved only for Himself). Another classification speaks of God's intransitive or immanent attributes, and transitive or emanant attributes (those attributes that remain within God's own being and those which go from and operate outside His being). To illustrate these three different classifications, one may use the attributes of infinity and love. Infinity would be classified as an absolute, incommunicable, or intransitive attribute. Love, however, would be a relative, communicable, or transitive attribute.

The presentation of the attributes of God in this text will follow a fourth classification—moral attributes and non-moral attributes. Moral attributes are those which have some inherent moral quality attached to them (e.g. love, justice). Non-moral attributes are those which, in and of themselves, have no inherent moral quality (e.g. power, knowledge). Power, for example, is morally neutral; it can be used for good or evil. This does not mean that God exercises these non-moral attributes in a vacuum or may exercise them for either right or wrong. Because of the moral attributes of God, His non-moral attributes are always expressed in a positive moral manner. The non-moral attributes of God are never immoral.

## The Non-Moral Attributes of God

1. *Spirituality*—God is spirit (Jn 4:24). As a spirit being, God is not corporeal. He does not have a body and is not composed of any material substance. Thus God is free from all the limitations and restrictions of those with a physical body. Without form and matter He is invisible (Lk 24:39; Jn 1:18; 1Ti 1:17, 6:15-16). God transcends created substance and forbids making forms and images to try to depict Him. Idolatry is denounced in light of God's revelation as an immaterial, incorporeal being (Dt 5:12-28; Isa 40:12-25). The emphasis is on making a clear distinction between God, the Creator, and His creation.

Throughout the Bible this invisible incorporeal God, who is without form or substance, is spoken of as having eyes and ears, hands and feet, and a face. He speaks, hears, sees, walks, and acts (Ge 3:2-3; Ps 34:15; Isa 66:1). These passages should not bring confusion or contradiction to the teaching that God is spirit. Depictions such as "the arm of the Lord" or "the eyes of the Lord" are called anthropomorphic expressions. They are in the "form of a man;" expressions related to a person or understandable in terms of a person to help explain an activity or attitude of God. For example, a person's arm is used to fight, to defend, to rescue, and symbolizes a person's strength. To express God's strong activity in rescuing and defending His people the biblical writer may speak of the "arm of God" even though in reality God does not have a physical arm.

God as spirit makes possible the truth that God is a personal being. It is sometimes mistakenly thought that spirituality automatically implies personality. The Brahman of Hinduism, for example, is the World Spirit in whom there is no personality or self-conscious identity. However, the God of the Bible is revealed as a personal spirit being who relates in a personal way to His creation. As a personal being He is self-conscious and capable of self-determination. The personality of God is revealed in the declaration of His name (character) to Israel (Ex 3:13-14). Some suggest that the Hebrew of the declaration "I am that I am" might better be translated "I am who I am," meaning "I am the God who exists as a self-conscious, self-determining personal Spirit."[4]

Spirituality also speaks of life. God is the true and living God (1Th 1:9). Having life in himself, God is vibrant, active, involved, and continuing (Jn 1:3; 5:26). He is the source of life and the sustainer of life for others. This living, personal God, not made with man's hands, stands in stark contrast to the false gods who are of wood and stone, and cannot hear or speak, and cannot give and share life.

2.  *Self-existence*—God is self-existent (Ex 3:14; 6:3). This concept often was expressed by earlier theologians as the "aseity of God."[5] All of creation has its ground of existence outside itself— God is the ground of our existence. However, God has the ground of His existence within himself. He is sometimes described as the "Uncaused Cause." It may be best not to say that God is caused by himself, but that God is uncaused. God always has been, is, and always will be. It is His nature to exist. God's existence is rooted in His nature not His will, so that God exists by necessity not contingency. God cannot will himself out of existence.

3.  *Infinity*—God is infinite (2Ch 2:6; Jer 23:24). Infinity refers to the limitlessness of God. He is unlimited and unlimitable. The infinity of God is often linked to the three concepts of omnipresence, omnipotence, and omniscience.

Omnipresence (sometimes called immensity) refers to God's infinite relationship to space. God is not limited to or bound by space (1Ki 8:27; Ps 139:7-12). He transcends the limits of space in that He is not determined by them. As a spirit being, He does not fill a certain number of cubic feet. Also, there is no space from which God is absent. God is present everywhere in His entirety. There are not parts of God or aspects of His nature scattered everywhere, but the whole of God's nature is present everywhere. His infinity is not merely extensive but intensive (Jer 23:23). The

---

[4] J. Oliver Buswell, *A Systematic Theology of the Christian Religion*. Vol. 1, 35.

[5] Augustus H. Strong, *Systematic Theology*, 256.

infinite God may be found everywhere and anywhere. He is not removed from His creation. The omnipresence of God may be either a fearful or comforting reality.

Omnipotence refers to God's limitless power. God is all-powerful. With God nothing is impossible. His arm is strong to save; He is the Lord of Armies; nothing is too difficult for Him (Gen 17:1, Jer 32:17, Mt 19:26). God has the power to act to accomplish His purposes. The infinite power of God should not be thought of as some boundless energy, or some uncontrollable force. God is in control of His power. The exercise of His power is determined by His will, which in turn is determined by His nature (Ps 115:3). Therefore the doctrine of God's omnipotence does not require God to do what is absurd, contradictory, or contrary to His moral nature. Also, omnipotence is not incompatible with God's gentleness, mercy and compassion, but is necessary for them.

Omniscience refers to God's infinite knowledge. God is all knowing. God knows himself—He is not some kind of unconscious ground of being. He knows perfectly all things external to himself—persons, places, and things (Ps 139:1-4). The hidden things are not secret from Him. He knows the very depths of the human heart (Ps 139:23). God's infinite knowledge is innate, immediate and simultaneous rather than learned, reasoned, and successive. It is complete and perfect. Through divine foreknowledge, God even knows contingent events (1Sa 23:10-13; Ps 81:14, 15, Mt 11:21). God's knowledge is both cognitive and experiential. Cognitively he knows the facts of all things at once. Experientially, however, God knows events as they happen. For example, God cognitively knew Christ as slain before the foundation of the world, but experienced Christ's death as He hanged upon the cross in history. The infinite wisdom of God also should be considered under the idea of the omniscience of God. Wisdom involves the application of knowledge. God's wisdom is the perfect application of His infinite knowledge to attain those ends which accomplish His will and bring Him ultimate glory.

4. *Eternality*—God is eternal. Eternality refers to God's relationship to time (Ps 90:1-2). God is not bound to time. By creating something outside himself, He indirectly created time. He is the

Alpha and Omega, the Beginning and the End, the First and the Last. God was before all time, exists in time, and will exist forever (Isa 44:6; Jude 25; Rev 1:8). With regard to His person, God is timeless because He does not grow or develop or change in His being or any of His attributes. All time is present to God; however, God is aware of the succession of points of time as they occur in human experience. There is also "successive order to the acts of God and . . . logical order to his decisions, yet there is no temporal order to His willing."[6] God transcends all temporal limitations and "possesses the whole of His existence in one indivisible present."[7] The Bible uses both terms "eternal" and "immortal" to describe God in His essential being. Immortality implies never ending or dying, therefore the term immortal may be applied in a conditional sense to humanity. However, eternity stretches both directions—God had no beginning and will have no ending.

5. *Immutability*—Immutability refers to the unchangeableness of God (Ps 102:26-27; Nu 23:19; Mal 3:6). There is no change in God's nature—neither quantitatively nor qualitatively. God cannot become better for He is already perfect; nor can He become less than He is, for then He would no longer be God. Unlike the view of process theology which makes God dependent on the processes of the world, the Bible presents Him as the God who guides the processes to accomplish His unchanging purposes. God's plans, actions, and promises are reflective of His immutable nature. One can depend upon the promises of God because they are grounded in His unchanging person. His purposes are forever settled. Those scriptures which speak of God "repenting" are not contradictory of those verses which speak of His immutability. Rather, studied in their context, they will be seen to be anthropomorphisms, anthropopathisms, contingency responses, or a new stage of constant purpose. It is helpful to remember that immutable is not the same as static or immobile.

---

[6]Millard J. Erickson, *Christian Theology* Vol. 1, 275.

[7]Louis Berkhof, *Systematic Theology*, 60.

The unchanging God is indeed active and dynamic in conformity with His perfect nature.

## The Moral Attributes of God

1. *Holiness*—The God of the Bible is a holy God. Many theologians have suggested that holiness is the supreme or regulating attribute of God. At least it is a quality of God that is frequently addressed by both Old and New Testament writers (Ps 99:3; Isa 6:1-4; Rev 15:4). Central to both the Hebrew (*qadosh*) and Greek (*hagios*) words for holy is the idea of separation. The attribute holiness carries with it two main areas of separation with respect to God's nature. First, God is separate from His creation and exalted far above them in infinite majesty (Ex 15:11). There is a qualitative difference between Him and all other beings. He is high and lifted up; His places are sacred; He inspires awe and reverence and worship (Ps 99:9). Second, holiness points to the perfection of God. He is without flaw, without short coming, without need. Specifically, God's absolute ethical and moral purity is highlighted. He is separated from any taint of moral evil or sin. The attribute of God's holiness serves as the source of one's own standard of morality. We are called upon to be holy even as He is holy (Lev 11:44-45). God hates sin and demands purity in His moral creation. He has revealed the holiness of His own nature by implanting its standard in one's own heart. It was enshrined in the moral law given in the Scriptures, and demonstrated by Jesus Christ, the "Holy and Righteous One" (Ac 3:14). God's spirit, the Holy Spirit, works the qualities of moral living in the heart of the believer.

2. *Justice*—God is just and righteous. Distinctions are often made between justice and righteousness, but for this study the terms will be used synonymously. Justice may be seen as an expression of God's holiness in reference to His moral creation. God's moral creatures are required to adhere strictly to God's moral law as a reflection of His own moral nature. God's justice assures that the treatment of His creatures conforms to the constant moral standard of that nature. In the administration of His moral government throughout the world, God is entirely fair and equitable. He has no respect of persons and shows no favoritism

or partiality. The godly man and the wicked man are both judged fairly according to the same standard. Since God's moral government includes promises of reward for obedience and threats of punishment for transgression, some theologians distinguish between remunerative justice (the former) and retributive justice (the latter) (Ps 58:11; Ro 1:32, 2:7; 2Th 1:8; Heb 11:26). At times, from man's perspective, it may seem that God is unjust. This is exemplified by the age-old question of why the wicked often prosper and the righteous suffer (Ps 73). The outworking of God's justice at times extends beyond this life. The doctrines of heaven and hell are indications of this extension of divine justice. Likewise, the death of Christ as the provision for man's salvation is necessitated by the justice of a holy God (Ro 3:21-26).

3.  *Goodness*—God is not only separated from moral evil, but also is positively good (Mk 10:18). Something is good if it conforms to what it ought to be. God is all that He should be in relation to Himself and to His creation. Men are called to seek God as the *summum bonum*, the highest good objectively and subjectively. Goodness is often used as a generic term to cover a number of characteristics of God taught in the Scripture. Four of these expressions of God's goodness are briefly considered below.

    First, the goodness of God is seen in His benevolence. Benevolence is the perfection of God that involves His bountiful and kindly dealings with His creation (Ps 145:9-16; Mt 6:26, 28). God cares for his creation's welfare. He blesses persons whether or not they are his children, causing the sun to shine and the rain to fall upon the just and the unjust (Mt 5:45; Ac 14:17).

    Second, the love (Greek, *agape*) of God involves His continual giving of himself to His creation. He communicates himself in affection and concern for our welfare. It was God's love that motivated the sending of Christ to be the savior of the world (Jn 3:16). God is love and serves as the source and motivation of reciprocal love to God and love towards one's fellow man (1Jn 4:8, 16). It is true that "we cannot do anything to make God love us any more or to love us any less." The love of God can best be seen in the love shown toward us even in our sins, by His sending Christ to die in our place (Ro 5:8). Such love is not capricious, but consistent and enduring, and from which nothing can separate us (Ro 8).

Third, the grace (Hebrew, *chen*; Greek, *charis*) of God is an expression of His goodness addressed to those who are unworthy of it. Popularly, grace is defined as the unmerited favor of God. It is no surprise that *Amazing Grace* remains a favorite hymn of the recipients of this grace (Ex 34:6). God in grace extends His goodness to those who do not deserve it and have forfeited it through sin. All the spiritual blessings that come to the sinner are the result of God's grace (Eph 1:6-8; Tit 3:24). Though mankind was under the sentence of condemnation, God's grace brought salvation to those who believe in His Son (Eph 2:7-9; Tit 2:11). If God gave salvation only to those who deserved it, no one would be saved. Yet, His grace offers salvation to all.

Fourth, the mercy (Hebrew, *chesed*; Greek, *eleos*) of God is the goodness of God communicated to those in misery. He is compassionate and tenderhearted to those in need (Ps 103:13; Mt 9:35-36). His lovingkindness reaches out to those in distress. God's mercy is abundant and enduring. Every verse of Psalm 136 ends with the testimony "His mercy endures forever." He is rich in mercy toward his children and to the sinner as well (Eph 2:4). The mercy of God restrains the punishment deserved by the wicked. This aspect of mercy is sometimes called the forbearance or the longsuffering of God. Because of His mercy, He is slow to anger and bears long with those who continue long in disobedience (Ex 34:6). The goodness of God expressed as mercy does not override His justice, but seeks to lead the sinner to repentance (Ro 2:4). Even abundant, enduring mercy does not cancel out the justice of a holy God if its offer in Christ continues to be refused.

4. *Truth*—God is true in the sense of veracity (Jer 10:10). If something is true it conforms to reality. God is what He claims to be and is to be distinguished from other so called gods who are false in their claims (Pss 96:5; 115:4-8; Isa 44:9-10). God's inner reality and outer expression always correspond. That which God says is also true in the sense that it conforms with reality as guaranteed by His omniscience. God cannot lie, for He is holy (Heb 6:18; Tit 1:2; Nu 23:19). God is also true to His covenants

and promises. He cannot deny himself. Heaven and earth may pass, man's word may fail, but the word of God abides forever (2Ti 12:13; Mt 5:18; Isa 40:8). God is also true in the sense of being faithful and dependable. Paul reminds us that "He who calls you is faithful, and He will do it" (1Th 5:24). Berkhof points out the great practical significance for the people of God, of knowing God as faithful and true. "It is the ground of their confidence, the foundation of their hope, and the cause of their rejoicing."[8]

God calls upon us to emulate His moral attributes. As His people we are to be loving and giving people who are concerned about our neighbor and our world. We are to act with grace and mercy towards all men. As a people called to holiness, we are to separate ourselves from evil and surrender ourselves to God's moral standard. We are to work for justice and speak the truth in love. God is the source of these spiritual qualities and it is He who works them in us by His Spirit.

Two other terms should be mentioned briefly when considering God's nature—transcendence and immanence. Transcendence refers to God's exalted position above all His creation. He is high and lifted up, the sovereign Lord over all, beyond human comprehension (Isa 55:8-9; Ps 113:5-6). Yet, God is also immanent, not far from any of us. He is near at hand, interacts with His creation, and indwells the believer (Ac 17:27-28; Ro 14:8; Mt 6:25-30; 2Co 1:3-4). Both the transcendence and immanence of God must be kept in balance.

Before leaving the topic of the nature and attributes of God, consider a helpful definition of God given as an answer to question four of the *Westminster Shorter Catechism*, "What is God?" "God is a spirit, infinite, eternal, and unchangeable, in his being, wisdom, power, holiness, justice, goodness and truth." Each of these three adjectives (infinite, eternal, and unchangeable) should be applied to each of the nouns of the definition. (For example, God is infinite in His wisdom, eternal in His wisdom, and unchanging in His wisdom). This simple but profound definition

---

[8]Berkhof, 70.

of God may be helpful to the reader in remembering God's attributes.

## God's Work of Creation

The Book of Genesis introduces one not only to the person of God, but also to God as the Creator (Ge 1, 2). God created both immediately (directly) and mediately (indirectly). Immediate creation is described as *ex nihilo*—creation out of nothing. God created the heavens and the earth out of no previously existing matter, but solely from the power of His word (Heb. 11:3). Mediate creation—creation from existing materials—was involved in other aspects of creation including the creation of humanity. God's triune work of creation is attested to throughout the Bible (Col 1:16-17; Heb 11:3; Isa 40:26; Ro 11:36; Ps 102:18). No part of the created order came in to being apart from God (Jn 1:3).

Several creation theories have been proposed by Bible scholars. The following four are the most common:

1. *Gap theory*—a long time span exists between the creation mentioned in verse one and the creation that follows from verse two of Genesis chapter one.

2. *Day Age Theory*—each creation day (Hebrew, *yom*) refers to a long creative period of time.

3. *24-Hour Day Theory*—creation was completed in six 24-hour days.

4. *Pictorial Day Theory*—the days of Genesis 1 are not literal but "pictures" of creative events.

Regardless of the view one may choose, it is best to keep in mind that it is a theory. It is best to stay with the specific teaching of the Bible about creation and acknowledge that information beyond that is speculation.

The main importance of the doctrine of creation is to affirm that God is the creator of all things including humankind. A person bears an inherent responsibility to God, as one's maker. God's creation was intrinsically good (Ge 1:10-13). Humanity has a cultural mandate to maintain, preserve, and use the environment in a way that honors God. Creation has been adversely affected by sin, but is included in God's plan for redemption (Ro 8:20-23).

## God's Work of Providence

The God of the Bible is not the God of Deism, a God who creates the world only to leave it functioning without His concern. Rather, God the Creator continues to be involved with His world through the work of divine providence. God's providential workings fall into two categories. First is His work of preservation. He continues to sustain and preserve what He has created. God does not constantly recreate the universe or periodically repair it, but divinely holds all things together by His word of power (Col 1:17; Heb 1:3). Creation would cease to exist if God did not continue to will its continuance. Part of God's work of preservation is supplying His creation with what it needs to perpetuate itself (Mt 6:26-33).

A second providential work of God involves His guiding or governing the world which He created. He directs the whole course of history toward the end He has ordained. Nature, persons, and governments all do His ultimate bidding (Da 2:21; 4:24-25; Isa 14:24-27; Ps 47:7-8). God's governing activity does not extend only to His people, but is universal in scope. However, His people are under His special care and will benefit greatly from the ultimate end of God's providential activity.

God's works of providence are the outworking of God's decrees (some would say decree, singular). God has decreed all that shall ever happen. His decrees are eternal and based on His infinite knowledge and wisdom. The ultimate purpose of His decrees is to glorify himself (Isa 14:24-27; Eph 1:4,11; 3:11). Other subordinate purposes, such as the happiness and sanctification of His people, are included within His decrees. God's decrees are often divided into the categories of efficacious decrees and permissive decrees. Efficacious decrees are those things God determines to bring about. Permissive decrees are things which God allows to happen within the larger scope of the efficacious decrees. Two important topics to consider in the light of God's providence and decrees are prayer and miracles. Persons and their world are significant in God's continuing activity—they continue to share in His goodness and power. Believers may live their lives with great confidence in the God who is from the beginning to the end.

## For Reflection and Discussion

1.  Choose one of the non-Christian concepts of God. Think of ways to effectively witness to someone who holds this view of God.

2.  List illustrations for each of the moral arguments for God's existence. Consider both the strengths and weaknesses of these arguments.

3.  Read about the Hindu Triad (Brahma, Vishnu, and Shiva). How is the Christian concept of Trinity different from this Hindu concept of God?

4.  Choose five of the attributes of God and think of practical ways in which they are important to the Christian life.

5.  When you think about God, what is the first thing which comes to mind? Why do you think this is the case? Set aside an uninterrupted fifteen minute period to think specifically about God's character.

# 3

# And God Said
## Genesis 1:26

THE ONLY THINGS WE KNOW WITH CERTAINTY ABOUT GOD and His relationship to us and our world are what God himself has made known to us. This knowledge is called divine revelation. Revelation is simply making something known that was previously unknown. Much of one's own understanding about God would be only guesses if God had not made himself known. Human ideas of God, apart from what He has revealed, are often vague, uncertain, speculative, and contradictory.

## Divine Revelation

Divine revelation is God's self-disclosure; the communicating of himself to His creation. In words and acts God makes known His person, His purposes, and His ways. The term "divine revelation" may be used in a narrow sense of a particular work or event used by God, or in a broad sense of the whole process of making himself known.

This self-disclosure was deliberate and at God's initiative.[1] No one discovered God accidently or through searching, apart from His willingness and desire to be known. God was not forced to reveal himself; He chose to do so. He alone is responsible not only for the fact of revelation, but also for the time, method, place, and recipients of that revelation. God has made himself known gradually and progressively. The manner in which He has revealed himself is greatly varied—angels, dreams, events, prophets, visions, voices and more. He revealed himself on mountains, in deserts, palaces, cities, temples—wherever He chose. Recipients of His revelation included kings, shepherds, fishermen, priests—whomever He determined.

God revealed himself for humanity's benefit.[2] Though God chose to reveal himself, such revelation does not reflect a need or compulsion on God's part. Rather, the self-disclosure of God is an act of grace toward His creation. God not only created humanity, but through revelation of himself, provided humanity with the opportunity of fellowship with Him. Graciously, He would be their God, and they would be His people (Lev 26:12). The knowledge of himself is God's greatest gift to humankind.

God's self-revelation is personal.[3] It is communication from a personal God to personal recipients. From His initial revelation, God makes himself known as a personal being rather than an object, cosmic force, or impersonal world-soul. He is to be understood as Lord, as Father, as King, as Shepherd, and other personal designations. He mocks "other gods" that are merely the workmanship of human hands. The personal God speaks, hears, loves, and helps.

---

[1] Carl F.H. Henry, *God, Revelation, and Authority* Vol. 1, 8.

[2] Ibid., 30.

[3] Ibid., 151.

Though divine revelation makes God known, it does not completely reveal Him nor exhaust the mystery of His person or His ways. God is greater than His own revelation of himself. His person and knowledge transcend His self-disclosure. He is the inexhaustible God (Isa 40:13, 28; Dt 29:29; Ro 11:33). Through all eternity it seems one's knowledge of God will increase as He unfolds new insights into His person and relationship to humanity (1Co 13:12; Eph 2:7).

Although one now knows only "in part," not exhaustively, that which is known now is valid and trustworthy. One does not have to know God fully to know Him truly. Divine revelation may be incomplete in the sense of not being exhaustive, but it is sufficient for acceptability before God and for doing His will. God has made known all that one presently needs to know, and it is entirely meaningful, reliable, and consistent. Also, since the revelation is made by the one God, though the forms, times, and methods of the revelation may be many and varied, the comprehensive unity of that revelation is assured.

Divine revelation is usually considered under the separate topics of General Revelation and Special Revelation. Natural theology and revealed theology involve the theological ideas arrived at through human reason and reflection as one views General Revelation and Special Revelation respectively.

## General Revelation

General Revelation involves God's making himself known indirectly (mediately) to humankind through history, the environment/nature, and human nature.[4] God has revealed himself in and through human history. God is the Master of His universe and is at work in the world. Moving towards certain goals, He guides the affairs of nations and acts in behalf of His people. The children of Israel constantly rehearsed the "acts of God" in their history (Ps 136). His redemptive acts are rehearsed in the creeds of the Church such as the Apostles' Creed—creation, incarnation, cross, resurrection, ascension, second coming, and judgment. There is a continuity of God's dealings with humanity as the God who is just and powerful in the course of

---

[4]Bruce A. Demarest, *General Revelation*. Demarest provides a thorough treatment of historical views and contemporary issues related to General Revelation.

history. All history comes under His governing purpose as He controls, guides, and personally acts within it.

God also makes himself known through man's environment—nature and the universe. A world of infinite variety, order, and beauty reflect a God who is infinitely wise and powerful. His glory and handiwork are declared in the heavens (Ps 19:1-6). The revelation of nature transcends all human language and propositional statement and extends to the ends of the earth. It is important to distinguish between a "talking cosmos" and divine General Revelation. God makes himself known through the natural order which He has created—one is not to listen to "Mother Nature" but to the "Creator God."

More personally, God reveals himself through human nature itself. Humanity has been created in the image of God (Ge 1:26). Though this image has been marred and distorted by sin, it has not been utterly destroyed. It remains a point of contact between God and fallen humanity. The remaining moral and spiritual qualities inherent in human nature point to a holy and good Creator. Humanity individually and collectively is universally aware of a basic connection with a moral God (Ac 17:24-29). Even without a formal, written religious law code, an inherent moral law is engraved by the Creator on the hearts of all humanity (Ro 2:11-15).

Though God's revelation of himself through history, nature, and the human heart may seem less obvious than other forms of revelation, such general revelation does have actual impact and is universally given and received. General Revelation brings *truth* about God that is *clearly seen* even by sinful persons. However, the sinner, being without excuse, suppresses this truth. Suppression of the knowledge of God incurs the wrath of God and leads to further sinful degradation (Ro 1:18-32).

General Revelation universally and continually brings a cognitive knowledge of God to all humanity. Thus it is the foolish person who says in his heart that God does not exist (Ps 53:1). However, sin obscures almost everything about God except one's knowledge of His existence in power and majesty and of His execution of moral judgment. Such knowledge only leaves one without excuse before God for willfully suppressing it, putting forth truth substitutes, and failing to live according to the moral standard written on one's heart. General Revelation has no power to redeem fallen humanity, only to condemn—but it condemns in order to point to a redeemer outside oneself. The insufficiency of General Revelation for salvation necessitates (from a human perspective) a Special Revelation from God leading to redemption.

## Special Revelation

Special Revelation involves God directly revealing himself to humanity. The God of might and majesty, of wisdom and morality, is made known to one more fully. God tells in great detail who He is, what His will is, and how He relates to humankind. Though Special Revelation preceded humanity's fall in the Garden of Eden, Special Revelation primarily deals with unfolding God's plan of salvation for the fallen race. Special Revelation is usually limited to God's particular self-disclosure through the incarnate Christ and the Holy Scriptures. This chapter will limit consideration to the Bible.

## Special Revelation through the Bible

It is reasonable to expect that God who has chosen to reveal himself would use a book in which to reveal himself more fully and clearly. Subjective experience is too obscure and variable as a means of sure revelation. An objective standard is provided by the written word. Likewise memory and oral tradition are untrustworthy for accurate transmission of God's revelation. Books have been the best method of preserving truth in its integrity and transmitting it from one generation to another. Also, God's revelation is progressive. God's special revelation has been written down at the various stages of its reception, making it possible now to have the whole of revelation. Thus today one has the revelation made to Moses, David, Paul, and others, revealing, centuries after the fact, God's will and complete plan of salvation.

By holding Special Revelation from God in a "permanent" form, the Bible is both a record and interpreter of God. Through it the historical truth of God's past revelation is brought into one's present.

The Bible is the Word of God in written form. Virtually all religions have their holy books, their sacred scriptures. However, though many of them may contain worthy moral teachings, Christianity has historically maintained that the Bible is uniquely and exclusively the Word of God. God's written Special Revelation is confined to the thirty-nine books of the Old Testament and twenty-seven books of the New Testament. The following are some of the evidences presented for identifying the Bible as God's Word.

1. There is a remarkable consistency in the varied content of the books of the Bible. The Bible was written over a period of approximately fifteen centuries by about forty very different writers. They came from varied backgrounds, confronted different experiences, and had their own strengths and weaknesses. They wrote in different places, and under varied circumstances. They wrote from different continents, in three languages, on hundreds of subjects. Yet, their writings combine to form a consistent whole which unfolds the story of God's relationship to humankind.[5]

2. The biblical writings set forth an ethical standard that surpasses what would be expected of a finite being. It calls one to a morality that exceeds one's own measure of righteousness. Adherence to an external code falls short of its demand for internal goodness. Both one's moral failure and moral redemption are understood only in terms of one's relationship to a holy God.

3. The Bible addresses every essential area of one's life. Though written centuries ago it speaks forcefully to human need in every generation. It correlates to complex human nature while providing reasonable answers to the ultimate questions of life. The penetrating revelation has a transforming power for those who embrace its message.

4. Prophecies which speak of future events, many of them centuries in advance, pervade the Scriptures. The accuracy of predictions, as demonstrated by their fulfillments, is absolutely remarkable.

5. The Bible has had an extraordinary influence on societies around the world. It has been printed in more languages and read by more people than any other book. Widely quoted as a source of wisdom, inspiration and ethical teachings, it has served as the foundation for the laws of many nations, for great social reforms, and for scientific inquiry.

6. The accuracy of the Bible in all areas, including persons, places, customs, events, and science, has been substantiated through history and archaeology. At times the Bible was thought to be in

---

[5]James Montgomery Boice, *The Sovereign God*, 68-69.

error, but later discoveries attested to its truthfulness. With great care the biblical writings have been copied and handed down to succeeding generations to preserve the accuracy of God's written message.

7. A very small percentage of ancient books survive from one generation to another. Yet the Bible has survived throughout the centuries in spite of organized attempts to destroy it. Rather than die out, the Bible has thrived in the midst of criticism and religious persecutions. Far more manuscript portions of the Bible have been preserved than any other piece of literature. As remarkable as the survival of the Bible may be, it is understandable from both the human and divine perspective if it is God's Word.[6]

8. Jesus Christ consistently and emphatically gives testimony to the Scriptures as being the Word of God. He commends the Pharisees for doing what the Scriptures teach, and condemns them for substituting their traditions for the *commandments of God* (Mt 15:3-6). He regarded the Scriptures as the final authority in matters of faith and conduct because their source was God (Mt 23:43; Mk 12:36). He proclaims that he did not come to destroy the Old Testament Scriptures but to fulfill them (Mt 5:17-20). As one who speaks for God, Jesus claims authority for His own writings, and claims special authority for those He commissioned as His witnesses endued with the Holy Spirit (Jn 7:15-17; 8:26-47; 14:10-26; 15:3-26; 16:12ff).

9. The Bible repeatedly makes the explicit claim that it is a special revelation, the very Word of God.

## The Inspiration of Scripture

While the term revelation refers to the activity of God making himself known, inspiration refers to the inscripturation (writing down) of that revelation. One must move from the revelational act/word to the written word of Scripture. Consideration must be given to what sense, or degree, or extent the writings of the biblical authors can be understood as God's Word or a special revelation from God.

---

[6]Henry C. Thiessen, *Lectures in Systematic Theology* revised edition, 45-46.

Many of the biblical writers claim to be eyewitnesses of the events of which they are writing (Ac 10:39-42; 1Pe 1:16-18; 1Jn 1:1-3). Likewise, they make the direct claim that their message was actually a message from God (Ac 4:24-25; 1Co 2:13; Gal 1:7,18; 1Th 2:13; 4:2,14; Heb 2:1-4; 1Pe 1:12; 2Pe 3:2). The Bible is replete with source identifying statements such as, "Then the Lord said to Moses . . ." (Ex 14:1), "This is the word that came to Jeremiah from the Lord . . ." (Jer 11:1). In the Old Testament alone expressions such as "Thus says the Lord" occur more than thirty-eight hundred times.

Jesus spoke of even the least of the biblical commandments as important and binding.

I tell you the truth, until heaven and earth disappear, not the smallest letter, not the least stroke of a pen, will by any means disappear from the Law until everything is accomplished. (Mt. 5:18)

Reward or judgment is predicated on one's relationship to the least of the commandments. Accused of blasphemy because of His claim to deity, Jesus appealed to the phrase "ye are gods" in Psalm 82:6. He builds the defense of His claim on the well accepted truth that even a relatively obscure phrase of Scripture cannot be broken. The reason it could not be broken was that, as a portion of Scripture, it was the authoritative Word of God (Jn 10:34-35).

The Apostle Peter describes the human authors of the Scripture as men carried along by the Holy Spirit. The result of the superintending of their activity by the Holy Spirit was a message not initiated by human design nor the product of mere human reason and research. Their words were to be regarded as a "more sure" word of prophecy because they were the words of God himself (2Pe 1:19-21).

Paul writes to Timothy that the Scriptures are able to make him "wise for salvation" (2Ti 3:15). The value of the Scriptures is derived from their source. Paul's testimony was that "All Scripture is given by inspiration of God" (2Ti 3:16). The term inspiration is the translation of the Greek word *theopneustos* which literally means "God-breathed." Paul is saying more than that all Scripture exudes or speaks of God. The use of the Greek passive form is to identify the source of all Scripture. It is breathed forth by God. He is the ultimate author. Thus all Scripture is the voice of God, the Word of God (Ac 4:25; Heb 1:5-13).

In the context of 2 Timothy 3:16, one understands that the Old Testament Scripture is in view. Thus the explicit claim is the whole of the Old Testament is an inspired revelation of God. Though the time frame for the writing of the New Testament prohibits such an explicit claim for the whole New Testament, there are enough specific statements by the writers of the New Testament to infer reasonably that the inspiration of all Scripture extends to the whole Bible. For example, in 1 Timothy 5:18 Paul quotes from Deuteronomy 25:4 and Luke 10:7, referring to both being Scripture. Also, Peter, in 2 Peter 3:15,16, speaks of the writings of Paul as Scripture.

## Mode of Inspiration

If the self-testimony of Scripture is accepted, the inspiration of Scripture is clearly taught. As the human authors wrote, in some sense God himself was involved in communication of their message. However, since in most cases the Bible does not reveal the psychology of inspiration, various understandings of the mode of inspiration have been suggested.

Some view inspiration as merely a natural insight exercised by gifted persons in spiritual matters. No special involvement of God is seen. Others suggest a special illumination by God to enhance or intensify one's religious perceptions. For many inspiration refers to a special guidance of the Holy Spirit to assure the trustworthy transmission of God's message as it deals with matters of religious faith and living. This special guidance of God's Spirit does not extend to details of history, science, geography and other non-religious matters. In an attempt to emphasize the activity of God in inspiration, some hold to a mechanical human reproduction of divine words as the Holy Spirit dictated them to the human writer. The most widely accepted evangelical understanding of inspiration is often called "verbal plenary inspiration."[7] In this view all (plenary) the words (verbal) of Scripture are derived from an infallible, supernatural superintendence of the human faculties of the writers whereby the Holy Spirit guaranteed the accuracy and completeness of *all* that was

---

[7]R. Laird Harris, *Inspiration and Canonicity of the Bible*. Harris presents a history of the doctrine of verbal inspiration and a defense against objections to it.

written. God motivated them to write, guided the process, and assured that there were no errors or omissions.

A proper mode of inspiration must include all the elements which the Bible posits in both the act of inspiring and the effects of the act of inspiring. It must give proper place to both God's activity and man's activity. Those views which regard inspiration as only some natural gift or illumination do not give proper attention to God's "breathing out" the Scripture. The view which sees matters of faith and life as inspired apart from other more mundane content leave no sure method of determining what is inspired and what is not. Nor does it address the explicit claim that *all* Scripture is inspired, even the most obscure of verses. A mechanical dictation view of inspiration does not give proper recognition to the human styles, expressions, and emphases of the writers. The Verbal Plenary view of inspiration avoids the pitfalls of those views which emphasize human contribution to the neglect of God's involvement or emphasize God's activity to the neglect of human participation. The whole of Scripture is inspired as the writers wrote under the direction and guidance of the Holy Spirit. Their writings were thus kept from error and omission as they communicated the message of God while accounting for variety in literary style, grammar, vocabulary and other human peculiarities. Verbal Plenary Inspiration was the view of the early church. During the first eight centuries of the Church no major church leader held to any other view and it continued to be the view of virtually all orthodox Christian churches till the eighteenth century.[8]

## Authority of Scripture

God is the ultimate authority for all that exists. However, since God is known to individuals only by His self-disclosure, His authority is addressed to them in and through His revelation. Therefore, Protestant Christianity has recognized the authority for humanity to be the inspired Scripture, rather than another person, human reason, or even the Church.

---

[8]In the ninth century, Scholasticism began to assert reason over biblical authority through the School Men such as John Scotus Erigena. See "The Church Doctrine of Biblical Authority," Jack B. Rogers, *The Authoritative Word*; Clark H. Pinnock, *Biblical Revelation*; "The View of the Bible Held by the Church: The Early Church Through Luther," *Inerrancy*.

The authority of Scripture is the authority of God himself. While the authority of Scripture is a derived authority, it is also an inherent authority because God is both the revealed one and the One who reveals. The Bible does not merely contain the Word of God, but is itself the very Word of God.

"Thus says the Lord" fills the pages of Scripture as the human authors consciously declared the authoritative will of God. Christ, himself the Logos of God, both in attitude and word, validated the Old Testament Scripture as divinely authoritative. He promised His apostles that the Holy Spirit would lead them in truth in giving testimony of Him. The New Testament writers did not hesitate to put their own writings on par with the Old Testament Scripture as they wrote authoritatively of the saving significance of Christ's life and work (2Co 12:19; 1Th 2:13). The sovereign God breathed out the Scriptures as the very Word of God, as the Holy Spirit superintended the human writers. Evidences, both internal and external, present the Bible as an authoritative work which predicts the future, changes live, and influences the course of human history.

Calvin emphasized that the ultimate testimony to the authority of Scripture is the internal witness of the Holy Spirit.[9] The Holy Spirit's witness is superior to human reason, the Church, and internal and external evidences marshalled in support of Scripture. Through this inward witness the Scriptures are self-authenticating, producing certainty and conviction that they are indeed the Word of God. One must be careful to understand the union of the Spirit and the Word. There is not one inward message of the Spirit and another external message of the Scripture. The authority of the Bible is not dependent on a person's acknowledgement of that authority. Rather than persons sitting in judgment of the Scripture, the Scripture calls all persons into judgment (Ro 2:16). To obey the Scripture is to obey the voice of God.

## Infallibility/Inerrancy of Scripture

Infallibility and inerrancy are terms used to speak of the truthfulness of Scripture. It does not fail; it does not err; but is entirely true in all that it affirms. An infallible Bible has historically been the view of orthodox Christianity. Though the terms may not have been

---

[9]John Calvin, *Institutes of the Christian Religion*, 1.7.4.

used, the early church fathers, the great Protestant reformers, and the modern day evangelicals all have affirmed a Bible that was entirely true without room for falsehood or error.

The accuracy of the details of Scripture is attested to by science, archaeology, and secular history. But of greater importance is the truthfulness of its message. The truthfulness of its message is inseparably linked to the character of God. Scripture is the revelation of the God who cannot lie (Nu 23:19). The God of truth would be expected to reveal himself truly and to speak truthfully about His relationship to humanity. Jesus asserts that heaven and earth will pass away before the smallest detail of Scripture would be found uncertain (Mt 5:17-19). Its absolutely binding character, which causes Him to state it cannot be broken, is based on the accepted understanding that whatever God says is always true.

An infallible Bible is vital if our faith in God is to be certain. The truthfulness of God's Word is an eternal, life and death issue. It is not sufficient to hope that its message is true. Certitude comes from acknowledging the unity of Scripture as one divine message which the Holy Spirit superintended to assure completeness, accuracy and truthfulness.

While the terms infallibility and inerrancy historically have been virtually synonymous for Protestant Christianity, in recent years many evangelicals have felt the need to distinguish between them. Thus for some, infallibility may be used to refer to the truthful message of the Bible without necessarily meaning that the Bible contains no errors. Sometimes this view is called "limited inerrancy" with the assertion of "no errors" relating only to those verses in the Bible which deal with matters of "faith and practice." Therefore, to affirm inerrancy in *addition* to infallibility is to affirm that the whole of Scripture is without error, even in such matters as history, names, geography, and science. At times a whole argument of a Scripture passage hinges on one word, or a verb tense.

Some prefer to use the term infallibility rather than inerrancy because of possible misunderstandings of what inerrancy means when applied to the Bible.[10] However, inerrancy allows that

---

[10]Paul D. Feinberg, "The Meaning of Inerrancy," *Inerrancy*.

approximations can convey truth. Modern technological precision in reporting statistics and measurements is not to be expected. Likewise scientific and historical data need not conform to modern scientific and historiographic methodologies. "Language of appearance" is often used in the Bible (Jos 10:12-13). Symbolic, metaphoric, and figurative language is widely used by the writers. The Bible uses parables, poetry, and proverbs. Inerrancy does not require verbal exactness in New Testament quotations of the Old Testament. It is expected that the writers and speakers would paraphrase much as is done today.

It is important to remember that infallibility/inerrancy is true only of the autographs—the original scriptural writings. This is not to disparage the truthfulness and certainty of our present biblical texts and versions. Errors have crept into the biblical texts as is true in the transmission of any writing from generation to generation. However, in the providence of God thousands of manuscript portions of the biblical text have been preserved. Through the science of textual criticism, biblical scholars are able to come very close to the inerrant autographs. To deny the infallibility/inerrancy of the original writings is to undermine the authority of our Scriptures today.

Belief in biblical infallibility and inerrancy does not guarantee evangelical orthodoxy. It is possible to believe in the truthfulness of the entire Bible, yet interpret the Scripture incorrectly. Proper hermeneutics must be applied for the correct understanding even of infallible truth. Even more important, understanding infallible truth is not the same as embracing it. The inerrant truth that God reveals about himself and His will must be accepted and lived.

## The Canon of Scripture

All religious literature—even the most helpful and widely read—is not considered Scripture. Only the sixty-six books in the Bible are worthy of this designation. These books are referred to as the "canon" of Scripture. The term comes from the Greek *kanon* which designated a carpenter's measuring rule. The books in the canon of Scripture are those that measure up to the standard which marks them as the Word of God. They alone are inspired by the Holy Spirit as the authoritative and infallible revelation of God.

The establishment of the canon was not the decision of the writers, or religious leaders, or a church council. Rather, the process of these particular books being accepted as Scripture was from the providential influence of the Holy Spirit upon the people of God. The canon was formed by consensus rather than decree. The oldest Christian list of the Old Testament canon which has survived comes from about A.D. 170.[11] The official "recognition" of a closed Old Testament canon is usually dated from the Council of Jamnia about A.D. 90-100. An ecumenical church council probably first recognized an undisputed New Testament canon at Carthage in 397. However, the Church did not decide which books should be in the biblical canon, but only gave recognition to those *already* recognized by God's people. God is the one who established the canon by inspiring certain writings to convey His eternal life-changing message.

## The Illumination of Scripture

Illumination is the term used to express the work of the Holy Spirit in His ministry of helping one understand the truth of the Scripture. The Holy Spirit who superintended the writing of Scripture is the same Holy Spirit who brings understanding of the Scripture to the believer (1Jn 2:27). Only believers can know the illuminating ministry of the Spirit, for the unregenerate person cannot know the things of God which are spiritually discerned (1Co 2:9-10). The god of this age has blinded the minds of persons to the gospel and the illumination of the Spirit is needed. The Spirit may work His illuminating ministry through various means; however, ultimately the link between God's Word and the human mind is the Spirit himself.

The illumination of the Spirit does not refer to some "new revelation" or "deep hidden meaning." The message of the written word is illumined. Illumination is not intended to be a shortcut to scriptural knowledge or meant to replace exegetical study. Rather, illumination primarily involves the reception of God's Word, allowing it to be heard by the "heart" as well as the intellect (Ro 10:17).[12] Only the Spirit of God can open one's heart to the Word of God.

---

[11]F. F. Bruce,"Tradition and the Canon of Scripture," *The Authoritative Word.*

[12]Millard J. Erickson, *Christian Theology,* 247-251.

## For Reflection and Discussion

1. Animism usually involves the worship of aspects of nature. Reflect on how this would relate to General Revelation. Could General Revelation serve as a bridge to witnessing to animists? How?

2. The Bible affirms the value of General Revelation. Yet, sin has impacted General Revelation in a negative way. How is General Revelation to be understood prior to the Fall of man, presently to sinful man, and presently to redeemed man?

3. The doctrine of the inspiration of Scripture does not require that the authors only mechanically transcribed what God wanted communicated. The writers retained their own particular literary style and form. Select two biblical authors and note some of their writing characteristics.

4. Both biblical prophecy and biblical archaeology have been appealed to as areas of evidence for the uniqueness of the Bible. Compile a list of biblical prophecies and their fulfillment and a list of archaeological discoveries that support biblical content.

5. The doctrine of biblical inerrancy refers to the biblical autographs. Since we do not have any of the autographs, how does inerrancy relate to the versions and translations of the Bible that we use today?

# What Is Man?
Psalm 8:4

FROM THE BEGINNING OF HUMAN HISTORY, men and women have searched for answers to some of the most basic questions of life: "Who am I?" "Where did I come from?" "Where am I going?" Many centuries ago, the Psalmist echoed similar sentiments by pondering his place in God's creation: "What is man that you are mindful of him, the son of man that you care for him?" (Ps 8:4).

The Christian doctrine of man, or anthropology, attempts to find meaningful answers for such questions. (It should be noted that the term "man" will be used in its generic meaning [both male and female] as a synonym for humankind in this chapter. This is supported by the primary biblical terms for man [Heb. *adam*, Gr. *anthropos*] which, although masculine in gender, are frequently used in a generic manner in Scripture.) Theological anthropology (as differentiated from scientific or cultural anthropology) deals with man in relation to God. Thus, the primary and only authoritative source of knowledge for this study is the Bible. This does not mean, however, that there is no overlap between theological and scientific/cultural anthropology. Indeed, there are many areas of human life that are not clearly addressed in Scripture, and one may turn to the behavioral sciences (sociology, psychology, etc.) to gain a greater understanding of certain aspects of human nature. While the Bible does not provide comprehensive information about man, nor does it replace all that can be learned about humanity from other sources, it does give a vital dimension to man's self-understanding which cannot be discovered any place else. The Christian doctrine of man attempts to interpret and integrate the material found in these other disciplines as it seeks an honest answer to the question of what it means to be human.

## The Origin of Man

There are countless theories on how humankind came into being. The modern scientific world has increasingly accepted the evolutionary theory (or perhaps "theories," since evolution is frequently presented in different ways) of the origin of the universe and humanity. Although evolutionary ideas about creation go back as far as the ancient Greek civilization, most modern theories of evolution can be traced to Charles Darwin in the nineteenth century.

Briefly presented, evolution is an attempt to account for the existence of the universe and its various forms of life through a totally naturalistic means. Evolutionary "purists" do not allow for any type of divine or supernatural activity at any point along the continuum of life. Man, as he is known today, is simply an extension of primitive forms of life that have gradually developed and become more complex over thousands (perhaps millions) of years. Many evolutionists accept Darwin's concept of "natural selection." Darwin believed that an over-production of any species of life would result in a struggle for existence. This struggle would in turn result in a variation of that species. Some would become stronger and more sophisticated and others would weaken and eventually die. This is often referred to as the "survival of the fittest." Thus, through this long process of natural selection and upgrading of species, humankind appeared. While humans are more complex and superior to previous forms of life, they have still not reached a final or "completed" form, as the evolutionary process always continues.[1]

A foundational principle in the evolutionary theory is that of strict continuity; that is, between the lower forms of life and humankind, there must be a natural continuum of process (which would also allow for positive mutations within a species). Any discontinuity or interruptions at any point along the evolutionary chain of development would be disastrous to the theory. There cannot be anything absolutely new or totally unpredictable in the overall process.[2]

It is at this point that differences emerge between the secular, naturalistic evolutionist and others who wish to harmonize the concepts of natural science with the biblical record. Such persons are variously designated as deistic evolutionists, theistic evolutionists, and progressive creationists. The deistic evolutionist maintains that God began the entire process of evolutionary development, creating the initial material of the universe and establishing the laws to govern that universe, and then withdrew from any further active involvement, assuming the role of "Creator emeritus."[3]

In a similar vein, the theistic evolutionist proposes that evolution is God's method of working. At a certain point, however, God intervened in the natural process to create the first human being. Some theistic evolutionists further qualify this by contending that man's material being (the body) has evolved from the lower forms of life, while his immaterial being (the soul or spirit) has been created directly by God.[4] Some Roman Catholics adhere to this latter idea, following the 1950 encyclical *Humani Generis*, in which Pope Pius XII declared, "The teaching of the Church leaves the doctrine of evolution an open question . . ." in regard to the development of the human body, but strongly asserted that the Catholic faith teaches "that souls are immediately created by God."[5]

---

[1]Cf. Charles Darwin. *The Origin of Species.* 1859.

[2]Cf. Louis Berkhof, *Systematic Theology*, 183.

[3]Millard J. Erickson, *Christian Theology*, 480.

[4]Berkhof, 184.

[5]Cited in Henry C. Thiessen, *Lectures in Systematic Theology, Revised Edition*, 151.

A more traditional Christian approach in viewing the Genesis creation story, including the origin of man, is to hold to fiat creationism, that is, creation by divine pronouncement ("Let there be . . . and there was . . ."). Every aspect of the creation was a direct, immediate act of God. Fiat creationists believe in a literal interpretation of the Genesis record (including literal twenty-four hour days of creation), and consequently reject any form of evolutionary development, attributing such teaching to an atheistic attack upon the Christian faith.[6]

A view which is similar to fiat creationism in that it stresses the divine, direct and immediate creation of man is progressive creationism. Unfortunately, this view is also occasionally confused with theistic evolution because it sees God's creative work as a combination of unique and new (*de novo*) creative acts along with a more natural process of "evolutionary" development. Progressive creationists allow for development and "change" within a given species of life, but not for any interdevelopment or "crossing over" between species.[7] It is significant to note that progressive creationists emphasize that man's entire nature (material and immaterial) was a special *de novo* creation of God.

While it is not the purpose of this chapter to explore in-depth all of the ramifications of the above views of man's origin, several observations are in order. Of the four stated positions, deistic evolution seems to have the least biblical support. Like its namesake, Deism, this view allows for no further involvement of God with the created order after its inception. Theistic evolution is somewhat similar, except that it does allow for the direct creation of man's soul or spirit by God. Its tendency to allegorize the spiritual truths of man's beginning and his fall into sin seems to weaken the importance

---

[6]Cf. Pattle P. T. Pun, "Evolution," in *Evangelical Dictionary of Theology*, 389.

[7]The more technical terms sometimes used by progressive creationists are "microevolution," referring to "intrakind" evolvement or change within a particular species of life, and "macroevolution," which indicates an "interkind" development or crossing over from one species to another. For example, while progressive creationists allow for general "evolvement" within the human species (people may become physically larger and stronger, be able to physically adapt to new geographical conditions, etc.), they do not allow for any human "evolvement" from lower, non-human forms of life. Cf. Erickson, *Christian Theology*, 482.

of these historic events. Fiat creationism, while on the surface appearing to support the biblical account by its literal interpretation, may extend such interpretations beyond their intended meanings. For example, the Hebrew term "day" (*yom*) does not always refer to a twenty-four hour, solar day, but can also refer to a longer period of undesignated length (cf. Ge 2:4; Ps 90:1-4) or a figurative period such as "the Day of the Lord" (Joel 2:31; Mal 4:5). Similarly, the fact that most forms of life were created after their "kind" (Heb. *min*) is often assumed by fiat creationists to refer specifically to species in which all variations were created directly by the Lord, but this term also is indefinite and can refer to other types of division (such as genus, family, or order).[8] Concerning this view of man's origin, Erickson notes that one "cannot claim that the Bible *requires* fiat creationism; nevertheless, it is clear that it most certainly *permits* it."[9] Finally, progressive creationism, which allows for more flexibility in interpreting the Genesis account (including day-age creation, microevolution within species, etc.) is still faithful to the biblical record, and demands that man's creation is a unique and immediate act of God. One Christian biologist notes, "The position of the progressive creationists seems to be able to maintain scriptural as well as scientific integrity."[10]

Before leaving this section on the origin of humanity, several implications of the Genesis account should be acknowledged. Scripture offers a brief, twofold account of man's creation: Genesis 1:26-30 and Genesis 2:7-8, 15-25. The first account is broad and general in scope, seeing the creation of man (*adam*, used here generically for male and female, 1:27) in relation to the rest of the created order. Mankind is the last and the highest act of God's creation, and is given authority and responsibility over the other forms of life. The second account (Ge 2) is much more detailed concerning man's beginning. The difference between these two narratives has led some to believe that they derive from different authors and are contradictory. A closer

---

[8]Walter C. Kaiser, "*Min* (Kind)," in *Theological Wordbook of the Old Testament*, Vol 1, 503-504.

[9]Erickson, *Christian Theology*, 480.

[10]Pun, 392.

examination, however, will reveal a complementary purpose of the two records. The first account is comprehensive in nature, whereas the second is specific; the first shows man's connection to the other facets of God's creation, while the second depicts their correlation to man.

Several truths may be derived from the Genesis account of man's origin. First, it is important to note that man's creation was an immediate act of God, in contrast to some of the other creative acts which may have involved some type of mediate (or processive) activity.[11] The fact that God had more direct involvement with the creation of humanity may signify that God intended this to be a special, more personal relationship than that which He would have with any other aspect of the creation. Second, man's creation was patterned after the likeness of God. More will be said later in this chapter about the implications of man being created in the image of God, but for now it should be asserted that there was something about the nature of God which provided the pattern for something within man, different from and superior to the rest of creation. Third, man's creation involved two separate elements: the "dust of the ground" and the "breath of life" (Ge 2:7). Man's body was "formed" (Heb. *asah*, taken from preexisting materials[12]) from elements which God had already created, possibly explaining the presence of common natural elements in the human body. Man's immaterial aspect (or "soul"; Heb. *nephesh*) was derived directly and uniquely from his Creator. This suggests at least a twofold (dichotomous) human nature (elaborated upon later in the chapter). Fourth, the woman (*ishah*) was also created directly by God, separately from and "taken out of man" (*ish*; Ge 2:23), in order to be a "suitable helper" for him (cf. Ge 2:18, 20b). Some older versions translate this as "helpmeet," but the Hebrew actually uses two words, *ezer* ("help," sometimes used to refer to the help of God) and *neged* ("corresponding to" or "equal to"). Thus, the implication of this term is not that the female was created to be

---

[11]"Immediate" acts of creation refer to those acts of God which were direct and without any previous pattern or prototype. "Mediate" creative acts are those which were also acts of God, but in which He possibly worked more indirectly in a processive manner (e.g., creating things "after their kind"). For example, the creation of man would be considered "immediate;" the creation of animals and plant life could be considered "mediate."

[12]Raymond M. Pruitt, *Fundamentals of the Faith*, 134.

inferior to the male, but rather to be a complementary coworker.[13] Finally, the Genesis account indicates that man was created to be in an exalted position, to have dominion over all lower forms of life and to be the "king" of the earth[14] (Ge 1:28-30, 2:15-17, 19-20). Perhaps this suggests that man should more seriously consider his ecological and environmental responsibility for the world in which God has placed him.

## The Nature of Man

The biblical question "What is man?" can also be employed to question the nature of the human constitution. That is, should the human being be analyzed in terms of "parts" (body, mind, soul, spirit, etc.)? If so, to what part(s) does God relate? Are some eternal and therefore more worthy of attention than others which are temporal and transient?

Historically, there have been several major views concerning the makeup of human nature, including the trichotomous, dichotomous, and monistic views. The trichotomous view was popular in the ancient Eastern church, and was revived among nineteenth century conservatives. It is still popular among many modern conservative Christians (including many Pentecostals). This position (also known as the trichotomist or tripartite view) suggests that man has three essential aspects: body, soul, and spirit. Scriptures such as 1 Thessalonians 5:23 (". . . May your whole spirit, soul and body be kept blameless . . .") and Hebrews 4:12 ("For the word of God . . . penetrates even to dividing soul and spirit, joints and marrow . . .") are often cited in support of the trichotomous position. There are various ways of differentiating between these three aspects, but usually it is believed by trichotomists that the body (Gr. *soma*) is the material or physical part of man's being; the soul (Gr. *psuche*) is the psychological element through which humans reason and relate to others; and the spirit (Gr. *pneuma*) is the religious aspect which uniquely enables man to comprehend things of the spiritual realm and relate to God. One Pentecostal writer indicates that the body is the "world-conscious" aspect of man, enabling him to relate to his environment by means of

---

[13]Cf. Erickson, 546.

[14]Cf. Erich Sauer, *The King of the Earth*, 1981.

the natural senses; the soul is the "self-conscious" aspect which provides for and governs the human personality (intellect, will, and emotions); and the spirit is the "God-conscious" aspect through which man is capable of spiritual relationship to God.[15]

The dichotomous (or dichotomist, or dipartite) view was popularized by the ancient Western church, and has been the most popular view throughout the history of Christianity. This view sees man as being comprised of two essential aspects, the material body, and an immaterial soul or spirit. The latter terms are used interchangeably by most dichotomists, but some prefer to make some minor distinctions, while still seeing soul and spirit as part of man's immaterial being. For example, Strong sees the *psuche* as that aspect of man's immaterial nature which is capable of animated and conscious life, while the *pneuma* is that part of the same immaterial nature which is susceptible to divine influence and indwelling. Strong declares that the soul is human nature "looking earthward" and the spirit is that same nature "looking Godward."[16]

Monism, in contrast to the above two views, states that human nature is indivisible. Man should not be perceived as being composed of "parts" (such as body, soul, or spirit) but rather that he is a radical unity, a "self." According to monism, there can be no "spiritual" existence, no "immortality of the soul," apart from a bodily existence, since all three concepts are used in reference to the entire human personality. The monistic view thus states that body and soul are not contrasting, but rather interchangeable and synonymous terms.[17]

A more recent understanding of human nature which on the surface bears similarities to monism is the Gestaltian view. This term (from the German, for "whole" or "complete") derives more from modern psychology than from historic theology, but many modern theologians are finding it useful. The Gestalt view agrees with monism that the biblical emphasis is not to divide human nature into various components, but to view the person in a holistic perspective. For

---

[15]William W. Menzies, *Understanding Our Doctrine*, 33-34.

[16]Augustus H. Strong, *Systematic Theology*, 486. Cf. the works of A. A. Hodge, L. Berkhof, and H. Thiessen for similar views.

[17]Erickson, 524-527.

example, the Gestaltian view agrees with the monistic that there are numerous biblical references in which the term "soul" (Heb. *nephesh*; Gr. *psuche*) is used to portray the entire person (cf. Ge 2:7, 12:5; Mk 8:35-37). Similarly, the Gestalt concept is in agreement with the dichotomist position that the terms "soul" and "spirit" (*psuche* and *pneuma*) are frequently used in the New Testament in an interchangeable sense, both referring to the life or being of an individual (cf. Mt 20:28, 27:50; Jn 12:27, 13:21). In a comparable way, the Gestaltian view may also be held by those of the trichotomist persuasion. The major difference between the traditional monistic view and the Gestaltian view is that the latter can accept that man's essential composition can have more than one aspect (such as material and immaterial). The Gestaltian emphasis, however, is that God does not relate to man in compartmentalized or fragmented terms, but rather as a person whose whole being is important to his Creator. Louis Berkhof, who is himself a dichotomist, is careful not to make an arbitrary or artificial separation between the elements of man's nature. Berkhof notes

> . . . the Bible teaches us to view the nature of man as a unity, not as a duality . . . . While recognizing the complex nature of man, it never represents this as resulting in a twofold subject in man. Every act of man is seen as an act of the whole man. It is not the soul but man that sins; it is not the body but man that dies; and it is not merely the soul, but man, body and soul, that is redeemed in Christ.[18]

To be certain, this is not one of the more "weighty" matters of theology; that is, there are sincere Christian believers who adhere to any one of the major theories concerning the constitution of human nature. On the other hand, it is not an issue that should simply be dismissed and ignored, as it does have a bearing on how one understands the relationship between God and man. For instance, many of the heresies that were especially prevalent in the ancient Eastern church were in part due to an arbitrary understanding of human nature being divided up into "parts," some of which were "spiritual" and good, and others which were considered "carnal" or "fleshly" and hence evil. Examples would include many Gnostic groups who held to a dualistic world view, believing that man's spirit

---

[18]Berkhof, 192.

was eternal and part of the divine essence, emanating from God, but only to inhabit an evil, physical body in this corrupted world. This led many Gnostics to extreme forms of ascetic activities in their attempt to conquer the flesh and regain the spiritual "knowledge" (or *gnosis*) which was necessary for salvation. Also the Apollinarian heresy taught that Christ's humanity consisted only of a body and soul, but that the human spirit was necessarily replaced by the divine Logos in order to keep Christ truly divine (and less than fully human). In the modern era, there are some neo-Pentecostals or Charismatics who teach that Christians can be partially "possessed" or controlled by demonic powers, allowing for Satan to have power over the more carnal aspects of man's nature (e.g., the body or the mind), but not over those which are under God's control (the soul or spirit). Such teaching is not consistent with the fundamental biblical teaching concerning the true nature of redemption in Christ, which applies to the entire person, not simply one or more aspects of that person (e.g., 2Co 5:17; 1Co 3:16-17, 6:19-20). Even those Scriptures which are often used to support a distinction between the components of man's nature might be better interpreted to emphasize the value which God places upon that entire nature. For example, the apostle Paul's emphasis in 1 Thessalonians 5:23 is not on the composition of human nature, but rather that God would "sanctify you *through and through* [*holoteleis*, "complete"]. May your *whole* [*holokleron*, "entire"] spirit, soul and body be kept blameless at the coming of our Lord Jesus Christ" (emphasis added). Similarly, the emphasis of Hebrews 4:12 is that the word of God is powerful enough to penetrate the whole being of man (not separating one "part" from another), with the effect that nothing "is hidden from God's sight. Everything is uncovered and laid bare before the eyes of him to whom we must give account." Erickson stresses that "The gospel is an appeal to the whole man. It is significant that Jesus in his incarnation became fully man, for he came to redeem the whole of what we are."[19] Thus the overall emphasis of Scripture is that God is concerned about every facet of man's being, and that there is no aspect of one's life that is outside His love and providential care.

---

[19]Erickson, 539.

## Created in the Image of God

In many respects, man is similar to all other forms of animal life: he is born, breathes, eats, sleeps, fights a losing battle with death, and returns to dust! The thing that makes man a distinctly *human* being, different from and superior to all other animals, is that he is created in the image of God (*imago Dei*).[20] The first biblical reference to this is found in Genesis 1:26-27:

> Then God said, 'Let us make man in our image, in our likeness, and let them rule over the fish of the sea and the birds of the air, over the livestock, over all the earth, and over all the creatures that move along the ground.' So God created man in his own image, in the image of God he created him; male and female he created them.

While most Christians would agree that humanity is created in God's image, they often differ over exactly what this means. This difference of opinion has a long history in Christian theology. While an in-depth study of this history is beyond the purpose of this study, a brief overview is in order.

In the early centuries of Christianity, most were agreed that the *imago Dei* included man's rational and moral characteristics. Some were even inclined to include his bodily traits. For example, Irenaeus and Tertullian (2nd-3rd century) believed that the "image" referred to physical characteristics, while "likeness" alluded to spiritual traits. Others, such as Clement of Alexandria and Origen (2nd-3rd century) rejected this distinction, and instead offered that the "image" denoted the essential human characteristics, whereas "likeness" suggested non-essential characteristics, which may be cultivated or lost.[21] Still others, such as Augustine (5th century) taught that the "image" referred to the intellectual faculties of man's nature, while the "likeness" related to the man's moral faculties. Generally speaking, theologians of the ancient Eastern church stressed the rationalistic basis as the ground of the divine image within man, while the Western theologians emphasized the moral aspects of this image.[22]

---

[20]Cf. Shirley C. Guthrie, Jr., *Christian Doctrine*, 188.

[21]Berkhof, 202.

[22]H. Orton Wiley, *Christian Theology* Vol. 2, 30.

In the Medieval period, the Roman Catholic theologians known as the Scholastics tended to continue making a distinction between the image and the likeness of God in man. The image referred to the natural attributes of God which could be seen to some degree in man (e.g., reason, will), and the likeness consisted of the moral qualities of God. The latter was a supernatural gift given by God to keep man's lower nature in check. This *donum superadditum* ("superadded grace") was lost in Adam's Fall, but was restored to man upon salvation to enable him to merit eternal life. The Scholastics taught that since man had lost this supernatural element (likeness) in the Fall he was morally corrupt, but since he retained the image of God he was still complete and had not lost the essence of human nature.[23] The implications of this apparently innocent distinction between the likeness of God being lost but the image of God being retained allows for the possibility of a rational or natural theology, which further allows for man to do good works to receive salvation, apart from the grace of God. It is upon such a rational system that the Roman Catholic doctrine of soteriology is based.[24]

With the Reformation came a rejection of this somewhat artificial dichotomy between image and likeness. Martin Luther correctly noted that the two terms, as used in Genesis 1:26, exemplify Hebrew parallelism and are really speaking about the same thing. Luther believed that all aspects of God's image in man have been corrupted by the Fall, so that only fragments or a small remnant of that image remains in man. John Calvin essentially agreed with Luther that the whole image was marred by sin, but Calvin emphasized that humans still have the ability to reason and in that way man can still know something about God.[25]

In the modern era, there are many who continue holding to variations of the views that have been propagated throughout the history of Christian thought. Suffice it to say that most Protestants (including most Pentecostals) adhere to the theology that has developed out of the Reformation era concerning the image of God. The

---

[23]Ibid. Cf. Erickson, 500; Berkhof, 202.

[24]Cf. David Cairns, *The Image of God in Man*, 114-120. Also cf. Erickson, 501.

[25]Cf. Erickson, 501; Berkhof, 203.

remainder of this section will attempt to delineate the meaning and implications of the biblical teaching that man is in the image of God.

As the Reformers suggested, the biblical record uses the terms image (*tselem*) and likeness (*demuth*) interchangeably. For example, both are used in Genesis 1:26, but only "image" is used in 1:27. Similarly, the term "likeness" is used in Genesis 5:1 but both terms are used synonymously in 5:3. The implication is that man was *created* in the image/likeness of God, and not that this was something with which he was later endowed or which he could merit. Berkhof suggests that God was the original, of which man was made a copy. Man not only *bears* God's image (cf. 1Co 15:49) but he *is* God's image (cf. 1Co 11:7).[26]

It would also seem that man, being in the image of God, was created with a rational and holy nature. Man was given an intellectual, volitional, and emotional nature which far surpasses that which can be evidenced in any form of animal life (which typically operates on instinct). Although these characteristics of human personality are marred by the Fall, they obviously are not completely destroyed, or man would cease to be human. Scripture seems to indicate this in passages such as Genesis 9:6 and James 3:9, which refer to humans bearing the image of God, regardless of their spiritual condition. Man is a rational creature who was created with a true character of holiness. This can also be referred to as a positive state of holiness, in that it was not simply a passive state of ignorance or moral innocence, but rather was characterized by an active sense of willful obedience to God. This was a *created* holiness, not something for which Adam was personally responsible. That is, Adam could not take credit for possessing holiness, and there was no reward or merit associated with it; however, he was responsible before his Creator for continuing in the state of holiness in which he was created.[27] Wiley notes that even in this pre-fallen condition of holiness, man was still dependent upon the presence and power of the Holy Spirit in order for his free will to respond faithfully and obediently to God.[28] While

---

[26]Berkhof, 203.

[27]Pruitt, 138.

[28]Wiley, 48.

man's fall corrupted this original condition of holiness, it should be noted that through the process of salvation, believers are being restored into this image of God (cf. Ro 8:29; 2Co 3:18; Eph 4:23-24; Col 3:10).

Another quality of man that is related to the image of God is spirituality. In fact, one theologian refers to spirituality as "the deepest fact in the likeness of man to God . . . and the ground of all other forms of likeness."[29] Whereas God in His essential nature is spirit (Jn 4:24), He has created humanity in such a way that man is not merely a physical, mortal creature that functions according to natural instincts, but also a being endowed with spirituality, who is capable of fellowship and communion with one's Creator. In relation to man's spirituality, the great nineteenth century theologian Charles Hodge has stated that man

> . . . belongs to the same order of being as God Himself, and is therefore capable of communion with his Maker. This conformity of nature between man and God, is not only the distinguishing prerogative of humanity, so far as earthly creatures are concerned, but it is also the necessary condition of our capacity to know God, and therefore the foundation of our religious nature. If we were not like God, we could not know Him.[30]

Related to man's possession of spirituality as part of the image of God, it is appropriate to speak of man's soul or spirit as immortal. Only God possesses the essence of immortality (1Ti 6:16), but man has a derived immortality in that he was created to have an everlasting existence. Since God is incorporeal, it is not accurate to say that man is in God's "physical likeness"; however, some suggest that the human body does constitute a part of the image of God in that God created man—not simply the soul or spirit of man —in His image, and this "living soul" (Ge 2:7) was not complete without the body. Perhaps it is best to say that God's image is found in man's body in the sense that the body was created to be the proper habitation or instrument for the self-expression of the soul.[31] This is further evidenced in the

---

[29]Ibid., 32-33.

[30]Charles Hodge, *Systematic Theology* Vol. 2, 97.

[31]Cf. Berkhof, 205.

resurrection of the righteous, when the immortal soul or spirit will be united with a glorified body and man shall dwell eternally in the presence of the Lord. The realization that humans have an unending existence (for the righteous, in the presence of God; for the wicked, separated from God), and that this earthly life is only a small part of that existence, should give one a different perspective on life. Most importantly, the recognition of this eternality should affect the manner in which one lives in this present life.[32]

An important implication of humanity being created in the image of God is that man is to reflect God; that is, just as a parent may be "imaged" in a child, so God is imaged in human beings. "Man is God's reflection upon earth: the mirror of God."[33] Williams notes three major ways in which this can be accomplished. First, man is to reflect God's dominion (cf. Ge 1:26; Ps 8:6). While man cannot control the operations of nature and the universe, which belongs solely to the sovereign power of God, he has been given a sense of "subdominion or vice-regency,"[34] which suggests a large degree of ability and responsibility for the care and stewardship of this world's resources. Second, man is to reflect God's being (Ge 1:26-27). God, who exists in Himself as Father, Son, and Holy Spirit, did not intend for man to exist in singularity, but as male and female. Williams declares, "The creation of man and woman in this ontological relationship is thus a creaturely repetition of the being of God, whose inner life is one of relationship and mutuality."[35] This is similar to the words of Karl Barth:

> God exists in relationship and fellowship. As the Father of the Son and the Son of the Father He is Himself I and Thou, confronting Himself and yet always one and the same in the Holy Ghost. God created man in His own image, in correspondence with His own being and essence. . . . Because He is not solitary in Himself . . . it is

---

[32]Cf. Millard J. Erickson, *Does It Matter What I Believe*, 65-66.

[33]J. Rodman Williams, *Renewal Theology* Vol. 1, 201.

[34]Ibid., 202.

[35]Ibid., 204.

not good for man to be alone, and God created man in His own image, as male and female.[36]

Thus the human desire for fellowship and companionship is grounded in man's social likeness to God. "Human love and social interests spring directly from this element in man's nature."[37] Williams correctly observes that the male alone was not made in God's image, but the male *and* the female (cf. Ge 1:27). Just as with God there is both unity (one God) and differentiation (three persons), so with man (unity) there are distinctions (male and female). The fact that God created man in this manner suggests that only in the proper differentiation and functioning of the two (male and female) is God's image truly evidenced in humanity. "Man and woman are made to complement each other . . . In mutuality and reciprocity they reflect the image of God."[38] Third, man is to reflect God's character. Just as God is perfectly holy, righteous, loving and true, so He desires man to emulate and reflect these characteristics in his relations with his fellow man. When man walks in such a manner, he conforms to God's will and images his Creator.[39]

As a final summation to this section, it may be stated that the only true picture of what it means for man to be in the image of God is evidenced in the Lord Jesus Christ, the one declared to be "the image of the invisible God" (Col 1:15; cf. 2Co 4:4; Php 2:6). Because the "Second Adam" was true to His own humanity and fulfilled what the first man and all other persons have failed to do or to be, one can learn what it really means to be human and hence to be in the image of God by observing the humanity of Jesus. Guthrie notes that the unique and decisive thing about Jesus' humanity (and His being in the image of God) was not simply some quality or attribute He possessed, but rather the way in which He lived. Jesus was the one person who has ever lived who was completely for God and in complete obedience to Him, and completely for His fellow men and in complete

---

[36]Karl Barth, *Church Dogmatics* III/2, 324.

[37]Thiessen, 157.

[38]Williams, Vol. 1, 204.

[39]Ibid., 206-208.

identity with them.[40] Similarly, Erickson notes that Jesus was the perfect example of what human nature is intended to be. Just as Jesus had perfect fellowship with the Father, fully obeyed the Father's will, and had a strong love and compassion for His fellow man, so it is God's desire that a similar sense of fellowship, obedience, and love should characterize man's relationship to God as well as to his fellow man. One may experience full humanity only when one is properly related to God.[41]

> Every human being is God's creature made in God's own image. God endowed each of us with the powers of personality that make possible worship and service of our Creator. When we are using those powers to those ends, we are most fully what God intended us to be. It is then that we are most completely human.[42]

## The Fall of Man

A theological study of the doctrine of man (anthropology) would not be complete without addressing the issue of the Fall and the doctrine of sin (hamartiology). Sometimes the two are explicated as man's *status integritas* (before the Fall) and man's *status corruptionis* (after the Fall). This section of the present chapter will briefly examine the latter category.

As noted earlier in this chapter, man was originally created in God's image, which included the fact that he was a rational creature with the freedom of choice, and that he was in a condition of true holiness, which allowed him unhindered access to God and a propensity to choose that which was good. For such freedom to be truly "free," however, meant that man also was given the choice to disobey and to do evil. The same free moral agency that enabled man to choose to serve God also enabled him to choose to serve himself. The question has often been raised why God did not simply create man "impeccable," without the ability to sin, and thus to enjoy unbroken communion with God forever. This, however, is to miss the point of man being in the image of God, which includes man's freedom to willingly love and serve God and for God to be truly

---

[40]Guthrie, 191-192.

[41]Erickson, 514-515.

[42]Ibid., 517.

glorified by man. Perhaps it could be said that man was originally created perfect, but that this included the potential for imperfection.

Genesis 3 presents the account of the first human sin, or what is commonly referred to as the Fall of man. Being tempted by the serpent to partake of the forbidden fruit (from the tree of the knowledge of good and evil; cf. Ge 2:16-17), the woman (Eve) and then the man (Adam) chose to disobey the command of God, and sin entered the human race (cf. Ro 5:12). Throughout Christian history there has been some debate over whom to "blame" for the existence of evil. Many have been quick to affirm that sin originated with Satan (the serpent). This, however, is only true in that Satan was the first of God's creatures to freely rebel against God and to fall into sin. The Genesis 3 account simply indicates that Satan tempted man to make the same type of negative choice which he had earlier made. Thus Satan introduced man to the enticement of sin, but Satan is not the "creator" of evil. From the opposite end of the spectrum are those who feel that since God is the supreme Creator of all things, then He must also be the Creator of evil. This view also goes against the teaching of Scripture, which indicates that all of God's creation is "very good" (Ge 1:31), and that God neither can be tempted nor does He tempt others to do evil (Jas 1:13; cf. Job 34:10-12).

The most logical and biblically supported response to the question concerning the origin of evil is that it stems from the abuse of freedom in free, intelligent creatures, whether angelic or human (cf. Ge 2:15-17, 3:1-6). This is essentially the view of the early Church Fathers (especially Irenaeus), who taught that human sin originated in the voluntary transgression and fall of Adam.[43] It should also be noted that neither God, Satan, nor man "created" evil, since evil is not a "thing" of substance which can be created. (This latter idea can be traced to medieval Roman Catholicism and the Scholastic theologians [e.g., Thomas Aquinas] who distinguished between venial [forgiveable] sins and mortal [unforgiveable] sins, measuring them according to their seriousness and ascribing them "appropriate" acts of penance). Rather, evil is a relationship that is entered into by those who freely choose to oppose the righteous commands of God and

---

[43]Cf. Berkhof, 219.

choose instead to follow their own ways. Pruitt agrees with this, noting that "sin has no ontological being, that is, it was not something which God made, but is a contradiction which came through the willful rebellion of His free and rational creatures."[44]

There were several immediate consequences of man's Fall. Perhaps the most inclusive is the total depravity of human nature (cf. Ge 6:5; Ps 14:1-3; Ro 7:18). Human nature became "totally" corrupted in the sense that depravity is universal and that it extends to every aspect of man's being. This does not mean that individual persons cannot become even more "sinful," nor that all persons are totally devoid of any "good" human qualities. It does, however, indicate that fallen humans are unable to choose the ultimate good (or God) without divine assistance. Resulting from the depravity of human nature was a loss of communion and open fellowship with God. Instead of desiring to be in God's presence, Adam and Eve were conscious of their guilt, attempted to hide from God's sight, and were continually making excuses for their sinful actions (cf. Ge 3:7-13). Such feelings and behavior are characteristic of those who sin against the Lord. Unger aptly states, "They [Adam and Eve] display the natural bent of fallen man to cover rather than confess their guilt, and to offer some sort of human activity or merit rather than trust in God's grace alone."[45] Other immediate consequences of the Fall in the Genesis account include the curse upon the ground (Ge 3:17-19) and implicitly upon all nature (cf. Ro 8:19-22); and death (Ge 2:17; 3:3). The death referred to seems to primarily indicate spiritual death (cf. Ro 5:12; 6:23), but also could allude to the possibility that the process of physical death had already begun within sinful man (cf. Ge 3:19; 1Co 15:21-22). Berkhof notes that Adam went from a state of *posse non mori* (possible not to die) to a state of *non posse non mori* (not possible not to die).[46] Although Christians are now removed from the curse of the Law (Gal 3:13), and the punitive element of death is removed (1Co 15:54-57), Christians are still subject to the consequences of the

---

[44]Pruitt, 155.

[45]Merrill F. Unger, *Unger's Commentary on the Old Testament* Vol. 1, 16.

[46]Berkhof, 226.

Fall (including the curse on nature and physical death) until that day when they shall be glorified in the presence of the Lord.

The Bible uses numerous terms to describe the concept of sin. Sometimes sin is referred to as an act of the will, and sometimes as a condition or state of being. There are both sins of commission (doing things that should not be done) and sins of omission (not doing things that should be done). Some biblical terms describe the causes of sin, while others relate more to sin's effects. While it is beyond the scope of this chapter to review all of the biblical concepts regarding sin, some of the more significant New Testament terms will be briefly examined.

The most common Greek word for sin is *hamartia*, which is popularly defined as "missing the mark." While this may on the surface convey the idea of accidental behavior or sins of omission and ignorance, the term *hamartia* denotes a more deliberate action on the part of the sinner; that is, one misses the mark because one has intentionally aimed at the wrong target (cf. Ro 6:1-2). It should be noted that *hamartia* is used not only in regard to acts of sin, but also to describe the state or condition of sin which results from such acts (cf. Ro 3:9, 5:12-13).

Other important New Testament words for sin include *parabasis*, an act of transgression or disobedience (Ro 4:15; Heb 2:2, 9:15); *asebeia*, "ungodliness" (Jude 15); *adikia*, defined as "unrighteousness" or iniquity (1Jn 5:17a); *anomia*, which literally means "no law," or lawlessness (1Jn 3:4); *agnoema*, literally "no knowledge," or ignorance (whether innocent or intentional; cf. Ac 17:30; Eph 4:18). Many other New Testament as well as Old Testament words for sin could be mentioned, but most would have similar connotations to the above.

Based on the biblical teaching concerning the nature of sin, many theological definitions of sin have been offered through the years. Several of the more common as well as some of the more perspicacious depictions of sin include:

*James Arminius (1560-1609)*—Sin is "something thought, spoken, or done against the law of God, or the omission of something which has been commanded by that law to be thought, spoken, or done."

*Westminster Shorter Catechism (1647)*—"Sin is any want of conformity to, or transgression of, the law of God."

*John Wesley (1703-1791)*—Sin is "a voluntary transgression of a known law."

*Soren Kierkegaard (1813-1855)*—Sin is the opposite of faith, or "unfaith." Whereas faith is purity of heart, to be a united person who wills only one thing, sin is *verzweiflung*, to be divided in two and pulled apart.[47]

*Karl Barth (1886-1968)*—Sin is more than simply a mistake, but is an expression of our entire human nature which wages an inward revolt against God, our Creator. No part of humanity is untouched by sin; rather, humans have a "midas touch," utilizing every aspect of their being in revolt against God.

*Paul Tillich (1886-1965)*—Sin is "the personal act of turning away from that to which one belongs." Instead of recognizing God as the ultimate concern of one's life, sin attempts to elevate anything secondary to the ultimate position.[48]

*Jurgen Moltmann (1926- )*—Sin is hopelessness, an unwillingness to trust God's promises. It is hanging on to the past, rather than entering into the future. Sin is being Lot's wife, rather than being Abraham.

Each of the above definitions has some important insights into the nature and character of sin. Perhaps one significant element which is implicit but not specifically stated in Tillich's definition is selfishness. This seems to be a basic characteristic of sin from the beginning (cf. Ge 3:5-6). In his prophecy concerning the future sufferings of the Messiah, Isaiah stated, "We all, like sheep, have gone astray, each of us has turned to his own way; and the Lord has laid on him the iniquity of us all" (Isa 53:6). A proper sense of self-respect or self-esteem does not imply selfishness. Jesus even taught His followers to love their neighbors as they loved themselves! (Mt 19:19). Rather, it is when this love of self becomes magnified and one begins to place self-interests above those of God that it can lead to sin. Simply put, sin stems from being self-centered rather than being a centered-self, whose true source and motivation is God. In contrast, Jesus

---

[47]The perspectives of Kierkegaard, Barth, and Moltmann concerning sin have been drawn from the class lectures of Theodore H. Runyon, Jr. "Contemporary Continental Theology." Emory University, Fall, 1977.

[48]Paul Tillich, *Systematic Theology* Vol. 2, 46-55.

exemplified during His earthly life what it meant to be selfless and sinless (cf. Jn 5:30; Mt 26:39, 42).

Another issue related to the doctrine of sin that merits discussion is the concept of "original sin," or what is sometimes referred to as the sinful nature of man. The origin of human sin as depicted in Genesis 3 has already been seen. The question now is why and/or how does Adam's sin affect the entire human race since the Fall? Scripture clearly affirms the universal fact of the sinful condition of human nature, and that this condition can be traced back to Adam's sin (cf. Ro 5:12: "Therefore, just as sin entered the world through one man, and death through sin, and in this way death came to all men, because all sinned . . ."). The Bible, however, is somewhat vague on the "whys" and the "hows" of this universal condition. Thus, several major possibilities have been proposed, which will be briefly examined.

Most of the early Church Fathers did not deal with this issue in their writings, but there were several exceptions. Many in the Eastern church followed the ideas of Clement and Origen (both from Alexandria, Egypt) and denied that there was any inheritance of a sin nature. Both believed that man was created with a free moral nature, and that this freedom was not affected by Adam's Fall. Origen, in particular, believed in the preexistence of the human soul; i.e., the soul eternally existed and could have freely committed sin prior to its union with a physical body. This, Origen believed, could help explain the disparity of conditions that exist on this earth—why some are born rich or impoverished, why some are physically strong or weak, etc. Thus, sin could indirectly affect individuals through the inheritance of physical corruption (as a "punishment" for sins in the soul's previous existence), but sins in this life were due strictly to the acts of the human will, not to Adam's personal Fall. In the late fourth century, Pelagius took the Eastern emphasis upon human free will and self-determination to the extreme. Pelagius taught that man has no form of inherited sin or racial depravity simply because he is a descendent of Adam. Pelagius' motto was "you ought, therefore you can," meaning that what God has commanded can be fulfilled by anyone who wills to do it. There is no sinful nature that hinders one's moral actions; rather, many commit sinful actions because they follow the bad moral examples of others. Thus, there are no "sinners," but simply individuals who commit sinful acts, but who could also will to obey God's laws.

The ancient Western Church largely followed the ideas of Tertullian and Ambrose in regard to the doctrine of original sin. Both men believed that all persons have inherited or derived a sinful tendency from Adam. This sinful "taint" has corrupted and weakened man's free will, but it has not totally destroyed it, so that fallen man may still have some "good" within him. Extending this view (and in reaction to the extreme view of Pelagius), the great Western church leader Augustine (354-430) declared that man's nature is totally corrupted by sin, and that since the Fall man has not had true freedom to will anything but evil.

In reaction to this East-West debate, a compromise position was offered in the fifth century by John Cassian. This view, later to be called Semi-Pelagianism (or depending on one's perspective, Semi-Augustinianism), stated that man's will is corrupted by the sin of Adam and that all persons since the Fall are naturally inclined to do evil. Semi-Pelagianism, however, also *denied* the *total* depravity of man and the *total* loss of the freedom of the will. Thus, even sinful man has some "goodness" and can still exercise his corrupted will to cooperate with the grace of God for salvation.

Throughout the Middle Ages and into the modern era, debate has continued on the issue of original sin, with most persons and church organizations adhering primarily to one of the above three doctrinal positions. In general, it can be stated that most of the Protestant Reformers (Luther, Calvin, etc.) followed Augustine's thinking that man's will was entirely corrupted by sin and therefore a person (the "elect") can only be redeemed by the sovereign grace of God. A left-wing theological group during the Reformation era known as the Socinians (forerunners of the modern Unitarians) adopted the Pelagian concept that there is no original sin, instead emphasizing the ability of man's free will to choose right or wrong. The Semi-Pelagian compromise was rekindled by the followers of James Arminius in the seventeenth century, and later modified by John Wesley in the eighteenth century. This position, which became popularly known as the Wesleyan-Arminian view, suggested that man's will is corrupted by the Fall, but that man still has the freedom to cooperate with God's primary or "prevenient" grace to respond to salvation. Many modern

Pentecostals adhere to this Wesleyan-Arminian understanding in regard to the doctrine of original sin. The implications of these positions will be further examined later in this book in the chapter dealing with salvation.

Those who follow either the Augustinian or the Wesleyan-Arminian view of original sin would agree that human nature is totally depraved because of sin. This would involve the inheritance or derivation of a marred and corrupted moral image which is predisposed toward evil (what some would call a "bent toward sinning"). They would agree that sinful man bears the legal guilt for Adam's sin before a just and holy God, who demands that sin must be atoned for. It is sometimes stated that man is not a sinner because he sins; rather, man sins because he is a sinner. Man's original ability not to sin (before the Fall) is now the inability not to sin (after the Fall). Because of this sinful or depraved nature, man is unable to naturally reach out to God for salvation or for any other spiritual attainment. Man is dependent upon the election and irresistable grace of God (from a Calvinist perspective) or upon the general, prevenient grace of God (from an Arminian standpoint) in order to respond to God's offer of salvation through Jesus Christ. More will be stated concerning the Calvinist/Arminian perspectives of grace and redemption in chapter 6.

A concept related to original sin is the imputation of sin; i.e., how and why has Adam's sin been transmitted from him to the entire human race? Scripture clearly indicates that sin is a universal fact (cf. Ro 3:23: ". . . for all have sinned, and fall short of the glory of God . . ."; also cf. Gal 3:22; Eph 2:3; 1Jn 1:8-10). The Bible depicts all humans as sinners in need of the redemption that can only come through Christ. The question, however, is how does Adam's sin continue to affect all of humanity? Scripture gives some general teaching regarding the imputation of Adam's sin (cf. Ro 5:12-19), however the Scripture does not give specific details. Therefore, several theories have arisen which attempt to address this issue.

The earliest theory, which stems from the period of the ancient Church Fathers, is known as the realistic theory of imputation. Augustine helped to popularize this view (hence it is also known as the Augustinian theory) which states that the entire human race was "in Adam" when he sinned. There are scriptural passages such as

Hebrews 7:9-10 which deal with persons being in the "loins of their fathers." These suggest that prior to one's birth, one shares in the actions of one's ancestors. Thus, when Adam sinned, all of humanity actually sinned because of having racial continuity with Adam and being substantially present in him. The realistic (or Augustinian) theory of imputation is associated with a view known as traducianism, that the soul of each person is biologically propagated from one's parents, their ancestors, etc., back to Adam. Many interpret David's words in a very literal fashion to support this notion: "Surely I was sinful at birth, sinful from the time my mother conceived me" (Ps 51:5).

A second major view, associated with many theologians in the Reformed tradition, is known as the representative (or federal, or covenantal) theory of imputation. This view is also linked with the concept of creationism, the doctrine that God creates each individual soul and that one does not "inherit" a soul from one's parents. The representative theory indicates that Adam served as both the natural and federal (legal) head of the human race. When Adam sinned, he was acting in this representative capacity and as a result, all humans share in the legal responsibility of that sin and now have a corrupted and depraved nature. To illustrate, when an American president declares war on an enemy nation, all Americans are considered to be at war with that enemy, even if there are some who did not originally support the president's actions. This is true because the president is the federal leader of all Americans. In a similar way, what Adam did affects all other humans who share in a covenantal relationship with Adam. Many who hold to this representative theory of imputation feel that Romans 5:12-19 supports this position, especially verses 18-19, which compare the effects of Adam's sin to the righteous work of the "Second Adam," Jesus Christ:

> Consequently, just as the result of one trespass was condemnation for all men, so also the result of one act of righteousness was justification that brings life for all men. For just as through the disobedience of the one man the many were made sinners, so also through the obedience of the one man the many will be made righteous.

Neither of these two theories are without problems. For instance, the realistic view does not adequately explain why Adam's descendants are accountable only for his first act of sin, and not for those which he undoubtedly committed later (not to mention those committed by all future generations whose sins would seem to have a cumulative effect). In a similar manner, the representative theory emphasizes the analogy between the effects of the sin of Adam and the salvation brought about by Christ. This analogy, however, is not one which is totally parallel. The sin of Adam is universally realized, but the salvation that Christ offers, while universal in extent, is limited in its application to those who receive it through faith. In addition to these two theories of imputation, there are other mediating positions. For example, Millard Erickson offers one of the better mediating views of the imputation of sin. Erickson suggests that all humans were involved in Adam's sin and have received a corrupted moral nature. The *guilt* of Adam's sin, however is only conditionally imputed, pending a conscious, voluntary decision on man's part to engage in personal sin. Thus, while there is a sinful nature, there is no condemnation until one reaches the age of moral responsibility and can exercise one's freedom to choose to accept or reject God's offer of salvation through Christ.[49]

Regardless of which theory of the imputation of sin that one accepts, one should never overlook the biblical fact that since the Fall of man, all humans have been deemed sinners in the sight of a holy God, and are in need of forgiveness. Although it is through Adam's sin that "the many were made sinners," one may rejoice that due to the obedience and righteousness of Christ those who respond to God's offer of salvation "will be made righteous" (Ro 5:19).

---

[49]Erickson, 639.

## For Reflection and Discussion

1. In what ways do the behavioral sciences (e.g. psychology, sociology) complement the theological study of anthropology? Are there any ways in which they are contradictory or opposed to the biblical perspective on the doctrine of man?

2. Discuss the major tenets held by natural evolutionists, theological evolutionists, fiat creationists, and progressive creationists concerning the origin of humankind. Which view do you accept, and why?

3. Discuss whether you believe the Bible presents man as a three-part, two-part, or holistic being. What are the implications of this in regard to salvation? in regard to death and resurrection?

4. This chapter has discussed the biblical belief that humanity is created in the image of God. What are the implications of this for modern life (e.g., how should this affect Christian social concern? race relations? etc.).

5. What does Jurgen Moltmann mean by suggesting that sin is being Lot's wife rather than being Abraham? Can you think of any way this has been illustrated in your own experience?

6. Both Calvinists and Arminians believe that because of the Fall, man is totally depraved. What do these groups mean by this, and in what ways do their interpretations differ?

# 5

# You Are the Christ!
## Matthew 16:16

THE PERSON OF JESUS CHRIST stands at the center of human history. From His birth the chronicling of human events is dated. Libraries are filled with His story; churches are filled with His praise; nations are filled with His disciples. Born into a poor Jewish family, Jesus received little honor or recognition from the religious and political leadership of His day. For a while the common people heard Him eagerly as His message of God was punctuated with miraculous doings. Not knowing that His kingdom was "not of this world," some tried to make Him their king (Jn 6:15; 18:36). His strange response was to speak of self-denial, discipleship, and the cross (Mk 8:31-35). Confused, many left Him or even turned against Him. Actually there were many things unusual about this person called Jesus. He was like them, yet different; He walked among them, yet spoke of coming from Heaven; He was a religious teacher, yet spoke as no other rabbi before Him. Throughout the land people were asking "Who is this?" "What manner of person is he?" (Lk 8:25). Friend and foe alike knew He was more than just a carpenter's son—He was God's son as well.

## Preexistence of Christ

Though both biblical and secular history attest to the existence of a person called Jesus, the Christ, who lived from around 4 B.C. to A.D. 29, it is clear that His birth in Bethlehem did not mark His beginning. Christ existed long before His birth to Mary, long before Jewish history, even long before the world was created. He is identified with the title of the God of the Old Testament indicating His existence is not only prior to Bethlehem but that He inhabits eternity with God (Mic 5:2).[1] Many believe that Christ actually appeared in human form during the Old Testament era as the Angel (Messenger) of Yahweh.[2]

The Early Church repeatedly affirmed Christ's preexistence. Jesus was God's Son sent from heaven (Mt 21:9-39; Jn 3:17-31; Gal 4:4). He was at the Father's side from the beginning prior to His being made flesh and tabernacling among mankind (Jn 1:14-18). In fact Paul and John record that His preexistence predates the creation of all other beings and things (Jn 1:1-2; Col 1:16-17). Yet He surrendered His rightful place in heaven to take the form of a man—though rich, for our sakes becoming poor (Php 2:5-11; 2Co 8:9).

Thus the Old Testament speaks of Him as already existing before Bethlehem, Jesus claims to have been sent by His Heavenly Father, and the New Testament writers present Him as one who came down

---

[1]For example He is identified with Elohim (Isa 9:6-7), Yahweh (Zec 12:10), and Adonai (Ps 110:1).

[2]In various Old Testament stories mention is made of a person distinct from Yahweh, yet to whom the titles, attributes, and works of God are ascribed (e.g. Ge 31:11-13; Ex 3:1-6; Jdg 2:1-5).

from heaven (Jn 16:28). This clear and repeated testimony of the pre-existence of Christ is inseparably linked to the claim of His deity. If Christ was not preexistent, then He could not be God—for God is eternal. However, a preexistent Christ is not automatically a divine Christ. The doctrine of His deity is an extension of His preexistence and must stand on its own merits.

## Incarnation of Christ

While it is important to affirm the preexistence of Christ, His historicity is also crucial to Christian doctrine. The Word (*Logos*) became flesh and lived and moved among mankind. This incredible event of God becoming man is called the incarnation. This is far more significant than any Old Testament theophany or mythical account of some avatar. For in the incarnation Christ does not merely come in the *appearance* of a man, but He becomes an *actual* man.

Through the incarnation the invisible God is revealed in human form. Those who saw Jesus saw the Father in the concrete expression of humanity (Jn 1:18; 14:9). His sinless life serves as an example of one's perfect devotion and obedience to God (2Co 3:18; 1Pe 2:21; 1Jn 2:6). Through Him the promise of a redeemer was fulfilled. Being "made like his brothers" He would destroy the works of the devil by doing away with sin through the sacrifice of himself (Heb 2:17, 9:26; 1Jn 3:8). Like no other priest, this high priest was both God and man.

## Virgin Birth of Christ

One of the most amazing facts of the coming of Christ to earth is the manner of His coming. Rather than arriving in great splendor as a noble adult, He comes in great humility as a helpless baby. His incarnation would include the human experiences common to the race—from birth to death. The creator God is born of a poor Jewish girl, Mary—a virgin Jewish girl!

Both Matthew and Luke provide accounts of this normal, yet miraculous birth. Matthew tells us that Joseph and Mary were betrothed or engaged. Engagement in that time and culture was legally binding and a first step in the marriage process (Mt 1:18-24). Though legally her husband, Joseph had no sexual relationship with Mary prior to the birth of Jesus (Mt 1:18,25). Therefore, when it was evident that Mary was pregnant, Joseph knew the child Mary was carrying was not his. Rather, her pregnancy is ascribed to the power of the Holy Spirit (Mt 1:18,20). In the genealogy that precedes the birth narrative, in the description, "Joseph, the husband of Mary, of whom was born Jesus, who is called the Christ," Matthew uses a genitive relative pronoun, *feminine* singular ("of whom") to ascribe the birth of Jesus to Mary and not to Joseph.

It is likely that Luke the physician would have been greatly interested in this medical impossibility of a virgin birth. As a historian he probably carefully investigated this event commonly held among the Christian community as a well developed doctrine of the middle of the first century. Luke attests to Mary being a virgin and emphasizes the extraordinary birth announcement for this extraordinary birth. The angel describes the child to be born as the "Son of the Most High," "the holy one," "the Son of God" (Lk 1:32, 35).

Without question Matthew and Luke describe the birth of Jesus to Mary the virgin. However, some have suggested that because the writers may have followed the Septuagint version of Isaiah rather than the Hebrew version the translation "virgin" is inaccurate. The Gospel writers refer to the expression "The virgin will be with child" which uses the Hebrew term *almah* for virgin. Critics say Matthew and Luke should simply have described Mary as a young woman rather than a virgin since this is the common rendering of *almah*. (The term *bethulah* is used to describe one who is in the sexual state of virginity.) However, none of the seven occurrences of *almah* in the Old Testament refer to a woman who is clearly not a virgin. An *almah* is a young woman of marriageable age. In that Jewish culture and age an *almah* would be assumed to be a virgin.[3] The technical Greek word for virgin is *parthenos*. The Septuagint as well as the Gospel writers correctly identify the *almah* as a *parthenos*. The young woman Mary, though engaged to Joseph, was a virgin.

Though Mary was a virgin one should not think that Mary contributed nothing to Jesus' humanity. God did not simply create Jesus' human nature and merely place it in Mary's womb to sustain it and give it birth. Jesus is the "seed of the woman" (Ge 3:15). The virgin both *conceives* and brings forth a son—one who is made of a

---

[3]See the Genesis 24 story of a bride for Isaac where the terms *almah* and *bethulah* are used interchangeably. Isaac certainly would have expected a virgin young lady.

woman (Mt 1:23; Lk 1:31; Gal 4:4). Jesus is a descendant of David according to His human nature (Ro 1:3).

The deity of Christ is directly connected to the doctrine of the virgin birth.[4] If born of two human parents, deity would not have been an aspect of His nature. The virgin birth is a truly miraculous and unique happening, but it is not an unnecessary and irrational happening. As is often pointed out, it would be virtually impossible to take a regular child born of two normal parents and convince one that the child is God. However, if this child Jesus is truly God, the virgin birth *is not* fanciful or strange, but to be expected as something wonderfully superordinary.

## Deity of Christ

The amazing belief that Jesus of Nazareth was also the eternal God became the prime theological interest of the apostles and early Christian theologians. Though the first followers of Jesus were predominantly Jews, and thus strict monotheists, they without hesitance or embarrassment confidently proclaimed that He was truly God.

Some have suggested that this startling acceptance of Jesus as God came about not only through what He did and said, but also because of a prevalent Jewish view of a divine Messiah. "There are few things which are more vigorously asserted . . . than that the doctrine of a superhuman Messiah was native to pre-Christian Judaism."[5] The writers of the New Testament often supported their assertions of Christ's deity by appealing to Old Testament passages which seemed to speak of a divine Messiah. For example the writer of Hebrews strings together a series of Old Testament quotations which portray the Messiah as not merely transcendent but actually deity. The Messiah rightly shares the divine designations of God, Lord, and Son of God and acts accordingly (Heb 1). The "Messianic Psalms" portray the Messiah in clearly divine terms (Pss 2, 45, 72, 110). The messianic figure presented in Daniel and other Old Testament apocalyptic writings is in some sense divine (Da 7; 23; Mic 5; Zec 9-12; Mal 3).

A puzzling parallel seemed to run throughout much of Israel's history. On the one hand Yahweh was to exercise universal reign; on

---

[4]Robert G. Gromacki, *The Virgin Birth*, 86.

[5]Benjamin B. Warfield, *Biblical and Theological Studies*, 87.

the other hand the Messiah was presented as a coming world-savior. Some viewed the Messiah as representative of and replacing the personal reign of Yahweh, however, the two streams of prediction were largely kept separate in the Old Testament. It was not until the advent of the person of Jesus of Nazareth that a personal synthesis was possible. In Him, God is with us (Immanuel) for He is both God and man.[6]

In the Gospels it is fascinating to see the dawn of acceptance by His early followers that Jesus was the promised Messiah. Such acceptance preceded His own ministry—Simeon and Anna recognized Him as the promised Messiah when Mary and Joseph presented Him in the temple soon after His birth (Lk 2:25-38). Nathaniel would have been representative of those who, hearing Jesus, recognized Him to be the Messiah promised to Israel (Jn 1:47-50). The Messiah was one who would come and heal the leper, give sight to the blind, raise the dead—Jesus performed such miracles (Isa 29:18-19; Mt 11:1-16). Peter declared "You are the Christ, the Son of the living God" (Mt 16:16). Rather than reject this profession of Peter, with an emphasis on his divine status, Jesus acknowledged this declaration of messiahship by saying that His Father had revealed this truth to Peter.

The pre-Christian conception of the Jewish Messiah involved ascribing to Him divinity. As the followers of Jesus began to accept Him as the Messiah, it meant also accepting Him as divine.

> When St. Mark tells us that St. John the Baptist was the herald of the advent of Yahweh, at the beginning of the Gospel, what else can he mean than that Jesus Christ, whose redemptive life is the theme of his Gospel, was very Yahweh.[7]

Jesus the Messiah was not merely "divine" in some abstract sense, but was deity in integrity and fullness.

## Evidences for Christ's Deity

Jesus is not presented in Scripture as the founder of another religion, but as Lord of all (Ac 10:36-42). The frequent designation "Lord" used by the biblical writers is clearly intentional. The Septuagint chose the Greek word *kurios* (Lord) as the equivalent for

---

[6]Franz Delitzsch, *Commentaries on the Old Testament*. See Delitzsch's treatment of Psalms 2, 45, 72, 110.

[7]Charles A. Briggs, quoted in Warfield, 103.

the Hebrew Yahweh. Knowingly applying this title (*kurios*) to Jesus strongly suggests the intention of declaring Jesus to be God. The declaration "Jesus is Lord" was probably the earliest of Christian confessions—it was a confession of Christ's deity.

The varied attributes of God are repeatedly applied to Jesus by the biblical writers (Jn 8:58; 16:30; Mt 18:20; Heb 13:8; Rev 1:8). Likewise, the Bible speaks of Him having the rights of deity, doing the works of deity, and holding the offices of deity. As God, He is the creator and upholder of all things (Jn 1:3; Col 1:16-17). He accepts worship and forgives sins as only God may do (Mt 9:2,6; Jn 20:25, 28). He is significantly linked with God the Father in such designations as the baptismal formula and Apostolic Benediction (Mt 28:19; 2Co 13:14). Jesus is Immanuel (God with us); the Son of God; the "exact representation" of God's being (Mt 1:22-23; Jn 10:36; Heb 1:3). Many of the statements of the Old Testament said of Yahweh are applied to Jesus in the New Testament (Isa 43:11; Ac 4:12; Zec 12:10).

Jesus is not merely a close replica, a clear refection of God, but is the very *morphe* (the true, exact form) of God (Php 2:5-6). In Him "all the fullness of the Deity lives in bodily form" (Col 2:9).

Repeatedly Jesus is explicitly called God in the Scriptures. Concerning His incarnation John says "No one has ever seen God, but God the One and Only who is at the Father's side, has made him known" (Jn 1:18). Confronted by the resurrected Christ, Thomas declared "My Lord and my God!" (Jn 20:28). This was no mere exclamation but a profession of faith. Paul shares "Christ who is God overall" with his Jewish brethren (Ro 9:5). While some see two persons, God and Christ, in this passage, both the context and the Greek construction favor the term God to be a description of Christ. Similarly, the expression "our God and Savior, Jesus Christ" speaks of *Jesus* as both our God and our Savior—the Greek grammar indicates only one person is being alluded to (Tit 2:13; 2Pe 1:1). The writer to the Hebrews tells us the Psalmist's declaration "Your throne, O God, will last for ever and ever" was spoken "about the Son" (Heb 1:8).

In the masterful prologue of his Gospel, John writes that not only was the *Logos* with God in the beginning, but also that "the Word was God" (Jn 1:1). Some, such as the Jehovah's Witnesses, have interpreted the Greek of this verse to mean that Jesus was only *a* god rather than *the* God. Their argument is based on the fact that no Greek definite article (the) precedes the word *theos* (God). Commonly the absence of the definite article means one translates the noun with the indefinite article (a)—in this case *a* god. However, Greek nouns do not always require the definite article, especially when they indicate a class, or quality of object or being. Thus *theos* may or may not have the definite article and still may be translated "God" or "the God." Sometimes the definite article is missing due to the grammatical structure of the sentence. In this verse *theos* is the first word of the clause. This is done in Greek for emphasis; and when definite nouns precede the verb they frequently lack the article. Placing a definite article before *Logos* but omitting it before *theos* lets the reader identify the subject of the sentence. In the whole prologue the question is not who God is, but who the *Logos* is. He is God—fully God. John used the only grammatical construction possible to distinguish between the two persons, Father and Logos, while indicating that the Logos was in nature deity. All one needs to do is read the Greek verses such as John 1:6, 12-13, 18 to see that *theos* without the definite article can and does refer to full deity for in these it refers to God the Father.

Jesus did not reject the opinion of others concerning His deity. Rather, His self-testimony reinforces this claim. One can hardly miss the unique manner in which He regularly referred to God as His Father (Mt 7:21; Jn 2:16; 14:20-21). An intimate filial relationship exists between the only begotten Son and His Father which transcends the spiritual relationship between God and His adopted children. His divine sonship was not just an earthly phase of existence, but an eternal relationship. Jesus was God's Son prior to the incarnation, brought that special relationship with Him from heaven, and was openly declared to be God's Son by a voice from heaven and by His resurrection (Jn 6:38-62, 7:28-29, 8:23-24; Mt 3:17; Ro 1:4). This special relationship as God's Son emphasized both His honor and equality with God (Jn 5:22-23, 14:23, 17:11). Thus the Jewish leaders "tried all the harder to kill him" because "he was even calling God his own Father, *making himself equal with God*" (Jn 5:17-18; emphasis added). Often Jesus spoke of himself in terms of "I am." Pointedly, such declarations alluded to the Old Testament identification of Yahweh as the "I Am" (Ex 3:13-14). Jesus was consciously making the claim of deity and the claim was readily understood by His Jewish audiences (Jn 8:58). Similarly, they understood that His claim "I and the Father are one" was a claim to deity. Jesus and the Father were not one person, but one essence or nature.[8] This is shown by the Jews' response who picked up stones to stone Him. "We are not stoning you for any of these [miracles] . . . but for blasphemy, because you, a mere man, *claim to be God*" (Jn 10:33; emphasis added).

## Humanity of Christ

The humanity of Jesus is more understandable than His deity, though no less amazing. God the Creator has become the human creation. The truth of Christ's deity must not detract from His true humanity.

Both Matthew and Luke provide natural human genealogies as a background for Christ's birth (Mt 1; Lk 3). Though the circumstances of His birth were unique, both gospel writers present His entrance into the world as a normal human birth (Mt 1:16-25; Lk 2:1-20). Every indication given in the Bible is that Jesus grew and developed as any other child (Lk 2:40, 52). His family, friends and others with whom He came in contact recognized Him and addressed Him as they would any other fellow human being. The Bible repeatedly refers to Jesus as a man (Ac 2:22; Ro 5:15; 1Co 15:21; 1Ti 2:5).

Jesus was not some docetic being with the mere appearance of a man. While both terms, soul and spirit, are applied to Him, He also had a true human body with the apparently normal appearance of a Jewish man (Mt 26:38; Jn 11:33; Lk 24:39; Jn 4:9; Heb 2:14; 1Jn 1:1-3). The normal physical senses also were experienced and exercised by Him. Likewise, the human psychological characteristics—intellect, emotion, and will—were evidenced in the life of Christ. He reasoned and understood; He displayed compassion and wept; He made conscious choices throughout His life. As a normal human person He grew weary, became hungry and thirsty, and was tempted in all aspects as any person is (Mt 4:2; 8:24; Jn 4:6; Heb 4:15).

An important distinction should, however, be made between Jesus and the rest of the human family. Concerning all of humanity, the Bible declares "all have sinned and fall short of the glory of God"

---

[8]The Greek word translated "one" is the neuter form *"hen"* rather than masculine *"hes"* or *"mia"* emphasizing nature or substance rather than person.

(Ro 3:23). However, the Bible clearly and emphatically testifies that Jesus was without sin, even though He experienced temptation (Jn 8:46; Heb 4:15; 1Pe 2:22; 1Jn 3:5). While His temptations were genuine, Christ demonstrated His impeccability. It is important to keep in mind that sin is not an essential component of human nature. Before the Fall, Adam was without sin. Yet he was completely human. Sin is an unnatural addition to integral human nature. Thus Jesus is completely human though He has never sinned. From His birth in Bethlehem's manger to His death on Calvary's cross, Jesus experienced life as a completely normal human being. As the sinless human person He truly died as the "just for the unjust" and became the Savior for all mankind (1Pe 3:18).

## Historical Views of Christ's Person

As one might expect, various opinions concerning the person of Jesus Christ began to be formulated and circulated. Who was this Jesus of Nazareth? The son of Joseph the carpenter, or God's Son? One of the human family, or not of this world? A Jewish teacher, or God with us? The Bible clearly witnesses to the truth of "all of the above" and many other puzzling, if not contradictory concepts. Thus in the early years of the history of the Church, a number of conflicting views of the person of Christ arose. A brief sketch of some of the more popular and widespread views follows.

Various Gnostic views of Christ were widely circulated during the first century. Some held that Jesus and the Christ were actually two different beings. Since the idea of matter being evil is a major tenet of Gnosticism, they could not accept the idea that God (who is spirit) would literally assume human flesh. They denied the reality of Christ's human body—some allowing for a "body" but one that somehow was not comprised of matter. Thus the Gnostics denied the true humanity of Christ, while also reducing or denying His full deity. Many Bible scholars believe that the seeds of Gnosticism were already present in the New Testament Church and that the biblical writers on occasion were writing to refute this early heresy (Col 3:9; 1Jn 4:2-3).

In the second and third centuries, "monarchian" views suggested the opposite, yet related, views of Christ's person. Both were concerned that the *monarchia* (absolute unity) of God be preserved. Therefore, they resisted the concept of a personal subsistence for God the Son that was separate from, or independent of, God the Father.

Dynamic Monarchianism viewed Jesus as simply a man whom God chose or "adopted" to be His son in a special unique way.[9] He had not true divine nature, but rather God's power (dynamic) communicated something of deity to Him. The time of this "adoption" is usually assigned to Christ's birth or His baptism. Though merely human, due to this adoption as God's Son, He provides an example of true godliness as He lives in the strength and guidance of God's Spirit. He is worthy of honor as God himself. Christ's true humanity is affirmed, but His true deity is denied. (Both the *logos* and the *pneuma* are impersonal attributes of God communicated to Jesus, rather than Jesus actually having a divine nature.)

Another prevalent form of Monarchianism which developed is called "modalistic monarchianism."[10] While dynamic monarchianism stressed Jesus' humanity, modalistic monarchianism emphasized His deity. There is only one God. This one God is spoken of as Father, Son, and Holy Spirit. However, modalistic monarchianism does not see these as three distinct persons as does the orthodox doctrine of the Trinity (one God manifested simultaneously as three persons). Rather, the Father is the same person as the Son and the Son is the same person as the Holy Spirit. God was not the Father, Son, and Holy Spirit at the same time, but He assumed three successive modes, or forms of manifestation. Therefore, Christ is indeed God (deity), but only had a distinct personality in His historical appearance as Jesus of Nazareth. However, the deity of modalistic monarchianism is not the deity of trinitarian orthodoxy.

A very important historical view of the person of Christ developed in the fourth century, primarily around the teachings of Arius. Arius was an influential teacher and presbyter in Alexandria who had been trained in Antioch. (The theological emphasis of Antioch was Christ's humanity, while the emphasis of Alexandria was His deity.) Arius had no trouble affirming the true humanity of Jesus. However, he wrestled with the seeming biblical contradiction that there is only one God, yet Christ is God. To solve the riddle, Arius

---

[9]See the views of such persons as Theodotus and Paul of Samosata.

[10]The best known expression of modalistic monarchianism was Sabellianism. See the views of Sabellius. A modern day version of Sabellianism is called the "Oneness" or "Jesus Only" view.

reduced the full deity of Christ by positing that the Son had a beginning while God the Father is eternal. The Father created the Son prior to all other beings and through the Son created all else. Thus Christ may be regarded as *a* god— sinless, exalted, and possessing many divine attributes—but He is less than *fully* God.[11] The main opponent of Arius was Athanasius, later Bishop of Alexandria. The issue of the full deity of Christ was so crucial to the Christian world, that the first ecumenical church council was called in A.D. 325 to debate the matter (Council of Nicaea). Arius presented his arguments for a Christ who was preexistent, but created and therefore less than fully God. Athanasius insisted that the Scriptures taught that Christ was eternal and of the same nature as the Father in all respects.[12] The council supported the position of Athanasius and adopted what is commonly called the Nicene Creed. In part it reads:

> We believe in one God . . . And in one Lord Jesus Christ, the Son of God, begotten of the Father as only begotten that is, from the essence of the Father, God from God, Light from Light, true God from true God, begotten not created, of the same essence [*homoousion*] as the Father, through whom all things came into being, both in heaven and in earth; Who for us men and for our salvation came down and was incarnate, becoming human. . . .[13]

This decision, made at Nicaea and reaffirmed in A.D. 381 at the Second Ecumenical Council at Constantinople, essentially remains the orthodox view on the doctrine of Christ' deity.

It would be a mistake to think that these important church councils determined the doctrine of Christ's person. It would also be a mistake to think that the decisions of these councils ended all conflict about Christ's person. From the outset Christianity believed Christ to be a Divine-Human redeemer. It is the Scripture that sets forth the testimony to both His deity and humanity and determines who Christ is for the Church. The value of the councils was the study

---

[11]Arianism's view of Christ is largely continued today in the view of Christ held by the Jehovah's Witnesses.

[12]Much of the controversy centered on the expressions *homoousion to patri*, "of the same essence as the Father," (Athanasius), *heterousion*, "of different essence," (Arius), and *homoiousion* "of *like* essence" (Eusebius of Caesarea).

[13]John H. Leith, ed., *Creeds of the Church*, revised edition, 30-31.

of the Scripture and the affirmation of what the Scripture teaches. By the fourth century it was generally held that the Bible taught both the deity and humanity of Jesus. However, continuing controversy swirled around the question of the relationship of these two natures. Debate over the "hypostatic union" dealt with the issue of the union of the divine and human natures in the person of Jesus Christ.

One of the early fourth century attempts to explain the hypostatic union was by Apollinaris, bishop of Laodicea. He suggested that the divine *Logos* actually served as the mind/spirit for the person of Jesus. Thus Apollinaris reduced the true humanity of Christ by simply having God clothed in human flesh not assuming an integral human nature. Apollinarianism was condemned at the Second Ecumenical Council of Constantinople in 381.

Nestorius, bishop of Constantinople, suggested another explanation of how Jesus could be both God and man at the same time. He proposed that Jesus Christ did have two complete natures, human and divine. However, these were not united in the one person of Christ. The divine *Logos* dwelled as a distinct person within the human person of Jesus. Thus while affirming full deity and full humanity, Nestorius admitted no true union in the one person Jesus Christ, but maintained two separate persons, one human and one divine, both housed in the human body of Jesus. Nestorianism was first condemned in 431 at the Third Ecumenical Council of Ephesus.

One of the main opponents of Nestorius was an Alexandrian monk named Eutyches. In his desire to champion the union of the two natures in only *one* person, Jesus, Eutyches went to the opposite extreme of Nestorianism. He insisted that after the incarnation there was only one nature, that of the Word made flesh. True deity united with true humanity but did not remain distinct and with integrity. Instead, these two natures formed one mixed third nature (a *tertium quid*). Thus, instead of two complete natures Jesus only had this one mixed nature. Both Christ's humanity and deity were reduced by Eutyches.

Eutychianism (and again Nestorianism) was condemned at the important Fourth Ecumenical Council of Chalcedon in 451. More importantly the Council set forth in the Definition of Chalcedon a positive view of the two natures of Jesus Christ, the God-man, which is consistent with biblical teaching. In part the Definition of Chalcedon reads:

[We also teach] that we apprehend this one and only Christ—Son, Lord, only-begotten—in two natures; [and we do this] without confusing the two natures, without transmuting one nature into the other, without dividing them into two separate categories, without contrasting them according to area or function. The distinctiveness of each nature is not nullified by the union. Instead, the "properties" of each nature are conserved and both natures concur in one "person" and in one *hypostasis*. They are not divided or cut into two *prosopa*, but are together the one and only and only-begotten Logos of God, the Lord Jesus Christ. Thus have the prophets of old testified; thus the Lord Jesus Christ himself taught us; thus the Symbol of the Fathers [N] has handed down to us.[14]

The conclusion of the Council of Chalcedon remains the orthodox view of the person of Christ.

## Unity of Christ's Natures

Jesus Christ is a theanthropic person—the God-man. He is unique in being only one person, yet having two complete natures—human and divine. To understand how these two natures are united and function in the person of Jesus goes beyond human comprehension. However, there are certain things the Scripture explicitly or implicitly teaches about this hypostatic union. Christ is a divine-human person who was first a divine person only. This divine person added a human nature (not a human person) in the incarnation. There is continuity of person—the person who was the divine preexistent *Logos* is the same person that is Jesus, the Christ. Jesus is not "humanized deity" or "deified humanity" but the one eternal person who now has two full, integral natures that are united but not mixed. Jesus was conscious of both natures even as He functioned as one person (speaking of himself He used "I" or "me" not "we" or "us"). The hypostatic union eliminates separate, independent personal subsistence of either nature. They function together. Emphasis should be on the one person, not on trying to divide the activities of the two natures. However, the two natures retain their own properties and effect the other.

---

[14]Ibid., 36.

As a result of the union of the human and divine natures, a three-fold communication takes place.[15] First, the properties of each nature are now considered to be the properties of the *person*. Thus the person of the God-man can be described as omnipotent, eternal, and immutable while at the same time described as weary, limited by time, and growing in knowledge. This communication of properties does not mean that characteristics peculiar to one *nature* are communicated to the other *nature*. Second, Christ's work of redemption is a divine-human work. Both natures, each in their particular operations, contributed to the work of the divine-human redeemer. It is proper to speak of the "blood of God" shed for man's redemption. Yet, Jesus is not merely a human robot, blindly obeying the wishes of a divine director. Gethsemane is genuine human struggle as Jesus prepares to lay down His life for His friends (Jn 15:13). Third, by virtue of the union of the two natures, the human nature is exalted and attributed with the value of the divine. Because of this union, the God-man becomes the object of praise and adoration—the Lamb, worthy to receive "praise and honor and glory and power, for ever and ever" (Rev 5:13).

It is important to remember that the hypostatic union is an indissoluble union. While this union began at the incarnation of Christ, it did not end with His ascension. Christ remains the God-man in heaven today and for eternity.

## Kenosis—Christ Emptied Himself

Although the decision of Chalcedon has remained the orthodox statement on the person of Christ, about the middle of the nineteenth century several variations of kenotic theories began to circulate.[16] These views center on the interpretation of the Greek verb *ekenosen* found in Philippians 2:7 and sometimes translated "he emptied himself." (The name of the view, kenosis, comes from this Greek word.) This passage of Scripture tells us that Christ who was in the

---

[15]Communication of properties, *communicatio idiomatum*; communication of operations, *communicatio operationum*; communication of grace, *communicatio charismatum*. See Louis Berkhof, *Systematic Theology*, 324.

[16]Representative historic proponents of different kenotic views include Charles Gore; H.W. Beecher; F. Delitzch.

form of God emptied himself and took the form of a man. The question of these kenotic theories concerns "of what did Christ empty himself?" Some have wrongly suggested that He emptied himself of at least some of His divine attributes. However, such a view ignores the immutability of God, destroys the doctrine of Trinity, and assumes a pantheistic conception of God. It wrongly attaches the verb *ekenosen* to the phrase "form of God" (*morphe theou*). The verb is better translated "made himself nothing" (RSV) and contrasts His position of equality with God. Rather than empty himself of divine attributes (an impossibility), He exchanged the glories and privileges of His position as God for the servant existence of humanity. Paul does not teach that Jesus who once was God, in the incarnation became a man instead. Rather, he teaches that though He was (and is) God, in the incarnation He *also* became a man. To accomplish the plan of redemption Christ also imposed a self-limitation of the *exercise* of some of His divine attributes. However, even in this self-limitation He always has been fully God.

Nearly 900 years ago Anselm asked, "If a sacrifice for man's sin must be made, why must Jesus the God-Man be it?" His own answer was contained in his theological masterpiece *Cur Deus Homo* (*Why the God-Man?*) He pointed out that God became a man in Jesus Christ because only one who was both fully God and fully man could achieve humanity's redemption.

## Work of Christ

The work of Christ will briefly be expressed by considering His offices of Prophet, Priest, and King. Jesus was the great Prophet whom Moses predicted would arise (Dt 18:15-18; Ac 3:22-23). Both the people who followed Him and those who simply witnessed His public ministry described Him as a prophet (Mt 21:46; Lk 24:19; Jn 6:14). Jesus even referred to himself as a Prophet (Mk 6:4). Jesus fulfilled the central role of a prophet, being God's messenger who speaks in God's name and with His authority. The message He brought from the Father was confirmed by the mighty miracles He performed (Jn 8:26-28; Mt 8, 9). Jesus was greater than the other prophets of God. Others were simply channels for the Word of God; Jesus was himself the Word of God. The whole of His person, life, and work revealed the Father (Jn 8:26, 14:19). He not only spoke the truth, but declared that He is the Truth and called men and women to follow Him (Jn 14:6).

The work of Jesus was also a priestly work. As a priest He was man's representative with God. The theme of the *Epistle to the Hebrews* is the superior priesthood of Jesus, the great High Priest. In the incarnation Jesus was made like His brethren so that he could be "a merciful and faithful high priest in service to God" (Heb 2:17). While earthly priests themselves were sinful, and had to offer sacrifice for their own sins, Jesus was sinless (Heb 7:26-27). As priest He made atonement for the people. However, He was both the one who offered the sacrifice and the sacrifice itself (Heb 9:11-14). All previous sacrifices for sin only had merit in that they prefigured this sacrifice of himself. The sacrifice of His own blood was both complete and eternal—He offered himself for sins once, forever (Heb 10:12-14). Jesus the priest continues to make intercession for His people. Such intercession is not supplemental to His work on the cross, but consequential to it (Heb 7:25). See Chapter 6 for a more complete discussion of Christ's work of atonement.

Jesus fulfilled the prophecies of a Messiah King (Isa 9:6-7; Da 7:13-14; Mic 5:2). Even at His birth, the Magi searched for the one who was born King (Mt 2:1-2). At His death Pilate placed a sign "King of the Jews" atop His cross (Jn 19:21). Much of His message centered on the Kingdom of God with He himself as the King (Mt 4:17). His kingdom is not of this world (Jn 18:36). It is a spiritual kingdom as He rules in the hearts and over the lives of those who accept His lordship (Mt 8:11-12, 21:43; Lk 17:21; Jn 18:36; Ro 14:17). Through spiritual birth one is translated from the kingdom of darkness to the kingdom of God's dear Son (Jn 3:3, 5; Col 1:13). The one who believes in Him already participates in the life of the kingdom. One day He will demonstrate His rule over all the earth as King of Kings and His followers will rule and reign with Him (Rev 5:10, 19:16).

## The Resurrection of Christ

The main purpose of the incarnation was for Christ to be that lamb of sacrifice to take away the sin of the world (Jn 1:29). His death brought redemption, forgiveness, and reconciliation to mankind. The wonderful blessings of Christ's atonement discussed in Chapter 6 are made sure through the event of Christ's resurrection. Not only was Jesus "delivered over to death for [on account of] our sins," but also

He "was raised to life for [on account of] our justification" (Ro 4:25).[17] The assurance that the believer has that God accepted the death of Jesus as the sacrifice for one's sin is that He also raised Jesus from the dead.

As is true of His death, the resurrection of Christ is an historical event. His resurrection is not merely a faith event, but an actual rising from the dead; not merely a spiritual happening, but a bodily resurrection. It was a body with flesh and bone which could be seen and touched, yet it was changed, free from normal limitations (Lk 24:37-39; Jn 20:19). Christ was not simply resuscitated, coming back to life as others before had miraculously done, but He was resurrected—made alive never to die again. His resurrection and "glorified" body prefigures and guarantees the believer's own resurrection (1Co 15:45-49).

Though Jesus had foretold His rising from the dead, it was more than His dejected followers could believe and expect (Mt 20:18-19; Mk 9:10). But they were soon convinced, for He spent forty days among them showing himself to be truly alive (Ac 1:3). Thus in the witness of the Early Church the message of Christ's resurrection was heralded as the natural conclusion to His redemptive act on the cross (Ac 4:10).

The credibility of the resurrection event is crucial to the gospel (1Co 15:3-4). If Christ did not rise from the dead the Christian's faith is in vain and humankind is left in their sins (1Co 15:14-17). However, as amazing as the resurrection is, it is a well attested event. The Bible records more than ten specific appearances after His resurrection (Mt 28:9, 16-17; Mk 16:12-13, 19; Lk 24:34; Jn 20:19, 24, 26, 21:1; 1Co 15:6-8). He appeared to individuals, to small groups, and to a crowd of more than five hundred at the same time. These appearances took place at different times, at different places, and under different circumstances. He had to convince the skeptical such as doubting Thomas—and convince them He did (Jn 20:26-30). They talked with Him, held on to Him, and ate with Him. By the time He ascended back into the heavens, there was no doubt that He was indeed alive!

---

[17]The most common translation of the preposition *dia* used with the accusative case is "on account of." The same Greek pronoun construction is used in both halves of the verse.

The tomb was empty! He had conquered death and the grave (Mt 28:1-7). Vainly critics have tried to explain away the empty tomb through theories of fraud, or a mistaken grave, or fainting rather than death. The Early Church knew He was alive and His followers were prepared to preach that truth at the risk of their own lives (Ac 2:33-34; 5:27-32). Though the early Christians were primarily Jewish and thus held the Sabbath sacred, in honor of Jesus' resurrection they began to meet on the first day of the week (1Co 16:2). The Lord of the Sabbath was also the Lord of Life!

## Christ's Ascension and Exaltation

Having completed His earthly redemptive mission, Jesus ascended to His Father again (Ac 1:9). He ascended as the God-man, retaining His human nature. His humanity remained full and true, but changed in that He ascended with a glorified, resurrected body. The believer's humanity will likewise be changed after this pattern (1Co 15).

The ascended Christ is the exalted Lord. The glory which He shared with His Father prior to the incarnation has been restored. His name is above every name and every knee will one day bow before Him and every tongue will confess that He is Lord (Jn 17; Php 3:21). Though physically localized in heaven, He is spiritually present everywhere and is at the center of man's worship (1Co 1:2; Jn 4:24). As the exalted Head of His Church He continues to work His will throughout all the earth (Eph 4:8-13). One day the ascended, exalted Lord will return for those who love Him and look for His appearing (Heb 9:28).

## For Reflection and Discussion

1. Reflect upon the marvelous miracle of the Incarnation. Try to think of a present analogy which would help convey the idea in some small way.

2. Why is it important to the Christian that Jesus is God? Do you think it is necessary for a person to believe in the deity of Jesus in order to be saved? Explain.

3. Think of several areas of living that are basic to humanity. Reflect on how Jesus, who was fully human, handled these areas of life.

4. Do a comparison study of the Arian view of the person of Christ with the view of the Jehovah's Witnesses.

5. The resurrection of Jesus is one of the most important Christian doctrines. Think of some possible ways of trying to communicate this unique event to modern man in secular, technological culture.

# Such a Great Salvation
## Hebrews 2:3

SALVATION! The very term evokes joy and hope in the hearts of those who are redeemed, and fear and uneasiness within those who do not know the Lord. Even among some, however, who experientially know the blessings of having their sins forgiven, there is often a lack of thorough biblical and theological understanding of what it means to be saved. It is the purpose of this chapter to delineate more fully for the reader the major components of soteriology, the doctrine of salvation.

It is sometimes suggested that the overall theme of Scripture is redemption. God's plan of salvation is interwoven like a thread through all the other great doctrines of the Bible, providing them with harmony and continuity of purpose. The proclamations of the Old Testament prophets anticipated, and the messages of the New Testament apostles further explicated, the primary purpose for the coming of the Messiah:

> For God so loved the world that he gave his one and only Son, that whoever believes in him shall not perish but have eternal life. For God did not send his Son into the world to condemn the world, but to save the world through him (Jn 3:16-17).

A proper starting place, then, for understanding salvation is to focus on the purpose of Christ's coming—to give His life as an atoning sacrifice for the sins of the world.

## Atonement

The doctrine of the atonement has frequently been referred to as "the heart of the gospel." This is given further meaning when one considers that Christ's sacrificial death on Calvary was a part of the eternal plan and purpose of God, and was not merely an "afterthought" in light of human sinfulness. Christ is described in Scripture as "the Lamb that was slain from the creation of the world" (Rev 13:8). It is the atoning death of Christ that provides the basis upon which God accepts His saving work and applies it to sinful humanity. It is through the atonement that God and humanity are brought together and their fellowship restored. In fact, the term atonement is sometimes popularly divided and pronounced as "at-one-ment," indicating that the work of Christ at Calvary provides the means for God and the sinner to be made "at one."[1]

Some have questioned why Christ's death was necessary for sinful humanity to be forgiven. Since God is omniscient and knew that Adam's Fall would occur, and since God is omnipotent and sovereign, could He not therefore have kept Adam from sinning, or at least provided another "out" for sinful humankind besides the death of His Son? The answer to such questions is, of course, that the atoning death of Christ was the only means by which God could forgive the world.

---

[1] It is normally grammatically erroneous to arbitrarily divide words in this fashion; however, in this case it is appropriate. The *New Oxford Dictionary* indicates that the term "atonement" is an Anglo-Saxon word which dates from the sixteenth century, and is taken from two separate words, "at onement," meaning to have a harmonious relationship with another.

As noted in the chapter on anthropology, God created humankind in His image, which included a free will that enabled humans to make moral decisions. Because of Adam's initial choice to sin, the entire human race is deemed guilty and deserving of punishment. On the other hand, God is a holy God who cannot tolerate sin and whose righteousness demands that justice be served; yet He is also a loving God, who desires to be merciful and pardon the guilty. Further, God is not like a human person who can experience an internal struggle to act in ways that are contrary to His nature. God's attributes are part of His very nature, and are not in tension with one another. Perhaps it could be said that it was *both* the love and the justice of God which caused the atoning death of God's Son. Christ's sacrificial death did not produce God's love for the world; rather, it was the greatest expression of that love. Similarly, Jesus' death most clearly exemplified that sin is intolerable to a holy and righteous God. Thus, God's justice and His love are not contradictory, but are complementary and operate in harmony. God's love is a just love; His justice is a loving justice. By sending His Son to die on the Cross, God's justice was satisfied in that the penalty for sin was meted out, and His love was manifested in that Christ bore the sins of the world, sparing the human race. Erickson notes that God's holy justice required a payment of the penalty for sin, and His love provided that payment through the atoning death of Jesus Christ.[2]

The nature of the atonement is depicted in Scripture through the use of several key terms. The word "atonement" in the Old Testament is usually translated from the Hebrew *kaphar* ("to cover, to propitiate"). The concept of atonement is frequently seen in the Old Testament sacrificial system. "Salvation by faith" was very much a part of the Old Testament ritual. It was through faith that the person offering the sacrifice trusted in a holy and loving God to accept the sacrifice as an atonement for sin, thus providing a "covering" both for the sins (cf. Pss 78:38, 79:9) as well as for the sinner (cf. Lev 4:20, 5:18). Several meaningful images are used in the Old Testament to indicate how the sincere believer trusted that Yahweh had indeed forgiven one's sins. In Isaiah's vision of the holy God, the prophet was assured "your guilt

---

[2]Millard J. Erickson, *Christian Theology*, 818.

is taken away and your sin atoned for" (Isa 6:7). Other references in the book of Isaiah indicate that God has cast one's sins behind His back (38:17); that God is the One who "blots out your transgressions, for my own sake, and remembers your sin no more" (43:25); and that God has "swept away" the offenses of the repentant sinner so that one's sins have vanished "like the morning mist" (44:22). In comparable fashion, the prophet Micah declares that when sin is atoned for God "will tread our sins underfoot and hurl all our iniquities into the depths of the sea" (7:19). Using a different image to convey the same extent of God's forgiveness, the Psalmist (103:12) asserts that "as far as the east is from the west, so far has he removed our transgressions from us." The point of each of these references is that when God accepts the offering for atonement, God *completely* forgives and pardons the transgressor so that the sin is remembered no more!

The New Testament uses several terms which convey a similar idea to the Old Testament word *kaphar*. The Greek term *hilasterion* is variously translated as "atonement," "propitiation," or "expiation" (a comparison of Romans 3:25 in the NIV, NASB, KJV, and RSV will illustrate this). The connotation of this term is to appease the wrath of God which is directed toward sin, and thus to provide the way for God and the sinner to be brought together. This is the image communicated by the translation of *hilasterion* in Hebrews 9:15 as "mercy seat" (or "atonement cover," NIV) , i.e., the place in the Old Testament Temple where the blood of the sacrifice was presented before God on the Day of Atonement (cf. Ex 25:17ff, 30:10). While the term *hilasterion* is sometimes translated as either propitiation or expiation, some theologians point out that these two words relate a slightly different perspective on the meaning of atonement. Most would agree that propitiation is directed toward God, appeasing or propitiating His wrath, whereas expiation pertains more to taking away the guilt and canceling the punishment of the sinner. Wiley states that "The wrath or displeasure of God is propitiated, the sin is expiated."[3] Williams agrees with this notion, but prefers the term expiation to propitiation (especially in the translation of Ro 3:25) because he feels the latter term may imply that God only becomes

---

[3]H. Orton Wiley, *Christian Theology,* Vol. 2, 295.

gracious and turns away His wrath after Christ's death, whereas he believes expiation portrays God as already gracious and that the sacrifice of Christ is His action to change the sinful human condition.[4] The New International Version seems to capture both of these aspects by translating the term *hilasterion* as "sacrifice of atonement" and adding in a footnote that the term portrays Christ "as the one who would turn aside his [God's] wrath, taking away sin" (Ro 3:25; cf. Heb 2:17; 1Jn 2:2, 4:10).

Another New Testament word which is closely associated with the Hebrew *kaphar* ("atonement") and the Greek *hilasterion* ("propitiation") is "reconciliation," from the Greek *katallage*. Perhaps the three terms could be related by saying that the atoning death of Christ is the cause of propitiation (turning away the wrath of God and bringing the sinner "face-to-face" with God) and effects in reconciliation (canceling the enmity and restoring the relationship between God and the pardoned sinner). Bancroft states it in this manner: "God is propitiated, and the sinner is reconciled."[5] The apostle Paul concisely summarizes this latter aspect in Romans 5:10-11:

> For if, when we were God's enemies, we were reconciled to him through the death of his Son, how much more, having been reconciled, shall we be saved through his life! . . . we also rejoice in God through our Lord Jesus Christ, through whom we have now received reconciliation [or, 'the atonement,' KJV].

In another letter, Paul indicates that "God was reconciling the world to himself in Christ, not counting men's sins against them" (2Co 5:19). It is significant to note that God has already been reconciled to humanity through the atoning work of Christ. It remains for humanity to be reconciled to God, through accepting the saving work of His Son (cf. 2Co 5:20: "We implore you on Christ's behalf: Be reconciled to God").

While there are numerous other New Testament words which relate to the meaning of the atonement, one final term which will be observed in this context is "redemption." Scripture indicates that in Christ "we have redemption through his blood, the forgiveness of

---

[4]J. Rodman Williams, *Renewal Theology*, Vol. 1, 360, n. 18.

[5]Emery Bancroft, *Christian Theology*, second revised edition, 115.

sins . . ." (Eph 1:7; cf. Col 1:14). The concept of redemption is from the Greek *lutrosis*, which signifies a buying back from captivity through the payment of a price. Paul alludes to this concept in 1 Corinthians 6:19—"You are not your own; you were bought at a price." The Bible clearly indicates that the price of redemption was of inestimable value—the very life blood of Christ. Comparing the voluntary and ultimate self-sacrifice of Christ to the priestly sacrifices which needed frequent repetition in the Old Testament, the writer of Hebrews states that Christ "did not enter by means of the blood of goats and calves; but he entered the Most Holy Place once for all by his own blood, having obtained eternal redemption" (Heb 9:12). As the noted theologian Dietrich Bonhoeffer declared, the grace which is provided through the redemptive act of Christ is always free, but it is never cheap.[6] This thought would certainly concur with Jesus' words found in Matthew 20:28, ". . .the Son of Man did not come to be served, but to serve, and to give his life as a ransom [*lutron*] for many."

## Theories of the Atonement

Throughout the history of Christianity, various theories have been offered in an attempt to fully explain the character and significance of Christ's atoning death. While an in-depth examination of these theories is beyond the scope of this volume, several of the more prominent views will be briefly discussed.

One of the oldest theories, dating back to the third century, is the Ransom Theory (sometimes also referred to as the Ransom-to-Satan Theory). Origen, a major proponent of this view, believed that fallen humanity was held captive by the devil and could not be liberated until the proper ransom was paid. Christ's death provided this ransom to Satan, who was essentially "deceived" in the transaction, thinking that he would now retain the soul of Jesus, a far more valuable prize. What Satan did not count on was that Jesus had not forsaken His deity and the devil could not prevent the resurrection of Christ. Thus, Satan lost possession of both the souls of humans who died before the Cross, and of the Son of God, whose death provided total deliverance. The problems with this view are many, including a lack of Scriptural support (especially in that it sees the atonement directed to Satan

---

[6]Cf. Dietrich Bonhoeffer, *The Cost of Discipleship*, revised edition.

rather than to God), a portrayal of deceptive actions on the part of Christ, and giving Satan more power (almost an evil, divine status) than Scripture allows. In spite of the theological difficulties with this theory, it held popularity for nearly a thousand years, and has been given renewed emphasis in some modern charismatic circles. To be certain, Scripture indicates that Christ did give His life as a ransom for many (cf. Mt 10:28; Heb 9:15), but the price of redemption was offered to propitiate God's justice, and not in any way to "bribe" or accommodate Satan (cf. Lev 4:35; Ro 3:25-26; 1Jn 4:10).

A popular theory in the Middle Ages was known as the Satisfaction Theory (also the Commercial Theory, or the Anselmic Theory, after its originator Anselm of Canterbury [1033-1109]). The emphasis here was that sin violated the honor and dignity of God, and deserved eternal punishment. In order to satisfy the demands of a majestic God, Christ went to the Cross, taking upon Himself the exact equivalence of the deserved sufferings of sinful humanity, thus allowing them to be pardoned. While this theory proved to be a more credible doctrine of the atonement than the Ransom Theory (and finally helped to diffuse its popularity), it was still less than complete. For example, it places great emphasis on the honor of God, but says nothing about His essential holiness and justice. This theory also minimizes the significance of Christ taking upon Himself the nature of humanity and living a sinless life. Further, it depicts the Cross event more as a commercial transaction (transferring the merits of Christ to humanity) than as the vicarious sufferings of the Savior for the sins of the world.

Two theories which are somewhat related in that both emphasize the primary purpose of Christ's death to be its influence upon humanity are the Moral Influence Theory and the Example Theory. The Moral Influence Theory was first advocated by Peter Abelard (1079-1143) in reaction to Anselm's theory, and was later popularized in America by Horace Bushnell in the nineteenth century. This view emphasizes that there was nothing within God's nature that demanded satisfaction for sin; likewise, Christ's death was not for the purpose of providing a propitiation for sin. Instead, God is a God of love, and Christ died in order to manifest that love to the world, so that the hearts of humankind would become responsive to God's love and repent of sin. In a similar vein, the Example Theory (also called the Socinian theory, after the sixteenth century group who became the forerunners of modern Unitarianism) taught that God does not need to have His justice satisfied in order to pardon humanity from sin, thus an atonement was unnecessary. According to this theory, Christ died as a martyr, being put to death by His enemies who resented His high ethical standards and principles. Thus, His death does not atone for sin, but rather serves as an example for others to learn true obedience and devotion to the ways of God. Both of these theories, in their attempt to morally and ethically persuade humans to follow the ways of God, fall miserably short of the biblical teaching concerning both the dreadful reality of human sin and the unfathomable virtue of a holy God.

The view of the atonement adhered to by most conservative theologians is commonly referred to as the Penal-Substitutionary doctrine. The emphasis of this view is that the atoning death of Christ was an objective act directed toward God in order to propitiate His justice. God's holy nature is offended by sin and results in wrath towards sinful humanity (cf. Ro 1:18-19; Eph 2:3). In order to satisfy the justice of God, the sinless Christ took the place of sinful humanity, becoming their "vicar" or substitute, and bore the sin and the penalty deserved by the world. Centuries before Christ, the prophet Isaiah spoke of the vicarious work of the Messiah, proclaiming that "the LORD has laid on him the iniquity of us all . . . he poured out his life unto death . . . For he bore the sin of many, and made intercession for the transgressors" (Isa 53:6, 12). After the fulfillment of this prophecy, the apostle Paul declared that "God made him [Christ] who had no sin to be sin [i.e., a sin offering] for us, so that in him we might become the righteousness of God" (2Co 5:21). Paul further encapsulates the truth of the Penal-Substitutionary atonement when he states:

> But God demonstrates his own love for us in this: While we were still sinners, Christ died for us. Since we have now been justified by his blood, how much more shall we be saved from God's wrath through him! For if, when we were God's enemies, we were reconciled to him through the death of his Son, how much more, having been reconciled, shall we be saved through his life! (Ro 5:8-10)

Thus the Penal-Substitutionary view of the atonement seems to adhere to the overall teaching of Scripture regarding the purpose and meaning of Christ's death. He suffered the penalty for the sins of the world by becoming the vicar of humankind, taking their place. No person or power "forced" Jesus to do this; rather, He voluntarily gave Himself to do what no other could do (cf. Jn 10:17-18, 15:13). Erickson insightfully remarks that because the Father and the Son are one, there is a true sense in which the work of Christ was also a work which involved the Father. In this way, "the Father did not place the punishment upon someone other than himself."[7] Through the atoning work of Christ, God is both the judge who passes the sentence, and the One who pays the penalty.

## Calvinism vs. Arminianism

As indicated above, most evangelical Christians would agree that salvation is made possible because of the atoning death of Jesus Christ. How that salvation is applied to individual persons, however, has been a matter of considerable controversy throughout the history of Christian thought. Since the Protestant Reformation of the sixteenth century, most Protestants (including Evangelicals and Pentecostals) have tended to identify their understanding of soteriology with one of two schools of thought: Calvinism or Arminianism.

John Calvin (1509-1564) was the recognized leader of the second generation of the Reformation, and one of the most influential theologians to emerge from that important era. Calvin's overall theology was expressed in his four volume *Institutes of the Christian Religion*. Throughout this work, Calvin placed great emphasis on the absolute sovereignty of God. Obviously, with such a thorough and complex theological system, it is difficult to condense Calvin's view of salvation into a brief form; however, many of Calvin's followers through the centuries have presented what they feel to be the major essentials of Calvin's understanding of salvation using a five point formula. Employing an acrostic format of the word "tulip," the five key points of Calvin's soteriology are summarized as:

> T—*Total Depravity*. This is the belief that the guilt of Adam's sin has been imputed to all persons, so that there is nothing one can do to effect one's salvation.

> U—*Unconditional Election*. Borrowing from Augustine's earlier doctrine of double predestination, Calvin taught that God

---

[7]Erickson, *Christian Theology*, 817.

has predetermined who should be saved and who should be lost. This "election" is unconditional in that there is nothing one can do to influence God's sovereign decision.

L—*Limited Atonement* (or as some Calvinists prefer, *Particular Atonement*). The death of Christ was vicarious only for the elect, and has no significance for the non-elect.

I—*Irresistable Grace.* This again pertains only to the elect, and indicates that they cannot continually reject the grace of God that leads them to a saving knowledge of Him.

P—*Perseverance of the Saints.* Those who have been predestined for salvation, for whom Christ died, and who could not refrain from submitting to the saving grace of God, can never lose their salvation, but are eternally secure in their election.

It should be emphasized that not all modern Christians who identify with Calvinism have identical beliefs in regard to salvation. While there are still some who adhere to what is popularly regarded as "five point Calvinism" (as stated above), many others have modified these views. For example, some "moderate Calvinists" believe that Christ's death was sufficient for anyone who responds in faith to be saved. They also teach that predestination is not arbitrary, and that it is possible to reject the convicting power of the Holy Spirit which leads to repentance. Most moderate Calvinists, however, hold firmly to points one (total depravity) and five (perseverance) of the above "tulip" doctrine.

In response to Calvin's teaching on salvation, a Dutch professor of Reformed theology named James Arminius (1560-1609) protested against the above five points. While agreeing with Calvin that God alone is sovereign, Arminius believed that Calvin did not allow enough room in his theology for the free moral agency of human beings. Arminius believed that humans have more choice to respond to God, whether positively or negatively, than Calvinism allowed. Arminius' essential teachings in response to Calvin's "tulip" theory may be seen in the chart following.

Although Arminius died before his views gained widespread recognition, his followers kept what became known as "Arminianism" alive. In particular, John Wesley (eighteenth century) adapted the Arminian view of salvation to the theology of Methodism, which in turn had a strong influence on the later Holiness and Pentecostal movements. It would seem accurate to say that most modern Pentecostals are more Armininan than Calvinist in their soteriology, although Pentecostals differ among themselves, especially in the area of sanctification.

| CALVINISM | ARMINIANISM |
|---|---|
| *Total Depravity*: All persons are sinful as a result of their racial continuity with Adam. There is nothing inherently "good" within humanity that can enable one to choose salvation; it is totally a work of God's grace. | It is true that all humans are depraved since Adam's Fall; however, even in this sinful condition humans are able to respond to the "primary grace" of God and can cooperate with God for salvation. |
| *Unconditional Election*: God sovereignly elects some for salvation and others for condemnation without condition. | "Election" is conditional, based on one's response to God in faith. God foreknows who will believe and be saved, but He does not compel them to believe. |
| *Limited Atonement*: Christ's death on the Cross is particular—only for those whom God has elected. | The atoning death of Christ is unlimited and available to all. |
| *Irresistible Grace*: The elect cannot forever resist the saving grace of God, but will eventually yield and be saved. | Because of their free will, humans can resist and reject God's gracious offer of salvation. |
| *Perseverance of the Saints*: The elect can never lose their salvation, but are kept eternally secure by the grace of God. | While God is faithful and able to sustain the saints in their Christian walk, it is still possible to reject Him after one has been saved and to lose one's salvation. |

## The Role of the Holy Spirit in Salvation

Later chapters of this book will deal with the person and work of the Holy Spirit. It would be remiss, however, to overlook the vital role which the Spirit performs in the process of salvation. As with the other persons of the Triune God, all three of whom always work in interdependence, the Holy Spirit has certain functions which might be considered "primary" to Him. In a broad manner, the Holy Spirit is usually depicted in Scripture as transmitting and applying to the believer the work of the Father and the Son. This is especially evident concerning salvation.

It is the Holy Spirit who convicts the unsaved of their sinful condition and prepares their hearts to receive the saving grace of God (cf. Jn 16:8-11). Thus the Spirit becomes the agent of salvation (Jn 3:5-8), mediating the reality of salvation to the newly born again believer. In this regard the Holy Spirit is referred to as the Spirit of Adoption (Ro 8:15-16), the One who confirms that the believer now belongs to the family of God. The Spirit is also the primary agent of sanctification, working in the believer's life and enabling the believer to become more conformed to the image of Christ (cf. Ro 8:13-14, 15:16; 2Th 2:13; 1Pe 1:2).

It is important to note that from the moment one becomes a Christian, the Holy Spirit indwells the life of every believer. Paul indicated that the born again believer is no longer controlled by the sinful nature, but by the indwelling Spirit of God. "And if anyone does not have the Spirit of Christ, he does not belong to Christ" (Ro 8:9; cf. Jn 14:16-17). This abiding and indwelling presence of the Spirit is often confused by non-Pentecostals with what the Bible terms the "baptism with the Holy Spirit." For example, Thiessen incorrectly asserts that "This baptism takes place at the moment of salvation."[8] As noted in chapter 8, Scripture clearly distinguishes between salvation and receiving the baptism with the Holy Spirit (e.g., Ac 2:1-4, 19:1-6). Such confusion, however, should not discourage the Pentecostal believer from recognizing that the fundamental bond of unity among true believers from various backgrounds is the indwelling presence of God's Spirit (cf. 1Co 12:13, "For we were all

---

[8]Henry C. Thiessen. *Lectures in Systematic Theology*, revised edition, 255.

baptized by one Spirit into one body . . .”). It is because the Spirit indwells all believers that they may have the assurance of being the children of God, and that they may have genuine fellowship with the Lord as well as with other believers.

## Conversion

In dealing with the doctrine of salvation, some theologians prefer to follow what is called the *ordo salutis*, the order, or way of salvation. This is an attempt to follow a logical sequence of events from the moment one is first saved to the time when the believer is forever in the presence of the Lord. The difficulty with this method, however, is that while it appeals to human logic it is rather artificially contrived and can become more confusing than helpful. Further, it is rare that two theologians agree on the precise arrangement of the *ordo salutis*. It should be noted that the Bible does not suggest a step-by-step chronological or sequential formula for salvation. Rather, the forgiveness of sins is instantly applied to the life of one who sincerely accepts Christ as Savior. It is important, however, to carefully examine the various aspects that are integral to the salvation process. Thus, while not proposing a detailed order of salvation, several of the more significant facets of salvation deserve closer inspection. The first of these is conversion.

Conversion represents the human response to the saving work of Christ. There are two primary elements which are essential for conversion to occur: repentance and faith. From a Calvinist perspective, conversion is possible because of the effectual calling of God, enabling the elect to repent and have faith for salvation. From an Arminian (and Pentecostal) perspective, conversion is possible because of the primary (or prevenient) grace of God,[9] made available to all persons through the redemptive work of Christ. In either case, it is important to note that God takes the initiative in salvation. Only God can enable one to repent and have faith to be saved.

---

[9]“Prevenient” grace (a term used by John Wesley) refers to the grace which “comes before” salvation, enabling the sinner to repent of sins and receive forgiveness. This is essentially the same thing meant by James Arminius’ term “primary grace,” and is obtainable for all persons (not simply the “elect”).

There are several biblical terms which convey the idea of repentance. Two of the more frequently used are the Hebrew *shub*, to turn away from sin and return unto God (cf. 2Ch 7:14; Eze 18:30-32), and the Greek *metanoia*, to have a change of mind or direction (an "about face"; cf. Mt 3:2; Ac 2:38). Such a moral change is inspired by the Word of God (Heb 4:12-13) and by the convicting power of the Holy Spirit (Jn 16:8-11). Such "conviction" will lead to "contrition" of heart (not simply regret, but a godly sorrow for sin and a desire to abandon it), and to "confession" of sin before God. Another frequently neglected but very important element of genuine conversion is "reformation" of character. While in a sense this is an ongoing process, related to sanctification, it is still pivotal that the repentant sinner not only turns away from sin, but turns toward and follows in the way established by God. Pruitt notes that well-meaning Christians who encourage others to "only believe" and be saved, without recognizing, confessing and turning from their sin, are in effect "trying to short circuit the plan of salvation by leaving out one of its most essential elements."[10] The omission of true repentance leads to what Bonhoeffer called "cheap grace":

> Cheap grace is the preaching of forgiveness without requiring repentance . . . Cheap grace is grace without discipleship, grace without the cross, grace without Jesus Christ . . . [Genuine] grace is *costly* because it calls us to follow, and it is *grace* because it calls us to follow *Jesus Christ*. It is costly because it costs a man his life, and it is grace because it gives a man the only true life.[11]

While the power or ability to repent is given to the sinner by the Holy Spirit, the act of repentance is still dependent on the personal choice of the individual. Such repentance is essential for true conversion (cf. Jesus' words in Lk 13:3, 5, ". . . unless you repent, you too will all perish").

A second indispensable aspect of conversion is faith. The New Testament concept of faith is taken from the noun *pistis* and is related to the verb *pisteuo* ("to believe"). This suggests that faith is not simply a passive, mental assent to the facts of the gospel, but rather is an

---

[10]Raymond M. Pruitt, *Fundamentals of the Faith*, 241.

[11]Bonhoeffer, 47.

active, positive response of one's total being to follow Christ. Thus, "believing" in the Lord involves an intellectual, volitional, and emotional change in the life of the Christian convert. As true in the case of repentance, so there is both a divine and human element involved in the faith that leads to conversion (what some would call "saving faith"). It is God's grace that provides faith sufficient for one to believe in Christ, but it is still requisite for one to exercise that faith. God will not "believe" for the sinner, nor can anyone "believe" for someone else. Faith is a personal trust and commitment of one's life to the Lordship of Christ, which entails both creed (correct beliefs) and conduct (correct actions). Erickson makes an interesting observation that unlike the New Testament, the Old Testament does not have a noun for "faith." Instead, several Hebrew verb forms are used to convey the idea of faith. This suggests that faith in the Hebrew mind-set was not something which one *has*, but rather something which one *does*.[12] This is consistent with the New Testament concept of conversion, that faith is an active exercise of one's total person to repent of sin and to believe in the atoning work of Christ for salvation.

Before leaving the topic of faith, a brief word should be stated concerning its relation to works. Arminians (and by extension, many Pentecostals) are sometimes accused of believing in salvation by good works instead of by grace through faith. This is an inaccurate assumption. Neither Arminian nor Pentecostal theology would teach that one is saved by works, but would wholeheartedly endorse the words of the apostle Paul that "it is by grace you have been saved, through faith—and this not from yourselves, it is the gift of God—not by works, so that no one can boast" (Eph 2:8-9). The confusion on this issue apparently stems from a misunderstanding of the Arminian and Pentecostal emphasis that one who is truly converted will live a productive life of service for the Lord. Thus, while one cannot be saved by works, it is true that good works will naturally spring from the life of one who is redeemed and living in union with the Lord. This is apparent in Paul's thought referred to above, as he continues (Eph 2:10), "For we are God's workmanship, created in Christ Jesus to do good works, which God prepared in advance for us to do." (Cf.

---

[12]Erickson, *Christian Theology*, 938.

also Jn 15:1-5 and Jas 2:18.) Martin Luther's close friend Philip Melanchthon stated it well: "It is faith, alone, which saves; but the faith that saves is not alone."[13]

## Regeneration

Whereas conversion deals largely with the human response to God's offer of salvation, regeneration is the work of the Holy Spirit in the human heart. Regeneration means that one has been spiritually reborn. It refers to the divine act by which one's sinful nature is transformed into one that is cleansed from sin and given newness of life in Christ.

Probably the most familiar biblical passage which deals with the concept of regeneration is John 3. Jesus declared to Nicodemus that "no one can see the kingdom of God unless he is born again" (v. 3). As a bewildered Nicodemus pondered how a grown person could be reborn in a natural sense, Jesus explained to the Jewish leader that He was talking of a spiritual rebirth. Jesus stated:

Flesh gives birth to flesh, but the Spirit gives birth to spirit. You should not be surprised at my saying, 'You must be born again.' (Jn 3:6-7)

Several items should be noted from this context. The Greek term translated as born "again" is *anothen*, which could also be rendered as born "from above" (cf. v. 31). Both of these ideas could convey a single truth, that the origin of the new birth experience is "from above," i.e. from God. In John 3:7, Jesus uses an imperative in speaking of the need for regeneration: "You *must* be born again." This is consistent with the previous verses (cf. vv. 3, 5) in which Jesus admonished Nicodemus that the new birth experience was the only means by which a person could enter into the sphere of God's kingdom and realize salvation. This truth is proclaimed elsewhere in the New Testament writings, sometimes using different terminology to express the same idea. For example, John earlier in his gospel refers to being "born of God" (1:13). Similar teaching can be found in 1 John 2:29, 5:1, 4. The apostle Peter states that "In his great mercy he [God] has given us *new birth* into a living hope through the resurrection of Jesus Christ" (1Pe 1:3, emphasis added). Peter also reminds his readers

---

[13]Quoted in Robert Shank, *Life in the Son*, second edition, 7.

that they "have been *born again* . . . through the living and enduring word of God" (1Pe 1:23, emphasis, added). In Paul's letter to Titus (3:5), the apostle affirms that God has "saved us, not because of righteous things we had done, but because of his mercy. He saved us through the washing of rebirth ["regeneration," NASB] and renewal by the Holy Spirit. . . ."

Williams indicates that a miracle such as the new birth or regeneration can occur only through the agency of the Holy Spirit and the implanting of the Word of God.[14] This idea would agree with the emphasis of the last two biblical passages (1Pe 1:23; Tit 3:5) cited above. Williams compares the believer's regeneration through the Spirit to the fact that Jesus' physical birth or "generation" was accomplished through the same Holy Spirit (cf. Mt 1:20; Lk 1:35). ". . . Christ as the one to be first born of the Spirit, hence supernaturally, becomes the precursor of all who after Him, and because of Him, will be reborn of the Spirit, thus also supernaturally."[15] Just as the Holy Spirit is the agent in the regenerative work of God in a person's life, so the importance of the role of the Word of God must not be overlooked. Jesus' parable of the sower (Mk 4:1-20) stresses the fact that the word ("the seed") which is sown on good soil will be productive and will bring forth new life. Emphasizing the same truth, James asserts that the Father's gift "from above" (Gr. *anothen*, 1:17) will result in regeneration, through the vehicle of His Word. "He chose to give us birth through the word of truth, that we might be a kind of firstfruits of all he created" (Jas 1:18).

Concerning the result of regeneration, Paul makes one of the most powerful statements found in Scripture:

Therefore, if anyone is in Christ, he is a new creation; the old has gone, the new has come! (2Co 5:17)

The believer may still look essentially the same and have the same natural abilities as before salvation, but there is a new quality to the believer's nature. Williams notes that the term used here for "new," *kainos*, does not mean the appearance of something which previously did not exist, but the making new or renovating of that which was

---

[14]J. Rodman Williams, *Renewal Theology*, Vol. 2, 37-40.

[15]Ibid., 37.

already present. This is in agreement with Thayer, who indicates that the term *neos* suggests something new or recent in reference to time, but *kainos* denotes something new or fresh in reference to quality.[16] Thus, the regenerated individual is a qualitatively different person—through salvation, something genuine has occurred within—the believer is transformed, or re-created! On the one hand, the "old self" and its sinful desires has been put to death; on the other, the "new self" is a "new creation" who desires to walk according to the ways of God (cf. Gal 2:19-20, 5:24-25; Ro 6:1-11). Once again, the apostle Paul aptly describes the character of the regenerate:

> You were taught, with regard to your former way of life, to put off your old self, which is being corrupted by its deceitful desires; to be made new in the attitude of your minds; and to put on the new self, created to be like God in true righteousness and holiness. (Eph 4:22-24)

Having a renewed mind, being like God in righteousness and holiness, is only possible for the one who has been regenerated and is truly a "new creature" in Christ. Such a one has learned and experienced (and continues to learn and experience) the exuberant truth of what it means to "count [oneself] dead to sin but alive to God in Christ Jesus" (Ro 6:11).

## Justification

Another integral aspect of salvation is justification. Justification is a declarative act of God by which He absolves the guilt of one's sin and accepts as righteous the one who has personally accepted the propitiatory sacrifice of Christ. Whereas in regeneration one receives a new nature in Christ, in justification one receives a new standing before the Lord.[17] Ladd asserts that

> The root idea in justification is the declaration of God, the righteous judge, that the man who believes in Christ, sinful though he may be,

---

[16]Ibid., 50, n. 72.

[17]One's "new" nature in Christ is not an additional nature which previously did not exist. Rather, as suggested in the previous section on regeneration, the believer has a redeemed and transformed nature, one that is qualitatively "new" or different.

is righteous . . . because in Christ he has come into a righteous relationship with God. [18]

The primary biblical words for justification (Heb. *tsadaq;* Gr. *dikaios*) convey the idea that justification is a declaration or act of God (not of human merit) in which the Sovereign Judge of the universe pronounces that one is "not guilty" of sin. A common way of expressing this is that justification means "just-as-if-I'd" never sinned. While there is a sense of truth to this slogan, Erickson points out that biblical justification means more than God simply pretending that one is righteous. He notes that the justified one's guilt or liability is no greater than if one had never sinned. However, there is a significant difference between never having sinned and having committed sin and paying the penalty (or in this case, having the penalty paid by another on one's behalf). The one who has sinned has experientially learned the meaning of forgiveness, and knows the immeasurable gratitude of receiving the righteousness of Christ, which one could never attain by one's own efforts.[19]

The only means by which one may be justified is by faith in the atoning sacrifice of Jesus Christ. Belief that "the just shall live by faith" (Hab 2:4; Ro 1:17; Gal 3:11) was one of the major factors which spurred Martin Luther to oppose a medieval church which sought salvation through works or merit, and it has appropriately become the motto of countless individuals and groups who have followed in the Reformer's steps. Such a view clearly permeates the teaching of the New Testament (cf. Ro 3:20; Gal 2:16; Eph 2:8-9). Justification, then, is totally a gracious gift of God, undeserved and unachievable through even the best of human efforts (cf. Ro 3:23-24: "for all have sinned and fall short of the glory of God, and are justified freely by his grace through the redemption that came by Christ Jesus"). It is important to note here that while faith is essential for justification, faith is not the meritorious ground of justification. Thiessen correctly states, "Faith is not the price of justification, but the means of appropriating it."[20] Instead, justification is based solely on the vicarious death of Christ

---

[18]George E. Ladd, *A Theology of the New Testament,* 437.

[19]Millard J. Erickson, *Does It Matter What I Believe,* 129.

[20]Thiessen, 278.

(cf. Ro 5:9—"Since we have now been justified by his blood, how much more shall we be saved from God's wrath through him!"), and subsequently His resurrection from the dead (cf. Ro 4:25—"He was delivered over to death for our sins and was raised to life for our justification")./Because Christ has paid (and not merely excused) the penalty for the sins of the world, God declares that the one who repents is acquitted (cf. Ps 32:1-2; Ro 4:7-8). Believers no longer are under condemnation (Ro 8:1, 33), but can rejoice with the apostle Paul that "since we have been justified through faith, we have peace with God through our Lord Jesus Christ, through whom we have gained access by faith into this grace in which we now stand" (Ro 5:1-2).

## Sanctification

The final facet of salvation to be explored in this chapter is sanctification, or as some translators prefer, holiness. The primary biblical terms for sanctification and holiness are the Hebrew *qadosh* (from a root word meaning to cut or divide) and the Greek *hagios*, frequently translated as "saint" or "holy one." Both terms convey the idea of separation (from that which would corrupt or defile). Thus, holiness or sanctification is commonly understood as being separated from that which is secular, common, or profane and consequently being dedicated and consecrated unto that which is spiritual, noble, or pure. Ultimately, sanctification means separation from sin, and consecration unto God.

The Scriptures are replete with emphases on the need to be sanctified. God has called His people to a life of holiness, one that is characterized by spiritual separation and moral purity. While most modern Christians would agree with this general concept, many are in a quandary concerning the specifics of how to relate sanctification to everyday living. Some, in their sincere desire to please and obey God, emphasize that humans are personally responsible for their own sanctification. These persons frequently refer to such biblical passages as Philippians 2:12, in which believers are exhorted to "work out your salvation with fear and trembling." While such attitudes may be propelled by genuine motives, such believers can easily find themselves entangled in a futile exercise in "works righteousness." From another perspective are those who recognize the inability of human effort to achieve holiness, and instead emphasize that sanctification must be exclusively an activity of the Holy Spirit.

References such as Hebrews 10:10 ("By [God's] will, we have been made holy through the sacrifice of the body of Jesus Christ once for all") are often cited to support this position, which can also be taken to such an extreme that one has little concern and puts forth no personal effort for one's own moral perfection. While both extremes contain some biblical truth, either of them can become overstated and can lead to a person becoming spiritually dysfunctional and falling short of a biblically balanced perspective on sanctification. As will be seen later in this chapter, biblical sanctification is a cooperative relationship between God and man.

The doctrine of sanctification is viewed from different perspectives by the various Pentecostal organizations. Some, such as the Church of God (Cleveland, Tennessee) and the Pentecostal Holiness Church, can trace their beliefs on sanctification to the Wesleyan-Holiness tradition. Following the soteriology of John Wesley, many such Pentecostals teach that sanctification is a "second definite work of grace," and that an experience of "entire sanctification" is attainable in this life. When believers place their "all on the altar" so that the "root of bitterness" within is eradicated by a special act of God's grace, they may know true holiness. While these Pentecostals emphasize that both the grace of God and personal responsibility are essential for sanctification, the primary focus is upon the latter. This is consistent with Wesley's own teaching, in which he often spoke of the need for believers to anticipate the moment when they would receive entire sanctification or "Christian perfection." Wesley stated:

> . . . it is infinitely desirable . . . that it should be done instantaneously; that the Lord should destroy sin . . . in a moment. . . . And so he generally does. . . . Expect it *by faith*, Expect it *as you are*, and Expect it *now!*[21]

It should be noted that some in the Holiness-Pentecostal tradition have misunderstood John Wesley's intention of "Christian perfection" to mean "sinless perfection." Wesley himself never used the latter expression in reference to sanctification, but some of his writings were ambiguous and could leave the reader with that misconception. For

---

[21]John Wesley, "The Scripture Way of Salvation", in *Creeds of the Churches*, 372.

example, in Wesley's most famous work on the subject, he stated "I do not contend for the term *sinless*, though I do not object against it."[22] Methodist historian Albert Outler explains that Wesley never understood "perfection" as being perfect*ed*, i.e. reaching a finished state of spiritual growth, but rather as perfect*ing* (*teleiosis*), through which the sanctified believer would always be striving for a fuller participation in the things of God.[23] In this manner, Wesley did not envision holiness as a moribund, dismal state of existence, but he emphasized that the holy life should be a happy and a complete life, one that Outler describes as life of true "whole-i-ness."[24]

Some Pentecostal groups are more closely associated with the Reformed-Baptistic tradition in regard to their understanding of holiness. Such groups would include the Assemblies of God, the International Church of the Foursquare Gospel, and the Open Bible Standard Churches. Such Pentecostals see sanctification as both instantaneous and progressive: at the moment of justification one is set apart unto God (cf. 1Co 1:2, 30; 6:11; Ro 15:16), but sanctification is actualized as one progresses and matures in one's Christian life. The emphasis among such groups is on this latter aspect, that sanctification is a continual process of spiritual development. While Christians may still contend with sin, they are no longer under the dominion of sin (cf. Ro 6:6-7), but instead have newness of life in Christ (Ro 6:4, 11). As one encounters and overcomes the normal spiritual struggles of life, one is becoming increasingly conformed to the image of Christ (cf. Ro 8:28-29). Reformed scholar Sinclair Ferguson notes that the goal of the sanctification process is to regain through Christ one's true humanity as God intended it to be. Ferguson declares, "Sanctification is radical humanization. It means doing the 'natural' thing spiritually, and the 'spiritual' thing naturally."[25]

Understood from this perspective, sanctification may be viewed as a process having twin dimensions. It begins at the moment one is

---

[22]John Wesley, *A Plain Account of Christian Perfection*, 112.

[23]Albert C. Outler, *Theology in the Wesleyan Spirit*, 71, 73.

[24]Ibid., 83.

[25]Sinclair B. Ferguson, "The Reformed View," *Christian Spirituality: Five Views of Sanctification*, 66.

justified, but continues to develop throughout one's Christian walk. Erickson aptly describes the distinction between justification and sanctification:

> Justification is an instantaneous occurrence, complete in a moment, whereas sanctification is a process requiring a lifetime for completion . . . sanctification is an actual transformation of the character and condition of the person. Justification is an objective work affecting our standing before God, our relationship to him, while sanctification is a subjective work affecting our inner person.[26]

Thus justification refers to one's objective righteousness (what God has declared one to be, positionally), whereas sanctification refers to one's subjective righteousness (what God is making one to be, in actuality). In a similar twofold manner, sanctification is premised upon the grace of God and the indwelling presence and work of the Holy Spirit, but also involves human responsibility and the exercise of the human will to actively respond to God's call unto holiness. Williams shares this perspective that sanctification has a parallel composition. He notes that "Sanctification is primarily the work of God: its source is in Him."[27] Properly emphasizing the necessity of God's role in the process of sanctification, Williams sees God the Father as the source of sanctification, Christ as the agent of sanctification, and the Holy Spirit as the energizer of sanctification. God does not work, however, without human involvement and cooperation. Holiness is not a "50-50" project, but a "both-and" arrangement; in Williams' words, it is "God all the way through man all the way."[28]

It is sometimes suggested that salvation has a threefold application. There is a sense in which one has been saved (or justified; cf. Eph 2:5, 8); one is presently being saved (or sanctified; cf. 1Co 1:18); and one shall in the future be saved (or glorified; cf. Ro 5:9-10). The continuing, present work of salvation, or sanctification, has both a positional nature (cf. 1Co 1:2—". . . to those who have been sanctified in Christ Jesus, saints by calling . . .;" cf. also 1Co 6:11; 1Pe 1:1-2), and it is especially characterized as having an ongoing, progressive nature.

---

[26]Erickson, *Christian Theology*, 969.

[27]Williams, Vol. 2, 101.

[28]Ibid., 101-102.

Examples of the continual work of "being sanctified" abound in the New Testament (cf. 2Co 6:17-7:1—" . . . come out from them and be separate . . . let us purify ourselves . . . perfecting holiness out of reverence for God"; the reader should also note the present emphases of passages such as Ro 8:13, 12:1-2; 1Pe 1:13-16). The above mentioned Scriptures will further reveal that sanctification is both a work of grace as well as one in which the believer is expected to exercise personal responsibility. It is incumbent upon believers that they persevere in their quest for holiness (cf. Heb 12:14: "Make every effort . . . to be holy; without holiness no one will see the Lord"). Concerning his pursuit of spiritual maturity, the apostle Paul relates his own realization of the "already-not yet" character of sanctification in Philippians 3:12-15:

> Not that I have already obtained all this, or have already been made perfect [*teteleiomai*], but I press on to take hold of that for which Christ Jesus took hold of me. Brothers, I do not consider myself yet to have taken hold of it. But one thing I do: Forgetting what is behind and straining toward what is ahead, I press on toward the goal to win the prize for which God has called me heavenward in Christ Jesus. All of us who are mature [*teleioi*] should take such a view of things.

It should be noted that the Greek words highlighted in the above passage are both forms of *teleios*, which means mature or complete. While Paul recognized that he had not yet "arrived" spiritually, he also knew that his endeavor to be sanctified was not in vain, but that he would continue to grow and mature in his spiritual pilgrimage until the day when he would stand complete in the presence of the Lord. Such a similar realization should help the modern believer to "press on toward the goal," knowing that the blessings of one's present salvation experience will be intensified and gloriously culminated when one is forever in the presence of the Lord.

## For Reflection and Discussion

1. Prior to reading this chapter, what was your understanding of the biblical word "atonement?" Now that you have finished the chapter, in what way(s) has your conception changed?

2. What did theologian Dietrich Bonhoeffer mean by "cheap grace?" Can you think of modern examples of how some persons have incorrectly perceived of saving grace?

3. What is the significance of saying that Christ offered the atonement to God the Father, and not to Satan?

4. What are the key differences between the Calvinist and Arminian views of salvation? Would you classify yourself as a Calvinist or Arminian? Why?

5. Pentecostals are sometimes falsely accused of teaching that salvation is by works. However, Pentecostals do believe that good works are an important aspect of the Christian life. How do these two positions differ? Discuss what you believe is the role of works in a Christian's life.

6. The apostle Paul taught that Christians are justified by faith (cf. Ro 5:1), and yet James taught that a person is not justified by faith alone (Jas 2:24). How would you "justify" the apparent disparity between these two ideas?

7. Discuss ways in which sanctification or holiness can be evidenced in one's everyday life.

# When the Spirit Comes
## John 16:13

THE HOLY SPIRIT IN THE CHURCH
THE PERSON OF THE HOLY SPIRIT
THE FRUIT OF THE SPIRIT
THE GIFTS OF THE SPIRIT

THIS TEXT HAS BEEN FAITHFUL TO THE CHRISTIAN CONCEPT of a trinitarian God—Father, Son, and Holy Spirit. Earlier chapters have discussed the person and work of the Father and the Son. This chapter will present a theology of the Holy Spirit (pneumatology) consistent with the Trinitarian formulation. The first portion of the chapter deals with assumptions important to a theology of the Holy Spirit, the second section will discuss the person of the Holy Spirit and the final sections will consider the fruit and gifts of the Spirit as they are presented in the Scripture and manifested in the Church.

## The Holy Spirit in the Church

It is the person and work of the Holy Spirit who authenticates the person and work of Jesus Christ in the world.[1] The Holy Spirit is always in relation to the history of the Father and the history of Jesus Christ. The Holy Spirit never functions in isolation. He is always in relation to the Father and to the Son.

It is true that the Church facilitates expression of the ministry of the Holy Spirit but it is crucial that the Holy Spirit is not seen as a "common spirit" or merely as an application or expression of grace found within the Church. This domestication of the Spirit would run counter to the authentic relationship of the Spirit to the Church and of God to creation. At no time does the Church own or manage the Holy Spirit. It is the Holy Spirit who empowers and enables the Church. This is a point meaningful to Pentecostal theology. Pentecostal theology recognizes the importance of the ministry of the Holy Spirit and also acknowledges the existence and ministry of the Church as a formation of the Holy Spirit.

The question which must be answered is, "What is the place of the Spirit as God's gift to the Church?" The Pentecost narrative details the transfer of the Spirit from Christ to the disciples.

> Exalted to the right hand of God, he has received from the Father the promised Holy Spirit and has poured out what you now see and hear. (Ac 2:33)

The Christ who became the bearer of the Spirit at his baptism becomes the giver of the Spirit at Pentecost. Basic to the gifts of the ascended Christ and the gifts of the Holy Spirit is the gift of the Holy Spirit as an expression of unity. It is the Holy Spirit who brings unity to the Church.

> Make every effort to keep the unity of the Spirit through the bond of peace. There is one body and one Spirit—just as you were called to one hope when you were called—one Lord, one faith, one baptism; one God and father of all, who is over all and through all and in all. But to each one of us grace has been given as Christ apportioned it. This is why it says:

---

[1] See the comments in the Introduction which discuss the ministry of the Holy Spirit as the expression of the Son which enables humanity to know the Father.

When he ascended on high,
he led captives in his train
and gave gifts to men. (Eph 4:3-8)

Unity is a creation of the Holy Spirit and as such is a notable expression of the Spirit within the Christian community. A Pentecostal theology of the Holy Spirit demands a life lived in and through the Spirit. The faith is not a philosophical position to be judged and debated nor only an intellectual posture to be espoused but the faith is an embracing of the person of Jesus Christ in his life, death, resurrection, and ascension. This allows for no philosophical polemics but demands a unity and cooperation which encourages reconciliation, fellowship, and worship.

It is within the community marked by unity that the Spirit, as the one who leads and guides into all truth, as the one who anoints the Word, as the one whose presence enlivens the sacraments, as the one who drives the members of the community out into mission to a needy world brings fulfillment to the ministry of the Lord. The unity created by the Spirit allows for and encourages interdependence among the members of the community.[2] It is this recognition of and dependence upon the Holy Spirit which characterizes the Pentecostal community. The attitude of competition is replaced by the attitude of cooperation, the desire to be served is supplanted by the desire to serve, the ministry by a few becomes the ministry of all. This is the Church which displays the Spirit as God's gift to the Church.

Weber states that "when we speak of the work of the Holy Spirit, we speak of God's work, the work of Christ."[3] The intent is that the Holy Spirit is not merely a force or power. He is not distinct or separate from God but is the Spirit of God. The Christian has, in the Holy Spirit, received the promise of the ascended Christ to be present both temporally and eternally. This is the robustness of the Pentecostal position. God in Christ is present to the Christian through the person of the Holy Spirit.

Pentecostal tradition and theology have rightly acknowledged the importance of both the objective and the subjective aspects of the faith.

---

[2]Michael Green, *I Believe in the Holy Spirit*, 100-122.

[3]Otto Weber, *Foundations of Dogmatics*, Vol. 2, 235.

That God in Christ is present to the Christian through the person of the Holy Spirit sustains the objective reality of the transcendence of God and at the same time maintains the subjective reality of one's personal relationship to God. It is in encounter with the Living God that one is liberated from sinful self-reliance and through continuing encounter with God through the "Life in the Spirit" that the Christian is free to live life as a disciple of Jesus Christ. Pentecostal theology appropriately recognizes the importance of utter dependence on God and continuing living out of oneself by living in Him.

The diversity and interdependence which defines the Pentecostal community enables the community to represent the Living Christ, through the Spirit, to the world. Within the Kingdom of God the Holy Spirit unites the present with the future and the Pentecostal life is a life lived under the presence of Jesus Christ through the ministry of the Holy Spirit.

This eschatological element is important and necessary to the Church as it understands and lives in the power of the Spirit. For it is as Christ, ascended to the Father, reaches into the present age and through the Holy Spirit empowers the Church that the purposes of God are fulfilled. The enlivening and empowering of the Church is a function of Jesus Christ through the Holy Spirit. Now, in time and space the Church assumes a servant order. Because the Church exists only within time and space the spiritual and the physical necessarily co-exist. They may never be separated but may be distinguished. As the Church orders its service and worship and as it grounds its message in the message of the historical Christ it must at the same time be sure to accommodate the presence of the Spirit and the order of the New Creation. God was historically transcendent in the Incarnate Christ and through living in the Spirit of God one experiences a "lived transcendence by which the reality of God impinges upon the world. . . ."[4]

---

[4]Ray S. Anderson develops this thought both in *Historical Transcendence and the Reality of God* and in the chapter "Living in the Spirit" in *Theological Foundations for Ministry*. While Anderson posits his argument from a non-Pentecostal perspective it seems that in fact the emphasis on the Holy Spirit for empowering the life of the Christian and the idea of the Holy Spirit as the mediator of the life of Christ to humanity is central to the Pentecostal message.

Because of the transfer of the Spirit at Pentecost (Ac 2:33) and the continuing presence of the Spirit the Church continues to do and teach those things which Jesus began to do and teach (Ac 1:1). The Pentecostal position is that the Holy Spirit empowers the Church in this mission. The attitude of the Church reflects the attitude of Christ. Costas conceptualizes this perspective when he states

the true test of mission is not whether we proclaim, make disciples, or engage in social, economic, or political liberation, but whether we are capable of integrating all three in a comprehensive, dynamic, and consistent witness.[5]

It is within this framework of proclamation, discipleship, and service that the Church is and becomes a charismatic community, a community of ministering members enlivened and empowered by the Holy Spirit. It is critical that a Pentecostal theology of the Holy Spirit be founded in the mission and message of Jesus Christ. Prior to the transfer of the Spirit and the experience of Pentecost the message which is now proclaimed by the Church was proclaimed by the Lord. The manifestation of God to the world in Christ is now present in the life of the Spirit-filled believer. This does not mean that the believer is a god or becomes a god because of the presence of Christ through the Spirit in the life of the Christian, but it does mean that the Christian is inextricably linked to Jesus Christ.

At Pentecost the Holy Spirit came in a new manner. Undeniably the Spirit was already present in creation and performed in the world and among humanity but at Pentecost the world was encountered by the Spirit in a distinctive way. Pentecost, as with all Acts of God, is unable to be addressed as a fact standing alone. It must be understood within the context of the many Acts of God. The Creation, Incarnation, Crucifixion, Resurrection, Ascension, Pentecost, and the Advent are each integral to the Gospel and together are the Gospel.

Who is the One for whom the disciples expectantly waited? There would be One coming who would empower the disciples to take the gospel into the lands and for this One the disciples waited. Continuing in prayer and in fellowship and in the teaching of the Lord they waited;

---

[5]Orlando Costas, *The Integrity of Mission: The Inner Life and Outreach of the Church*, 75.

when the Day of Pentecost came, they were all together in one place. Suddenly a sound like the blowing of a violent wind came from heaven and filled the whole house where they were sitting. They saw what seemed to be tongues of fire that separated and came to rest on each of them. All of them were filled with the Holy Spirit and began to speak in other tongues as the Spirit enabled them. (Ac 2:1-4)

This new era maintains a continuity with that which precedes it. The community of disciples carries on the ministry of the gospel as heirs of the message proclaimed by Jesus Christ. There is a fundamental continuity between the times of Israel, Jesus, and the Church. The presence of the Holy Spirit in the Church does not mean that a new message is preached but that the message previously preached continues with the Church as the vehicle for the message. It is the ministry of the Holy Spirit to bring attention to Jesus Christ who in turn witnesses to the Father. Thus, the Trinity is sustained, humanity as objectively related to God comes to a self-understanding of its need for God, and the gospel is carried into the reaches of the world.

## The Person of the Holy Spirit

The Holy Spirit is a person and not a mere force or power. This position is foundational and requisite to a belief in the Trinity. Holdcroft notes the difficulty of defining the person of the Holy Spirit in a manner which is easily apprehended.

> Only by careful investigation can it be seen that the characteristics of the Spirit do entitle Him to be considered personal. Although humans ordinarily experience personalities in interaction with others who are corporeal and visible, neither visibility nor corporeality are essential attributes of personality. A real person is not the physical body, but the spirit and/or soul within that body. Although in human experience personalities reside in physical bodies, the Holy Spirit, in not being incarnate, has no need for such an association.[6]

One must be careful not to reduce the Holy Spirit only to a power or force. It is also necessary to realize that the use of the term "person" or "personality" is to "refer to rather than to define the distinct identities of the Father, of Jesus Christ, or of the Holy Spirit."

---

[6]L. Thomas Holdcroft, *The Holy Spirit*, 35.

The Holy Spirit is often referred to by personal pronouns. The word *pneuma* (spirit) is neuter but is used with the masculine personal pronoun *ekeinos* in John 16:14. The implication is that Jesus' reference to the Spirit is a reference to a person.[7] In addition to direct reference to the Holy Spirit by the use of personal pronouns there are many instances in which personal characteristics are ascribed to the Holy Spirit. Holdcroft affirms the common characteristics of personality to include intellect, will, and emotion.[8]

The Holy Spirit is linked with the Father and the Son. This is the case in the familiar passage of the baptismal formula in Matthew 28:19, ". . . baptizing them in the name of the Father, and of the Son, and of the Holy Spirit." This connection is also present in the biblical benediction of 2 Corinthians 13:14, "May the grace of the Lord Jesus Christ, and the love of God, and the fellowship of the Holy Spirit be with you all." In John 14-16 the Holy Spirit is directly linked both to Jesus Christ and to humanity. Concerning humanity the Holy Spirit is to be a *paracletos*, one who will stand with and alongside of the believer. The *paracletos* is referred to as *allos paracletos*, another comforter of the same kind. The meaning is that the Holy Spirit will follow Jesus as comforter and will function in a manner like Jesus. The going of Jesus is directly joined to the coming of the Holy Spirit.[9]

The Holy Spirit also engages in acts and ministry which are generally ascribed to persons. In the Scripture the Spirit is characterized as performing acts such as teaching, interceding, commanding, regenerating, testifying, guiding, restraining, and leading.[10] These actions portray the Holy Spirit as a person.

The conclusion is that the Holy Spirit is much more than a force or power. The Holy Spirit as a person is a distinctive member of the Trinity. This is not meant to allow for the reduction of the Spirit to human dimensions but rather to offer a means of understanding God

---

[7]Additional scriptural references include: John 14:16; Romans 8:16, 28; Ephesians 1:14.

[8]Holdcroft, 41-42.

[9]For additional references which identify the Holy Spirit as a person see: Mt 3:16-17; Ac 2:33, 38; Ac 15:28; Ro 15:16; 2Co 1:21-22; Gal 4:6; 1Pe 1:2.

[10]Lk 2:26; Jn 14:26; Ac 8:29; Ro 8:26; 1 Th 5:19; 2 Th 2:7; Re 2:7.

and the interactions of Father, Son, and Spirit within the Godhead and with humanity.

Closely related to a discussion of the Spirit's person is the issue of the deity of the Spirit. To assert the deity of the Holy Spirit is to assign to Him the same attributes that characterize the Father and the Son.[11] Holdcroft lists six biblical evidences which establish the deity of the Spirit.[12]

First, the Spirit is referred to as God. The Holy Spirit is designated as holy and therefore shares the perfection of the Father and the Son. There are several references which acknowledge the interchange of terms which refer to God, Lord, and Spirit (Ac 5:3-4; 1Co 3:16, 12:4-6; 2Co 3:17).

Second, the Holy Spirit possesses divine attributes. These include: omnipotence (Ro 15:19), omniscience (Jn 14:26), omnipresence (Ps 139:7), eternity (Heb 9:14), and self-existent life (Ro 8:2).

Third, the Holy Spirit performs divine works. These works include: creating (Ge 1:2), convicting (Jn 16:8), delivering (Mt 12:28), and regenerating (Jn 3:5-6). It is in the course of activity in the world that the Holy Spirit is active in the performance of these divine works (Ge 2:7, 1Pe 1:2).

Fourth, the Holy Spirit is clearly identified with the Father and the Son. Participation in the Trinity excludes both subordination and modalistic existence. It is one God conterminously existent in three persons (Mt 28:19, Lk 3:21-22, 2Co 13:14, Heb 9:14).

Fifth, Scripture declares the Holy Spirit to be God. Holdcroft notes the interchangeability of terms as biblical writers frequently ascribe the same act or function to different persons of the Trinity (Ex 17:7 & Heb 3:7-9; Ge 3:6 & 1Pe 3:20).

Sixth, The Holy Spirit proceeds from the Father (Jn 15:26). The procession is not to be interpreted as meaning the Holy Spirit is created by the Father but rather as meaning the Spirit "goes forth from" the Father and from the Son.

---

[11]Holdcroft, 47.

[12]Ibid., 48-56.

## The Fruit of the Holy Spirit

But the fruit of the Spirit is love, joy, peace, patience, kindness, goodness, faithfulness, gentleness, and self-control. Against such things there is no law. (Gal 5:22-23)

The discussion of the fruit of the Spirit precedes the discussion of the gifts of the Spirit for in the life of the believer the fruit of the Spirit is foundational for proper operation of the gifts of the Spirit. The fruit of the Spirit as defined in the passage cited above is not meant to be an exhaustive inventory of the characteristics of the Christian life but rather is a contrast to the previously cited "works of the flesh" (Gal 5:19-21).

The fruit of the Spirit defines the cohesive character which the Spirit produces and the Christian manifests. It is this character which provides the concrete ways by which the Christian is able to express the love of Christ in the world.[13] In contrast to the various gifts of the Spirit which are distributed to each person as the Spirit wills (1Co 12:11), the fruit of the Spirit is a singular and thus indivisible work of grace resident in the life of the Christian. It is not that one demonstrates love, another goodness, another self-control, etc., but that each Christian is called to live a life led by the Spirit and hence demonstrative of the fruit of the Spirit.

The contrast between "the works of the flesh" and the "fruit of the Spirit" is not to be interpreted to mean that the Christian is to passively wait for the manifestation of the fruit of the Spirit through one's life. The fruit of the Spirit brings with it an ethical mandate for the Christian to recognize the work of God in one's life and to actively express the fruit through one's lifestyle.[14] Paul is making an intentional contradiction between the "works of the flesh" and the "fruit of the Spirit." The Christian lives a life directed by the Spirit as opposed to a life defined by human efforts to fulfill the edicts of the law. In spite of the intentional adversarial relationship between "works of the flesh" and "fruit of the Spirit" in no sense is Paul's intent to describe a "dualistic view of the world in which two equal

---

[13]Charles B. Cousar, *Galatians* Interpretation: A Bible Commentary for Teaching and Preaching, 139-141.

[14]Richard C. Longenecker, *Galatians* Word Biblical Commentary, Vol. 41, 259-267.

forces are locked in a struggle with the final outcome still in doubt."[15] The final outcome is certain (1Co 15:24). The Spirit is at work in the life of the Christian. There are many claims on the life of the Christian but the ultimate claim is that one which binds the Christian to the Living God. It is the fruit of the Spirit which distinguishes the Christian and provides a context for the gifts of the Spirit. In the list cited in the Galatians passage love is that aspect of the fruit which heads the list. It is particularly significant that the characteristic which most lucidly displays the relationship between God and humanity and the redemptive gift of the Father to a lost people begins the description of the fruit of the Spirit.

God's love revealed in Christ (Ro 8:38) becomes the quintessential motivation for human relationships (1Co 13). Fung powerfully depicts the importance of love in the Christian life in the following manner. Love is the

> atmosphere in which believers are to conduct their lives (Eph 5:2), the garment they are to put on (Col 3:14), the consistent motive of all their actions (1Co 16:14), the secret of unity (Col 2:2), . . . the way to Christian maturity Eph 4:15) . . . accompanied by practical action (2Co 8:7f) . . . [and] keenly perceptive (Phil 1:9f).[16]

While the remaining characteristics of the fruit of the Spirit are not mere subsets of love the pursuit of love will ensure joy, peace, patience, kindness, goodness, faithfulness, gentleness, and self-control and those who have been transformed by the power of the Spirit and now belong to God will live by the Spirit and overcome the "works of the flesh."

## The Gifts of the Holy Spirit

The discussion of spiritual gifts in First Corinthians and Romans is couched within the greater context of Christian ethical behavior. This is clearly indicated in Paul's discussion of love (1Co 13) as a "necessary ingredient for the expression of all spiritual gifts."[17]

---

[15]Cousar, 141.

[16]Ronald Y. K. Fung, *The Epistle to the Galatians* The New International Commentary on the New Testament, 262-263.

[17]Gordon D. Fee, *The First Epistle to the Corinthians* The New International Commentary on the New Testament, 572.

Spiritual gifts are certainly for the benefit of the community and not for one's personal exaltation. Life in the Spirit is life within the Kingdom of God. The life that the Christian now lives is based in the life which is to be lived in the consummated Kingdom. Therefore the ethic by which the Christian orders one's life is the ethic of the coming Kingdom. As Christ is the guarantee of the future He has sent the Holy Spirit to guide and empower the Christian in living in the Spirit and in living out the Kingdom ethic.

Spiritual gifts are neither only natural nor only spiritual. It is the ministry of the Holy Spirit through the human vessel which provides the means for the operation of the gifts. Lim acknowledges the incarnational nature of the gifts. The gifts' true nature is found "at the point where the supernatural (all of God) meets the natural (all of man)."[18] Because the gifts are incarnational they are not a sign of spiritual attainment or spiritual maturity. The gifts are gifts *of* the Spirit communicated through a human messenger. Neither are the gifts of the Spirit to be thought of as items possessed by a person. The gifts of the Spirit are evidences of God's grace. They are *charismata*, gifts of grace freely given. The ascended Christ has given the gift of the Spirit and the Spirit gives the gifts. The human vessel is a recipient of both the gift and the gifts.

There is often a tendency to attempt to systematize the gifts of the Spirit but if one is to do this it requires that the lists of gifts presented in the New Testament passages be viewed as a comprehensive compendium of spiritual gifts. Within the contexts in which these passages are found (1Co 12-14, Ro 12, Eph 4) it is apparent that the emphasis is not upon the establishment of a comprehensive list but upon the empowerment of the church and the importance of right relations and ethical behavior as one lives the Spirit-filled life. At the same time it is clear that Paul desires that Christians acknowledge the presence of the gifts and have a proper understanding of the gifts and their use (1Co 1:7, 12:1).[19] The interaction of doctrinal teaching and ethical action is necessary for the church to fulfill its commission to carry the gospel to the world.

---

[18]David Lim, *Spiritual Gifts: A Fresh Look*, 44.

[19]Stanley M. Horton, *What the Bible Says About The Holy Spirit*, 206.

In the passages cited above (1Co 12-14, Ro 12, Eph 4) the ethical tension demonstrated in the contrast between the "works of the flesh" and the "fruit of the Spirit" is continued. In contrast to the sinful and carnal ambition to be recognized for one's individuality Scripture presents the ethical mandate to recognize the oneness, the fellowship, the communion of believers. It is not the many members as parts of the whole, being fit together to form the whole that is the focus of the diversity of gifts. In the diversity of gifts each one must recognize the other and in this recognition the "One Body" is made evident. The true fellowship which is essential to the Church is only evident as each person recognizes the giftedness of the other persons. Here, Pentecostal theology stands to offer a great contribution to the doctrine and practice of the Church.

> These passages reveal what the Church is through the expressions of gifts. They teach the context, the preconditions, and understandings that can set a church free to exercise gifts. Rather than emphasize only the spectacular gifts, the essential nature of all gifts and their regular exercise must be seen.[20]

It is not enough to understand the gifts and it is not enough to experience the gifts. Pentecostal theology unites understanding and experience, doctrine and reflection, theory and practice.

This ethical mandate may be seen in Paul's admonition to the Corinthians (1Co 12-14) to recognize the unity and diversity present in the Body of Christ. After declaring his desire that the Corinthians be knowledgeable concerning the spiritual gifts (1Co 12:1-2) Paul immediately states the single source of the gifts (God) and the diverse purposes of the gifts.

> There are different kinds of gifts, but the same Spirit. There are different kinds of service, but the same Lord. There are different kinds of working, but the same God works all of them in all men.[21]

---

[20]Lim, 184.

[21]Gordon Fee, in his commentary, *The First Epistle to the Corinthians* (581-589), rightly recognizes the necessary interrelationship of diversity and unity. It is diversity within unity manifested in the Church that re-presents Christ to humanity. Importantly, Fee also recognizes the one source of all spiritual working—it is God who works all things in all people.

In the following verse (v. 7) Paul announces that the gifts are given and utilized for the common good and for the building up of the community.[22]

At this point the foundation for the understanding and operation of spiritual gifts is clearly established. The foundation includes the following major considerations:

1. The workings of God are set within the Trinitarian construct of God. The implication of this is that while Systematic Theology may separately consider various areas of theological study all the areas are directly interrelated. Christology is related to ethics, pneumatology is related to ecclesiology, etc.
2. The diversity and unity found within the Triune God is a paradigm for understanding the work of the Spirit.
3. The "each one" is understood only within the community. Diversity and unity coexist.
4. The ethical mandate to live in proper relationship within the Church is integral to the life of the Church.
5. The gifts are manifestations *of* the Spirit. This indicates that they are not owned by any person.

Paul proceeds to offer a list of manifestations of the Spirit which may operate through the life of the Christian. Even in offering the listing Paul makes note that it is through the Spirit that the manifestation occurs. It is important that this is noted. If it is through the Spirit that the spiritual manifestations are given it is not possible to develop a comprehensive list of spiritual gifts. To do this would necessitate limiting the Spirit. Therefore, in considering the lists provided in Paul's letters one must consider the list to be representative rather than comprehensive.

Horton addresses the ways in which the gifts have been categorized. Some distinguish between public and private, some between functional and official, others between extraordinary and ordinary, some more supernatural and less supernatural.[23] Others also note

---

[22]Chapters 13 and 14 continue Paul's line of thought that the concern of the Spirit is for the building of the community and that within the building of the community the individual will also experience spiritual development.

[23]Horton, 262.

some of the various attempts at grouping the gifts.[24] The emphasis in 1 Corinthians 12:8-11 is not on the gifts themselves but on the fact that the gifts are supernatural; they are manifestations of the Spirit.

In keeping with the purpose of this text to provide an introduction to theology from a classical Pentecostal perspective one cannot neglect considering some of the gifts listed in the New Testament. Following will be brief discussions of several of the manifestations of the Spirit/spiritual gifts.

Mentioned first in Paul's Corinthian passage is the message or word of wisdom (*logos sophia*). The title aptly describes this gift for it is an utterance, declaration, or proclamation, which is "full of wisdom" and inspired by the Spirit. The wisdom by itself is not the *charisma* but it is the utterance of wisdom which is the spiritual gift. The Pentecostal community recognizes this manifestation to include both a word of insight given in a time of need and the message of Christ crucified as God's true wisdom.[25]

Along with the message of wisdom the message of knowledge (*logos gnosis*) would certainly have been meaningful to Paul's Greek audience. Many Pentecostal writers, including Donald Gee and Stanley Horton, link the message of knowledge with teaching the truths of the Word of God. This is most likely a spiritual proclamation which is revelatory in nature. This does not exclude the message of wisdom from being present in either teaching or preaching. The essential characteristic of the message is that it is consistent with the plan and purpose of God.[26]

Recorded in the Gospel of John is the promise of Jesus that the Holy Spirit would testify of Him, teach, and guide into all truth (Jn 14:26, 15:26, 16:13). Horton comments, "There can only be one conclusion. A word of knowledge comes as a declaration of gospel truth or the application of it."[27] The message of knowledge may occur in many different contexts and appear in several various forms

---

[24]For example see the discussion and notes by Fee in his commentary on First Corinthians, 590.

[25]Fee, 592 (including note 48).

[26]Lk 21:15; Ac 6:1-10, 15:13-21; Ro 11:33; 1Co 2:6-16; Jas 1:5.

[27]Horton, 272.

but it is always a supernatural illumination of the truths of the Word of God.[28]

Listed third in the First Corinthians passage is faith (*pistis*). The manifestation of the gift of faith is different from saving faith and from faithfulness as the fruit of the Spirit. This is a supernatural manifestation of faith given for a specific situation. The gift of faith is often in concert with the following two gifts, the gifts of healings and miracles. At the same time there is a sense in which every act performed in dependence on God requires this faith. Hebrews 11 chronicles examples of the gift of faith in action.

The gifts of healings are discussed in depth in Chapter 11 and therefore it will be given the briefest of attention in this chapter. There is no evidence that every sick person Jesus or the apostles encountered was healed nor is there evidence that the gifts of healings were permanently resident in any person.[29] Within the context of the community of believers is the environment in which the sick are healed, the bereaved comforted, and the afflicted relieved.[30]

A manifestation closely related to these two gifts is the workings of miracles or literally miraculous powers (*energemata dunameon*). Certainly healings are included but because Paul does differentiate, this gift likely portrays other kinds of supernatural manifestations. Lim states

> The Gospels record many miracles, all in the context of the manifestation of the messianic kingdom, the defeat of Satan, the power of God, and the person and work of Jesus. The Greek word for "miracle" in John emphasizes its sign value to point to belief.[31]

Prophecy (*prophetea*) is Spirit-inspired speech to the people of God. The purpose is to edify the Church and because of this potential benefit all are encouraged to seek the gift of prophecy. This does not mean that all are prophets. Prophecy in the New Testament is neither connected to a frenzied mode of delivery or a message of judgment.

---

[28]Ac 3; Eph 1:17-23; Col 1:9-10; Heb 10:26.

[29]Horton, 273-275.

[30]See the discussion of this gift by Lim, 75-78, for a more thorough explanation of the incarnational and ethical dimension of the operation of the gifts of healings.

[31]Lim, 78.

Rather prophecy is intelligible speech delivered to the congregation of believers in a manner that the assembled can be edified and/or encouraged. In order to maintain order prophecy is to be judged by the community of believers.[32]

Distinguishing between spirits (*diakriseis pneumaton*) suggests that there is a judgment to be made. The judgment is usually understood to refer either to the testing of spirits (1Jn 4:1)[33] or to the evaluation of prophetic utterances (1Co 14:29).[34] It is possible that the meaning may convey both alternatives. The context of 1 Corinthians 12-14 must be seriously considered if one is intent on attempting to describe this gift as it is presented by Paul. Because the context refers to the gathering of believers and to proper operation of the gifts it is possible that Paul considers this gift to play a part in the leadership function of guiding and leading the congregational meeting.

The final two gifts are very closely linked. Different kinds of tongues (*hetero gene glosson*) is a Spirit-inspired utterance addressed to God. Paul implies that tongues is not necessarily a known earthly language and is generally unintelligible to both speaker and hearer (1Co 14:1-5, 10-12). The interpretation of tongues (*hermeneia glosson*) is to accompany the manifestation of different kinds of tongues. The interpretation is not to be confused with word-for-word translation. Without the gift of interpretation the gift of tongues does not edify the Christian community.

Following this list of manifestations Paul again refers to the source of the manifestations (1Co 12:11) and to their place in the Christian community (1Co 12:12-1Co 14:40). All of the workings are of the Holy Spirit and are distributed and manifested as the Spirit chooses. The Pentecostal community must properly understand and rightly practice the operation of the manifestations of the Spirit. In order to do this the community must reflect not only on the operation of the gifts but on the purposes of the gifts. It is important to seek the Giver of all gifts and to consider the ethical mandate to live in the

---

[32]Ro 12:6; 1Co 14.

[33]Horton, 276-277.

[34]Fee, 596-597.

Spirit. In this way the Kingdom of God which is to be consummated in the future is also manifest in the present.

There are two other significant passages which provide biblical instruction on the purposes and practice of spiritual gifts. Ephesians 4:11-13 states

> It was he who gave some to be apostles, some to be prophets, some to be evangelists, and some to be pastors and teachers, to prepare God's people for works of service, so that the body of Christ may be built up until we all reach unity in the faith and in the knowledge of the Son of God and become mature, attaining to the whole measure of the fullness of Christ.

Again it is evident the gifts are given by God for the purpose of building up the Church. This remains true to the premise that the practice of the gifts is to occur within the context of practical Christian living.

The final section to be considered is Romans 12:1-8. Paul's remarks in verses 1-2 lay the foundation for the discussion of manifestations of the Spirit. In these early verses it is clear that the practice of the Christian life is of utmost importance. This section is not to be viewed as opposition to justification by faith but as an exhortation to obedience which is essential to the life of faith.[35] The "living sacrifice" is a demonstration of life in the Spirit.

Subsequent to the foundational remarks Paul discusses how these principles might look when lived out in the Christian community. Romans 12:3-8 declares

> For by the grace given me I say to every one of you: Do not think of yourself more highly than you ought, but rather think of yourself with sober judgment, in accordance with the measure of faith God has given you. Just as each of us has one body with many members, and these members do not all have the same function, so in Christ we who are many form one body, and each member belongs to all the others. We have different gifts, according to the grace given us. If a man's gift is prophesying, let him use it in proportion to his faith. If it is serving, let him serve; if it is teaching, let him teach; if it is encouraging, let him encourage; if it is contributing to the needs of others, let him give generously; if it is leadership, let him govern diligently; if it is showing mercy, let him do it cheerfully.

---

[35]C.K. Barrett, *The Epistle to the Romans*, 230.

To each one in the body of Christ is given grace. This demands that each one acknowledge not human ability but God's grace. Human recognition of the grace of God curtails human arrogance and encourages ethical practice within the Christian community. Pentecostal life with its integral recognition of the Spirit of God and the manifestations of the Spirit rightly acknowledges the ethical mandate to live in right relation with one another.

The great distinctive of Pentecostal theology is the attention which it gives to the person and work of the Holy Spirit. Is the Holy Spirit God? Yes! Does the Spirit manifest himself in the Christian community? Yes! It is incumbent on the Pentecostal Church to be sure the message of Pentecost is made known. The ascended Christ has sent another Counselor into the world, One who empowers and guides the Christian, One who convicts the world of unrighteousness, One who enables the Church to represent Christ to the world. Life in the Spirit, the Pentecostal life, is a glimpse of that which is to come. It is the age to come breaking into the present age. That which will one day be normative is now seen in part.

> I have much more to say to you, more than you can now bear. But when he, the Spirit of truth, comes, he will guide you into all truth. He will not speak on his own; he will speak only what he hears, and he will tell you what is yet to come. He will bring glory to me by taking from what is mine and making it known to you. All that belongs to the Father is mine. That is why I said the Spirit will take from what is mine and make it known to you. In a little while you will see me no more, and then after a little while you will see me.[36]

---

[36]Jn 16:12-16.

## For Reflection and Discussion

1. Explain the ministry of the Holy Spirit as a member of the Trinity. Be sure to consider the ministry of the Spirit in relation to the person and work of Jesus Christ.

2. What does it mean to the contemporary Church that "the Spirit has been transferred to the Church?"

3. Discuss the person of the Holy Spirit. Give special attention to the place of the Spirit within the Trinity.

4. How is the fruit of the Spirit manifested in the life of the Christian? Contrast the "works of the flesh" with the "fruit of the Spirit" and the implications of each for the Church.

5. Discuss the proposition that the gifts of the Spirit presented in 1 Corinthians 12-14, Romans 12, and Ephesians 4 are a representative list and not a comprehensive list.

6. Discuss 1 Corinthians 12-14 in light of the idea that this passage considers the gifts of the Spirit within the context of an ethical tension which exists in the Church.

7. Write a one page *credo* on "The Holy Spirit in the Church: A Contemporary Response to Pentecost."

# All of Them Were Filled
Acts 2:4

PENTECOSTAL OR CHARISMATIC CHURCHES are often distinguished by their belief in an experience commonly called "baptism in/with the Holy Spirit," which is accompanied by a phenomenon called "glossolalia." This Spirit baptism experience is described by various biblical expressions including "filled with the Spirit," the Spirit "poured out," the "Promise of the Father," the "gift of the Holy Spirit," "endued with power," and the Spirit "fell upon." These varied descriptions seem to depict the divine presence of the Spirit manifesting himself in a new, vibrant, relationship.

Like non-charismatics, Pentecostals recognize that every true believer receives the Holy Spirit at salvation (Jn 3:5-6; Gal 3:3; Ro 8:16; 1Co 12:13). One is born of the Spirit at regeneration and the indwelling of the Spirit of holiness begins to produce the fruit of Christian character. However, the Bible speaks of another experience of the Spirit which is in addition to and subsequent to salvation which has become identified as "baptism in the Spirit." Sometimes confusion is caused when Pentecostals refer to this subsequent Spirit baptism as the "baptism of the Holy Spirit." "Baptism *of* the Spirit," may properly be used to describe the Spirit's work in salvation. The Spirit baptizes the believer into the body of Christ (1Co 12:13). It is preferable to speak of this subsequent experience as "baptism *with* or *in* the Holy Spirit." Christ is the agent who baptizes *with* or *in* the sphere of the Spirit one who is already a believer. This does not mean that at salvation one receives "part" of the Spirit and at Spirit baptism more of the Spirit is received. Rather, baptism in the Spirit refers to a new experience of the Spirit through which the believer is empowered for witness and service.

> And the Pentecostal feels this presence, this power, this spiritual imprimatur, not because it is contained in a declaration or mere promise—even in Holy Scripture—but because it is an experience; a tangible, even physical, confirmable, personal experience.[1]

The early disciples were instructed by Jesus that as a result of the experience of being filled with the Spirit they would receive power to be witnesses throughout the whole world. The unfolding of this Spirit-enabled witness is chronicled in the Book of Acts. Both in the Scripture and in current church history, where believers are baptized in the Spirit there is subsequent expansion of the Church. Prior to beginning His ministry, Jesus was annointed with the Spirit; prior to the ministry of the members of His Church, they are to wait for the promise of the Spirit (Mt 3:16-17; Lk 24:49; Jn 3:34; Ac 1:4-5). The Spirit's power for witness includes but is not limited to the proclamation of the good news of Christ.

## Promises of Spirit-baptism

The prophet Joel spoke of a day when God would pour out His Spirit upon all flesh—men and women, sons and daughters, and young and old (Joel 2:28-29). To the multitude who asked what was happening to the disciples of Jesus who had gathered in the upper room on the Day of Pentecost, Peter explained that "this is what was spoken by the Prophet Joel" (Ac 2:16-17).

---

[1]Frederick Dale Bruner, *A Theology of the Holy Spirit*, 22.

A number of New Testament passages also anticipate the Pentecostal event of a special outpouring of the Holy Spirit. All four Gospels record John the Baptist teaching his followers that though he baptized in water, Jesus would baptize His followers with the Holy Spirit (Mt 3:11; Mk 1:8; Lk 3:16; Jn 1:26, 33). In a post-resurrection appearance of Jesus to His followers, He alludes to this statement of John the Baptist.

> Do not leave Jerusalem, but wait for the gift My Father promised which you heard me speak about. For John [*hoti*] baptized with water, but in a few days you will be baptized with the Holy Spirit (Ac 1:4-5).

The Greek conjunction *hoti* should not be regarded as causal, meaning "for" or "because" in the sense that John's baptism is the reason the disciples should await the promise of the Father. Rather, it is a reference to a particular fact—"seeing that." To reduce the act of John to a mere water ceremony is to miss the important fact that both baptisms are spiritual baptisms. John's baptism was a baptism of repentance for the forgiveness of sins (Mk 1:4). But entrance into the family of God is only a spiritual beginning. The disciples were going to be baptized or overwhelmed by another experience with the Holy Spirit in just a few days, namely on Pentecost. This promise of John serves as a prime source for referring to this special experience with the Spirit as a "baptism in/with the Holy Spirit."

In the above passage (Ac 1:4-5) Jesus mentions that His disciples had heard Him speak of this Spirit baptism in terms of the "promise of the Father." At the end of his Gospel, Luke links the promise of the Father with a promise of power.

> I am going to send you what my Father has promised; but stay in the city until you have been clothed with power from on high (Lk 24:49).

Luke identifies these same concepts of promise and power as marks of the baptism in the Spirit which he writes about in the first chapter of Acts (Ac 1:4, 8).

Probably Jesus' reference to prior discussion concerning the future descent of the Holy Spirit includes the paraclete passages of John 14-16. The Spirit's coming is the promise of the Father as the Spirit proceeds from both the Father and the Son (Jn 15:26). Also, the Father had promised the outpouring of the Holy Spirit through the Old Testament prophets.

Many Pentecostals regard the public announcement which Jesus made on the last day of the feast of tabernacles as prophetic regarding the baptism in the Holy Spirit. "Whoever believes in me, . . . streams of living water will flow from within him" (Jn 7:38). John parenthetically gives explanation of this graphic pronouncement. "By this he meant the Spirit, whom those who believed in him were later to receive. Up to that time the Spirit had not been given, since Jesus had not yet been glorified" (Jn 7:39). This experience of the Spirit is seen as subsequent to salvation. After the glorification of Christ the Holy Spirit would be poured out on those who had believed on Him. On the Day of Pentecost His disciples were not drunk with wine but flooded by a river of the Spirit which had been sent from their ascended Lord.[2]

## The Spirit Given at Pentecost

Pentecostals believe that the above mentioned promises of the special descent of the Holy Spirit upon the Church were fulfilled on the Day of Pentecost. The feast of Pentecost celebrated the completion of harvest. Why would God choose to send the promised Holy Spirit on this particular day? The selection of such a prominent yearly feast would assure a large audience of Jews from all parts of the land. Some probably would be the same ones who had been at the Passover and had seen Christ's crucifixion. They would now witness the bestowal of the Spirit by the risen Lord. The feast that marked thanksgiving for harvest would look forward to the great spiritual harvest which would be reaped through the operation of the Spirit in the field of lost humanity already ripe for harvest.

The Holy Spirit was outpoured when the Day of Pentecost "was being fulfilled" (Ac 2:1). The use of the verb as a present passive infinitive with *ento* (when) is peculiar to Luke in order to designate the arriving of a particular period or point of time. The idea expressed is that the arrival of a particular day or span of time begun at an earlier point is brought to completion. In Acts 2 the phrase reflects upon the earlier promises concerning the coming of the Holy Spirit. The arrival

---

[2]For a more detailed exposition of this view see: Stanley M. Horton, *What the Bible Says About the Holy Spirit*, 115-116.

of the Day of Pentecost fulfills the span of time envisioned when those promises were made.

As the group of about one hundred twenty followers of Jesus was gathered in the upper room, suddenly God broke in upon them with a sound like violent wind. This announced the arrival of the promised Holy Spirit, for whom they had been waiting. Some would argue that the disciples were not expecting the Holy Spirit. They do so by claiming that the word "suddenly" (Ac 2:2) means unexpectedly. This Greek word (*aphno*) is used three times in the New Testament, all by Luke.[3] In each passage, suddenly is just as appropriate a rendering, if not better, than unexpectedly. Even if the word meant only unexpectedly, that which would have been unexpected would not have been the arrival of the Holy Spirit, but the extraordinary signs with which He came. They were anxiously waiting for the Spirit—that was the whole purpose behind their stay in Jerusalem for the past ten days. Suddenly, that is in a captivating manner, the Holy Spirit filled their dwelling place as He came to fill their lives.

A visible sign accompanied the audible sign of the wind. Tongues of fire came to rest upon them (Ac 2:3). John the Baptist in his prophecy of this event had alluded to the symbolism of fire (Lk 3:16). These tongues of fire were distributed to those present. The word *diamerizomenai* carries the general idea of apportionment—the appearance of tongues of fire was distributed to each member in the room. While they were collectively gathered to await the Spirit's coming, each individually was a recipient. The baptism in the Spirit is an intensely individual, personal experience.

As appropriate as the manifestations of wind and fire were, the emphasis is certainly upon the fact that all were filled with the Holy Spirit (Ac 2:4). Of the multiplicity of terms used to describe the baptism in the Holy Spirit (came upon, poured out, baptized, etc.) the term "filled" best denotes the difference between the pre-Pentecost and post-Pentecost experience of the Spirit. The Holy Spirit exists from eternity and operated from the creation of the world (Ge 1:2). Indeed He moves throughout the events of the Old Testament. However, one should notice how He operated in relation to persons before Pentecost.

---

[3]Acts 2:2, 16:26, 28:6.

"The Spirit of the Lord came upon" Othniel; "the Spirit of the Lord began to stir" Samson; "the Spirit of the Lord came upon [clothed] Gideon"; "I have filled him [Bezalel] with the Spirit of God"; "the Spirit of the Lord came upon David."[4] Many similar occasions are recorded, most using the verb "came upon." Before Pentecost the Holy Spirit would come upon an individual to accomplish through that person some particular task for God. When the task was completed the Spirit lifted in that particular relationship. Even the instance where the individual is said to have been filled with the Spirit, the filling was for a particular time for a particular task. Bezalel was given special wisdom and gifts qualifying him to direct the construction of the tabernacle.

After Pentecost, the term "filled with the Spirit" took on a greater meaning. The initial experience of Pentecostal baptism is expressed by the word "filled" which is then followed by the related adjective "full." Full suggests a state of being, a condition resulting from the prior experience of having been filled.[5] The power of the Holy Spirit in this new relationship with the believer has come to stay. There is a conscious abiding presence of the Spirit for witness. Jesus had returned to heaven, but He promised that He would send another Paraclete "to be with you forever" (Jn 14:16). Filled also indicates the liberality with which the Spirit has been given. There is no need for spiritual deprivation, scarcity of joy, or meagerness of power, for the Spirit has come that one might be completely immersed in Him.

Another difference in the work of the Spirit post-Pentecost is the enlarged field of candidates for His work. All who earnestly awaited His coming were filled with the Holy Spirit (Ac 2:4). Previously the Spirit singled out relatively few people of God to come upon and to fill. Now the commission has been given to all to go into the whole world and preach the Gospel (Mk 16:15). The power to accomplish such a great task is now made available to all. Jesus declared that His followers would be witnesses to Him throughout all the world, after the power of the Spirit came upon them (Ac 1:8).

---

[4] Judges 3:10, 6:34, 13:25; Exodus 31:3; I Samuel 16:13.

[5] For a detailed discussion of "one or many" fillings with the Spirit see Stanley Horton, *What the Bible Says About the Holy Spirit,* and Howard Ervin, *These Are Not Drunken As Ye Suppose.*

As a result of being filled with the Holy Spirit they all began to speak in a language other than their own (Ac 2:4). Speaking in tongues as an evidence of one being baptized in the Holy Spirit has been a hallmark of Pentecostal doctrine. The technical term, "glossolalia," has been coined from *glossai* (tongues) and *laleo* (to speak). As the Holy Spirit enabled them, those filled with the Spirit began to speak languages previously unlearned and unknown to them. The nature of at least some of the glossolalia on the Day of Pentecost was the languages of persons in the multitude who had been attracted to this amazing spectacle.

> Utterly amazed, they asked: 'Are not all these men who are speaking Galileans? Then how is it that each of us hears them in his own native language? . . . we hear them declaring the wonders of God in our own tongues!' (Ac 2:7-8,11).

Some have without warrant described this event as a miracle of hearing, rather than of speaking. Such an interpretation avoids the most natural understanding of verses eight and eleven and completely ignores the *speaking* in other tongues of verse four. Although it may not be true of every individual who had been filled with the Spirit, on this occasion the glossolalia of at least some of them were known foreign languages of the day. It is without warrant to conclude that all glossolalia express known languages. Often it is reported that even today an utterance in tongues is a foreign language known by someone in the audience. At times glossolalia is spoken of as a "heavenly language" supposing there is a language of heaven presently known only to God. Glossolalia may be a language no longer in operation, or one of a thousand obscure languages few are familiar with, or possibly even a language unrelated to communication among persons. However glossolalia may be defined, it was verbal expression given by the Holy Spirit to those who were filled with Him. No one had to instruct them on how or what to speak, but the Spirit most naturally gave them the language.

While glossolalia may have accompanied the preaching of the Gospel, the purpose of speaking in tongues was not to enable one to preach in a foreign language. At Pentecost, though the multitude heard those filled with the Spirit speaking the wonders of God in their own languages, it was necessary for Peter to preach to them beyond the glossolalic utterances.

Speaking in tongues has long been at the center of debate and dialogue regarding Pentecostals and charismatics.

> The great stumbling block in the [Pentecostal] Movement is of course, the manifestation of "other tongues." If only this obstacle could be overcome, many orthodox sections of the Christian Church would be pleased to have greater fellowship with Pentecostal believers.[6]

Though this quotation of Howard Carter was written decades ago, the sentiment largely continues today. Glossolalia still is often the dividing line. Many from almost every church denomination have now embraced the doctrine of baptism in the Spirit. This charismatic inroad into non-Pentecostal denominations has been applauded as bringing new joy and enthusiasm, greater commitment to ministry, deeper devotion to Christ, and renewed interest in the Word, yet is often looked upon with suspicion, mild tolerance, or even disdain. Speaking in tongues remains difficult to accept and embrace. It seems the multitude of Pentecost, and possibly the disciples themselves, were likewise amazed at the phenomenon of glossolalia. Even among Pentecostals and charismatics there is lack of unanimity regarding glossolalia. Classical Pentecostalism maintains that:

> The baptism of believers in the Holy Ghost is witnessed by the initial physical sign of speaking with other tongues as the Spirit of God gives them utterance (Ac 2:4).[7]

Thus, when a believer is baptized with the Holy Spirit the person speaks in tongues. Boldness in witnessing, holiness of life, greater love for God, new interest in the Scripture and other similar evidences may be present, but glossolalia is *always* the initial physical evidence of Spirit baptism.

While classical Pentecostals view glossolalia as *the* evidence, many charismatics hold that glossolalia is only *one of many* possible evidences. Some would say a person may be baptized in the Spirit and never speak in tongues, while others believe one who is baptized may not speak in tongues immediately but will at some later time.

---

[6]Howard Carter, "The Pentecostal Movement," *The Pentecostal Evangel* (May 18, 1946), 3, 7-8.

[7]"Statement of Fundamental Truths," Constitution of the General Council of the Assemblies of God, Article V, Section 8, revised 1969.

Research has shown that most charismatics, the longer they have been involved in the movement, have moved in the direction of classical Pentecostalism. It is generally conceded that if glossolalia is not immediately present at Spirit baptism, that almost always it will be manifested at a later period. To ease this controversy, it has become common to speak of glossolalia in terms of the expected "result" rather than the "evidence" of the baptism in the Holy Spirit.

## A Normative Experience

Briefly the biblical accounts from which the belief that glossolalia is the evidence of baptism in the Spirit will now be considered. The dramatic signs of wind and fire were unique to the Pentecost event, but the experience of speaking in tongues continued as early church believers were baptized in the Spirit.

About ten years after the Jerusalem outpouring of the Spirit at Pentecost, Peter accompanied by other Jewish brethren went to preach to a Roman centurion named Cornelius and his household. As he was preaching "the Holy Spirit came on all who heard the message" (Ac 10:44). The Jewish brethren were astounded that "the gift of the Holy Spirit had been poured out even on the Gentiles" (Ac 10:45). When Peter returned to Jerusalem, he defended what had taken place as an event similar to the one he and the others had experienced on the Day of Pentecost.

> As I began to speak, the Holy Spirit came on them as he had come on us at the beginning. Then I remembered what the Lord had said, "John baptized with water, but you will be baptized with the Holy Spirit." So if God gave them the same gift as he gave us, who believed in the Lord Jesus Christ, who was I to think that I could oppose God? (Ac 11:15-17).

The expressions "as he had come on us," "the same gift," "as he gave us," as well as a reference to John baptizing with water and another baptism with the Holy Spirit, present a pointed parallel between what was experienced on the Day of Pentecost and that now experienced in Caesarea.

How did Peter and the others know that Cornelius and his household had been filled with the Spirit after believing on Christ as Savior? Luke explains

> The circumcised believers who had come with Peter were astonished that the gift of the Holy Spirit had been poured out on the Gentiles.

For they heard them speaking in tongues and praising God (Ac 10:45-46).

The Greek word *gar* (for, because) is always used to introduce the reason or explanation for a previous statement. The reason Peter and those with him knew the Holy Spirit had been poured out on Cornelius and family was that they heard them speak in tongues, as they themselves had done when they were filled with the Spirit on Pentecost. Although the spectacular signs of wind and fire were absent, this did not hinder their identification of what had taken place. Because of glossolalia they were convinced that these Gentiles had now received the same gift (*heise dorea*). It was "the same gift, equal in quality or quantity," as the one thundred twenty had received at Pentecost.[8]

Nearly twenty-five years after the Jerusalem Pentecost, Paul met with twelve disciples at Ephesus. He asked them "Did you receive the Holy Spirit when you believed?" To which they replied, "No, we have not even heard that there is a Holy Spirit" (Ac 19:2). Upon further questioning he discovered that they were disciples of John the Baptist. Paul explained that the ministry of John was to point persons to Jesus. The Ephesian men accepted Paul's message and believed in Jesus Christ. Whereupon they were baptized in water in the name of Jesus. Paul then laid His hands on them and "the Holy Spirit came on them, and they spoke in tongues and prophesied" (Ac 19:7).

> This recurrence of the glossolalia of Pentecost occurred in the Province of Asia, under the ministry of one who had not even been present on the Day of Pentecost, to persons who could not have anticipated the experience for the very reason that they had never heard of it.[9]

Thus glossolalia continued to accompany the baptism in the Spirit, long after the initial outpouring of the Spirit at Pentecost.

Since these were disciples of John the Baptist, who had to be introduced to the message and work of Christ, it has been questioned whether the reception of the Spirit refers to their conversion or a subsequent experience of the Spirit. Pentecostals hold that the Holy

---

[8]Joseph Henry Thayer, *Greek-English Lexicon of the New Testament*, 307.

[9]Charles W. Conn, "Glossolalia and the Scriptures," *The Glossolalia Phenomenon*, 49.

Spirit came upon them as a separate experience, though very soon after their conversion. The grammatical construction of the question "Did you receive the Holy Spirit when you believed?" involves a Greek verb (received) with an aorist participle (having believed). While the question may be translated "Did you receive . . . *when* you believed?", it may be preferable not to view the two actions of "belief" and "receive" as coincident. The general rule for translating the aorist participle is: "Antecedent action relative to the main verb is ordinarily expressed by the aorist or perfect."[10] Thus the question would be "Did you receive . . . *since* (or after) you believed?" A receiving of the Holy Spirit *subsequent* to salvation is also supported by the context. When Paul discovered these Ephesians were John's disciples and not followers of Christ, he taught them of Christ and exhorted them to believe on Him. Then in Acts 19:5 these new disciples are baptized in water in the name of the Lord Jesus. Presumably they were baptized by Paul or one of his co-workers. Before he would have baptized them Paul certainly would have been satisfied that they had truly believed and were converted. Not until they had believed and were baptized in water did Paul lay hands on them and the Holy Spirit came upon them. At this subsequent experience of the Spirit glossolalia was again manifested. One would hardly argue that glossolalia accompanies the receiving of the Spirit at salvation, but it does accompany being filled with the Spirit.

In addition to the three Scripture passages mentioned above which explicitly link glossolalia with baptism in the Spirit, the following two passages provide implicit support for tongues as evidence of Spirit baptism. First is the account of the Samaritan revival under the ministry of Philip (Ac 8). As the Church scattered under persecution, Philip carried the Gospel to the people of Samaria. Many of the Samaritans believed on Christ, many were healed, and there was great joy throughout the city. Even a local sorcerer, Simon, was purported to have believed. News of the great revival spread to the apostles at Jerusalem. Peter and John were dispatched to Samaria to see what was happening.

---

[10]H.E. Dana and Julius R. Mantey, *A Manual Grammar of the Greek New Testament*, 230.

When they arrived they prayed for them that they might receive the Holy Spirit, because the Holy Spirit had not yet come upon any of them; they had simply been baptized into the name of the Lord Jesus. Then Peter and John placed their hands on them, and they received the Holy Spirit (Ac 8:15-17).

Though many had believed and were baptized in water, none of them had yet experienced this *subsequent* experience of being filled with the Holy Spirit. "Here the coming of the Holy Spirit is clearly removed in time, and thus differentiated, from their conversion."[11] This was another distinct experience from conversion in which the Holy Spirit would come upon them.

When Simon saw that the Spirit was given at the laying on of the apostles' hands, he offered them money and said, 'Give me also this ability so that everyone on whom I lay my hands may receive the Holy Spirit.' Peter answered: 'May your money perish with you, because you thought you could buy the gift of God with money' (Ac 8:18-20).

When the Samaritans received the Holy Spirit, Simon desired that he might also have power to impart this gift. He even offered money to obtain the ability. It is most probable that Simon was greatly impressed by some clearly distinguishable manifestation that accompanied the Spirit baptism experience.

The context leaves us in no doubt that their reception of the Spirit was attended by external manifestations such as had marked His descent on the earliest disciples at Pentecost.[12]

Many non-Pentecostal commentators explicitly suggest here "that those who received the gift of the Holy Spirit spoke with tongues."[13]

A second passage that implicitly supports tongues as the evidence of baptism in the Spirit is the account in Acts 9 of Paul's being filled with the Spirit. After Paul's dramatic conversion on the road to Damascus, at which time he was blinded by the light from heaven, Ananias declared that Jesus had sent him to Paul that he might receive

---

[11]*The Person and Work of the Holy Spirit*, A study paper presented to the General Assembly of the Presbyterian Church in the United States, 1971. p.8.

[12]F.F. Bruce, *Commentary on the Book of Acts*, 181.

[13]A.T. Robertson, *Word Pictures in the New Testament*, III, 107. See also: Adam Clarke, William Barclay, R.C.H. Lenski, F.J. Foakes-Jackson, A.S. Peale, Herman Olshausen, R. Tuck.

his sight and "be filled with the Holy Spirit" (Ac 9:17). Again there is the pattern of conversion followed by the baptism in the Spirit. Paul was converted to Christ; three days later he was healed of his blindness and baptized in the Spirit. While the context does not indicate whether or not Paul spoke in tongues at this time, it is certain that he did at a later time. His own testimony was "I thank God that I speak with tongues more than all of you" (1Co 14:18). Since Paul did speak with tongues and we have a pattern of glossolalia accompanying Spirit baptism it is reasonable to conclude that, following the pattern, Paul began to speak in tongues when he was filled with the Spirit.

Thus Acts provides us with a sufficient context regarding five occasions when persons were baptized in the Holy Spirit. Three of those five occasions explicitly state that glossolalia accompanied the experience (Ac 2, 10, 19). In Acts 10 glossolalia alone is mentioned as the reason Peter and others knew that the household of Cornelius had been filled with the Spirit. In the other two passages (Ac 8, 9) glossolalia is strongly implicit. This scriptural support, along with the corroborative testimony of tens of millions of believers who have been filled with the Spirit, is the reason classical Pentecostals hold to tongues as the *initial physical* evidence of baptism in the Spirit.

Briefly, the common arguments against glossolalia will now be considered. First, it is questioned whether the Book of Acts which deals with the *history* of the Early Church should be used to teach doctrine. However, Paul teaches us that all Scripture is God-breathed and is useful for *teaching* [doctrine] (2Ti 3:16). In recent years a number of biblical scholars have recognized the theological character of Luke's historiography. Roger Stronstad in particular builds a strong case for Luke intentionally dealing with theological issues while writing his history of the church.[14]

A second objection is the lack of supporting information in other books of the New Testament. However, a matter taught in the Bible need not be dealt with repeatedly before it is to be accepted as true. Other New Testament writings which deal with other topics would not automatically be expected to insert teaching concerning baptism

---

[14]Roger Stronstad, *The Charismatic Theology of St. Luke.*

in the Spirit. The Bible does not shy away from mentioning glossolalia when it fits the context—e.g. Mark 16:17, 1 Corinthians 12-14.[15] References to glossolalia in relation to the baptism in the Spirit would be expected only if that is the theme of the passage.[16] Lack of repetition that tongues accompanied Spirit baptism does not mean that tongues did not occur—rather the opposite may be true. Today when a Pentecostal speaks to another about someone being baptized in the Holy Spirit it would not be the expected to say "He was baptized in the Spirit and spoke in other tongues." To say "He was baptized in the Holy Spirit" would suffice, since if he had been baptized one would automatically assume that he had spoken in tongues.

Certain Bible passages have led some to believe that while glossolalia was operative in New Testament times, not all who were baptized in the Spirit spoke in tongues or that glossolalia ended with the era of the Apostles. In his letter to the Corinthians, Paul asks "Do all speak in tongues?" (1Co 12:30). The Greek construction indicates a negative reply is in order—"no, all do not speak in tongues." Therefore, some have suggested that even in the Early Church some spoke in tongues and others did not. This would at least mean that not everyone who is baptized in the Spirit needs to speak in tongues. However, examining the context of 1 Corinthians 12, one readily notes that Paul is addressing the topic of the gifts of the Spirit. One of the gifts of the Spirit is glossolalia. While this glossolalia may be similar in nature to that of glossolalia which evidences baptism in the Spirit, they are to be distinguished as to purpose.[17] All do not have the "gift of tongues" but all baptized in the Spirit have the evidence of glossolalia.

Paul also makes the statement, "Where there are tongues they will be stilled" (1Co 13:8). Again the context tells us that Paul is speaking

---

[15]Although Mark 16 may be a disputed canonical passage it would likely reflect the practice of the time. The glossolalia mentioned in Corinthians would primarily relate to spiritual gifts.

[16]Some Pentecostals suggest a number of other verses which may relate to Spirit baptism, though it would not necessarily be the emphasis of the passage. Acts 4:31; Romans 8:26-27; Ephesians 1:13-14, 6:18; Jude 20.

[17]"Statement of Fundamental Truths," Article V. Section 8.

of tongues as one of the spiritual gifts, not the evidential tongues at baptism in the Spirit. Also, the time element at which tongues will cease is specified by Paul. They will cease along with the other gifts at the end of the age when that which is perfect comes (1Co 13:10).

It should be emphasized that Pentecostal theology does not emphasize tongues as a goal in and of itself. While glossolalia may be inherently valuable, the overriding concern is the importance of the believer being filled with the Spirit for power to be an effective witness for Christ.[18]

The continuance of the Pentecostal baptism in the Spirit is the very heart of Pentecostalism. To compromise this issue is to give up the Pentecostal movement's reason for existence.

It is axiomatic to charismatic Christians that the baptism in the Holy Spirit did not expire with Pentecost, nor even the close of the Apostolic Age. They believe it is the birthright of every Christian, and represents the Biblical norm for the Spirit-filled life.[19]

The baptism in the Holy Spirit is viewed as a normative Christian experience.

This in no way is meant to imply that those not baptized in the Spirit are incomplete or second class Christians. One is fully Christian simply through faith in Christ as Savior. Neither is there an automatic parallel between holiness of life and Spirit baptism. The fruit of the Spirit may be worked greatly in the heart of one who has not had this Pentecostal experience. However, Pentecostals do proclaim the baptism in the Holy Spirit as a new dimension to one's Christian life. This experience is available to all Christians and should be sought by all.

Briefly, baptism in the Spirit is considered a normative experience because it fits the teaching of Scripture. One of the signs that were to follow those who believe is that they will speak in new tongues (Mk 16:18). Speaking of the gift of the Spirit witnessed by the multitude on the Day of Pentecost, Peter declared, "The promise is for you and your children, and for all who are far off—for all whom the Lord our God

---

[18]See Carl Brumback, *What Meaneth This?*, for suggested reasons God chose glossolalia to evidence baptism in the Spirit.

[19]Ervin, 37.

will call" (Ac 2:39). In the context of Acts, the terms "promise," "gift," and "receive" used in Acts 2:38-39 are used to identify baptism in the Spirit. This promise of the Holy Spirit extends not just to those present on the Day of Pentecost but to their descendants—those far off in time and distance—even as many as God continues to call. If one has been called to salvation, that one also may claim the promise of the Father, the baptism in the Spirit. The biblical pattern demonstrated in Acts is that it is expected that the next experience of the Spirit after salvation was to be filled with the Spirit. Those at Samaria who believed, the converted Saul of Tarsus, the household of Cornelius who accepted the Word of Christ, the Ephesian disciples who embraced the message of Christ—for them all the next step was baptism in the Spirit. The prophecy of Joel which Peter identifies with the Pentecostal experience points to a continuing outpouring of the Spirit which would extend to the end of the "last days." Peter saw Pentecost beginning a continuing fulfillment of Joel's prophecy.

The Bible nowhere limits the experience of baptism in the Spirit to a certain age or group. Nearly twenty centuries after the initial outpouring of the Spirit at Pentecost, more than three hundred million believers in this generation claim to have received the "like gift," the baptism in the Holy Spirit.

"Have you received the Holy Spirit since you believed?" (Ac 19:2).

## For Reflection and Discussion

1. Baptism in the Spirit is supposed to be a "normative" experience for the Christian believer. However, the Pentecostal movement is dated from the turn of the twentieth century. What do you think about this?

2. Classical Pentecostals believe glossolalia is the initial physical evidence of Spirit baptism. What is the need to speak of any *evidence* at all of baptism in the Spirit?

3. Why do you think God chose glossolalia to accompany the Spirit baptism experience?

4. Though the Classical Pentecostal Movement has dated only from the beginning of the twentieth century and the Charismatic Movement from the second half of the twentieth century, Pentecostals/Charismatics comprise a major segment of Christianity. Do some research to help understand the phenomenal growth of this movement.

5. Since baptism in the Spirit is distinct from salvation, and is not required for one to go to heaven, and since there are many wonderful Christians who have never had this experience, why should this be regarded as such an important doctrine?

# I Will Build My Church
## Matthew 16:18

ONE OF THE MOST IMPORTANT, and yet most often neglected areas of Christian theology is the study of ecclesiology, or the doctrine of the Church. The Church is something that many Christians take for granted. In some areas, there seems to be a church on every street corner, and whether one has belonged to a church for many years or never has attended a service, there tends to be a perception among many that they "know" what the Church is all about because it has always been a part of their culture and/or life experience. It is not surprising, therefore, that many have not seriously examined the theology of the Church. Questions such as "what is the Church?" "when did it begin?" "why does it exist?" "what are its beliefs and practices?" "how does it apply to my life?" and other related questions will be explored in the contents of this chapter.

## The Term "Church"

In Matthew 16:18, Jesus proclaimed, "I will build my church." This is the first of over 100 New Testament references which use the term *ekklesia*. This Greek term is compounded from the preposition *ek*, "out," and the verb *kaleo*, "to call." Hence *ekklesia* refers to a group which is called out and gathered or assembled together for a specific purpose. While the first century Christians adopted this word to identify their spiritual gathering, they were not the first to make use of the term. *Ekklesia* was used in a secular Greek context to refer to any assembly of Greek citizens who were "called out" of their homes, businesses, etc., for the purpose of convening a public assembly. One can even see usages in the New Testament, such as in Acts 19:32, 41 in which *ekklesia* refers to the angry mob which "assembled" in Ephesus to protest the results of the apostle Paul's ministry. Even the Septuagint (LXX) translation of the Old Testament uses *ekklesia* nearly 100 times (usually as a translation of the Hebrew *qahal*), sometimes referring to a religious assembly, but often denoting a gathering for secular and even evil purposes. (Perhaps this serves as a good illustration of the need to be cautious of employing what may be called "concordance theology," the misconception that the same biblical word means the same thing in every context!) It should be noted that the majority of New Testament references to the "Church" have the specific intention of a Christian assembly which has been called together to worship and serve the Lord.

## The Church—Local and Universal

In modern language, the term "church" is used in a variety of ways. Sometimes it refers to a place of meeting ("I'm going to church"), or to one's local organization or particular denomination ("my Church believes"). Some churches started out and some still exist as a group officially adopted by a specific region or an entire nation ("the Church of England"). At times the term church is used with reference to all born again believers, past or present, regardless of race, nation, or denominational affiliation.

Some of this ambiguity of semantics stems from the differences between what has historically been called the "invisible" or universal church, and the "visible" or local church. There are numerous New Testament references to the universal Church (for example, this is inferred by Jesus' statement in Mt 16:18; also cf. Eph 5:25, ". . . Christ loved the church, and gave Himself up for her"). Thus, the universal church encompasses all true believers, who are truly "called out" from the world by Christ unto Himself. It is important not to confuse this with other frequently heard terms such as "ecumenical" or "catholic," both of which can be defined as "universal" but which have a different connotation from the way that "universal church" has been expressed above.

The local or "visible" church (the church organization on earth) should ideally be a smaller scale replica of the church universal; that is, it should be composed of people from all backgrounds, races and walks of life who have committed their lives to Christ. It is obvious, however, that this is often not the case, nor was it in biblical times (cf. the problems with personality cliques, inappropriate moral behavior, false prophets, etc., in the Corinthian church!). Thus, while all members of the local church unfortunately may not be sincere in their faith and therefore may not belong to the universal church nor to the kingdom of God, there is no question that the universal church is comprised exclusively of the truly redeemed.

## The Church and the Kingdom

In addition to its teaching on the Church, the New Testament often speaks of the kingdom of God (*basileia tou theou*). In fact, while there are only three usages of the term "Church" in the gospels (all in statements of Jesus, recorded in Mt 16 and 18), the primary teaching point of Jesus' ministry was the kingdom of God. While there is a connection between the two, there are also differences. The term *basileia* or "kingdom" is often defined as the rule or realm of God, or the sphere of God's influence. As such, it includes all of those who acknowledge God's rule and obey Him as their Sovereign. This would include all unfallen heavenly creatures and the redeemed of humanity.[1] By contrast, the Church consists specifically of those human persons who have been spiritually reborn through the work of Christ. The Church also has a definite beginning point, and it will

---

[1]Emery H. Bancroft, *Christian Theology*, second revised edition, 286.

have a definite culmination at the Second Advent of Christ, whereas the kingdom of God transcends earthly time, and is concurrent with the universe. From this broader perspective, the kingdom of God is made up of the redeemed from all ages (Old Testament saints, New Testament believers), but the Church is limited to those who have been redeemed since the resurrection of Christ. Thus it could be stated that one may be in the kingdom of God without being in the Church (in a technical sense, there will be "non-Christians" in heaven!), but all of those who belong to the Church are simultaneously citizens of the kingdom. As individuals are converted to Christ and become members of the church, they are "brought into the kingdom" and the kingdom of God is enlarged.

## Origin of the Church

"When did the New Testament Church actually begin?" has been a matter of considerable debate in theological circles. Some have felt that the Church has existed as long as humanity, that it includes all of those who have ever exercised faith in the promises of God, beginning with Adam (Ge 3:15).[2] Others still opt for an Old Testament inauguration of the Church, but associate its beginnings with the covenant relations of God with his people, whether during the patriarchal era or during the Mosaic period.[3] Still others, including at least one Pentecostal scholar, believe the Church had its conception during the days of Christ's earthly ministry, when He called out His twelve disciples.[4] There are a variety of other opinions, but it seems fair to say that the majority of scholars, whether pentecostal, evangelical, or non-conservative, believe the biblical evidence favors the Day of Pentecost in Acts 2 as signaling the true origin of the New Testament Church.

There is no clear evidence that the Church is found in the Old Testament period, and it has already been noted that when Jesus made the first New Testament reference to the *ekklesia*, He was speaking of the future ("I *will* build my church"). Throughout the New

---

[2]R. B. Kuiper, *The Glorious Body of Christ*, 21-22.

[3]Cf. Charles Hodge, *Systematic Theology* Vol. 3, 549; cf. also Louis Berkhof, *Systematic Theology*, 570.

[4]Raymond M. Pruitt, *Fundamentals of the Faith*, 350.

Testament, the Church seems to be presented as a new work of God which was initiated in the New Testament era. By the very nature of the Church as the body of Christ, it is vitally dependent upon the finished work of Christ on earth (His crucifixion, resurrection, and ascension), and the subsequent coming of the Holy Spirit.[5] In relation to this, it is notable that Luke never refers to the term *ekklesia* in his Gospel, but employs it twenty-four times in the book of Acts.[6] Following the Day of Pentecost with the outpouring of the Holy Spirit upon the disciples, the visible Church is formed and proceeds to follow the order of propagating the gospel as stated by the risen Lord in Acts 1:8. From that time until this, the Church has continued to develop and expand through the power and direction of the same Holy Spirit.

## Biblical Images of the Church

The nature of the Church is far too exhaustive to be grasped by simply understanding the definition of *ekklesia*. The Bible itself uses many metaphorical descriptions for the Church, each of which contains different aspects of the true nature and function of the Church. In fact, Paul Minear has indicated that there are as many as one hundred New Testament images which delineate the meaning of the church.[7] It would be impossible to fully cover each of these here, but several of the more prominent designations will be briefly explored.

The apostle Paul quoted from the Old Testament description of Israel and applied it to the New Testament church when he spoke of God's action to make believers His own people: "As God has said: 'I will live with them and walk among them, and I will be their God, and they will be my people.'" The Church is truly depicted as the people of God, a people for His own possession (cf. Dt 10:15, Hos 1:10; 1Pe 2:9-10). The Church's beginning, its history and its destiny are all founded upon the divine initiative and calling of God. As one has noted, the Church "is a people called forth by God, incorporated into

---

[5]Robert L. Saucy, *The Church in God's Program*, 57-58.

[6]Millard J. Erickson, *Christian Theology*, 1048.

[7]Paul S. Minear, *Images of the Church in the New Testament*.

Christ, and indwelt by the Spirit."[8] As such, the Church comprises the "elect" of God, those in whom His Spirit is actively at work in the process of sanctifying and conforming each member to the image of Christ (cf. Ro 8:28-29).

As the people of God, members of the Church are referred to by many very meaningful expressions: (1) "saints"—from the same term which is translated as "holy" (*hagios*), the Church consists not simply of those whose conduct could be depicted as "perfect" or "saintly," but rather of those who have been called and set apart by God for Himself, and in whom the Spirit of holiness is actively administering His work; (2) those who are "in Christ"—that is, those who share in the benefits of His saving work, and who share in common the corporate privileges and responsibilities of being called God's people; (3) "Christians"—similar to the above, this term (*Christianous*) was first coined by the pagans in Antioch (Ac 11:26), very likely as a derogatory expression for those who followed the teaching and way of Christ. Interestingly, although this word is widely used today, it is only found in two other New Testament references (Ac 26:28, used by King Agrippa; and 1Pe 4:16, used by the apostle); (4) "believers"—from *pistoi*, "the faithful ones," this term emphasizes the fact that the people of God are those who not only have believed and given mental assent to the saving work of Christ, but who live continuously in the attitude of faith and commitment to the Lord; (5) "brethren"—a generic term (*adelphoi*) which is often employed by the New Testament writers to express the mutual love and fellowship that is inherent among the people of God; (6) "disciples"—from the Greek term *mathetai*, which means "learners" or "pupils," this word suggests not only listening to the information conveyed by the Teacher (Christ), but also emulating His life. As theologian Dietrich Bonhoeffer has noted, true discipleship necessitates a willingness to die to self, and to give all to Christ. Bonhoeffer stated that genuine discipleship is only possible through what he declared to be "costly grace." In his words,

Such grace is *costly* because it calls us to follow, and it is *grace* because it calls us to follow *Jesus Christ*. It is costly because it costs

---

[8]Saucy, 19.

a man his life, and it is grace because it gives a man the only true life.[9]

Discipleship is never pictured in the New Testament as being "easy" (for example, cf. Jesus' words in Lk 14:26-33), but it is essential for those who claim to be the people of God.

A beautiful biblical metaphor for the Church is the "body of Christ." The apostle Paul frequently made use of this image in his writings, using the analogy of the parts of the human body and comparing their functions and interrelationships with members of the Church. This image depicts the essential unity that is required in the Church (1Co 12:12: "The body is a unit, though it is made up of many parts; and though all its parts are many, they form one body. So it is with Christ"). Paul goes on to say that Christians are "all baptized by one Spirit into one body" (1Co 12:13). While there must be unity among the members of the body of Christ, it is not contradictory to also emphasize that there is a needed diversity among the members of the body. For example, Paul again says in 1Co 12:14, "Now the body is not made up of one part, but of many." He also acknowledges in Romans 12:4 that ". . . each of us has one body with many members, and these members do not all have the same function . . . "and the application is made to members of the body of Christ. As Gordon Fee notes, unity "does not mean uniformity . . . there is no such thing as true unity without diversity."[10] The importance of this diversity for the proper functioning of the body is stressed throughout 1 Corinthians 12, and is particularly evidenced in relation to the spiritual gifts that are so essential for the ministry of the Church (cf. 1Co 12:7-11, 27-33; cf. also Ro 12:4-8). A significant emphasis of this metaphor is that there must be a mutual interdependence of the members of the Church. In suffering with those who suffer and rejoicing with those who are honored (1Co 12:26), in helping one's brother or sister in Christ to carry their burdens, one is enabled to truly fulfill the law of Christ (cf. Gal 6:2), and thus fulfill one's function in the body of Christ. Just as the physical body is dependent upon the brain to govern its activities, so the spiritual body of

---

[9]Dietrich Bonhoeffer, *The Cost of Discipleship*, second edition, 47.

[10]Gordon D. Fee, *The First Epistle to the Corinthians*, 602.

believers is dependent upon its relation to Christ, who is the Head of the body (cf. Eph 1:22, 5:23). As the members of the body of Christ are arranged and function as God desires (1Co 12:11, 18), and consistently follow the leading of Christ, the Head of the body, the Church will be nourished and sustained and will develop and mature "as God causes it to grow" (Col 2:19).

A third New Testament image for the Church is its depiction as the Temple of God. The biblical writers use several symbols for the building of this temple that correspond to the building composition of an earthly structure. For example, any building needs a foundation. The primary foundation of the Church is the historical person and work of Christ (1Co 3:10-11). Yet there is also a sense in which the apostles and prophets are foundational (cf. Eph 2:20) in that they were used by the Lord to establish and undergird the first century church with the doctrine and practice which they received from Christ, and which is communicated to Christians today through Scripture. Another vivid image which is closely associated with the foundation is the cornerstone. Whereas today a "cornerstone" is more symbolic than integral, it was a very important aspect in ancient building, as it was a larger than normal stone which helped to control the proper design of the building, bringing symmetry to the remainder of the edifice.[11] Concerning the spiritual "temple of God," Christ is described as the cornerstone, through whom "the whole building is joined together and rises to become a holy temple in the Lord" (Eph 2:20-21; cf. 1Pe 2:6-7). Not only was the cornerstone an essential component, but quite obviously there was a need for the regular stones to complete the building project. The apostle Peter describes believers as "living stones, [who] are being built together into a spiritual house. . . ." The term used by Peter in this metaphor is *lithos*, a common word for stone, but unlike other familiar synonyms *petros* (a loose stone or pebble) and *petra* (a larger stone or boulder), this term suggests a "worked stone," that is, one which has been hewn and shaped by the master builder for a proper fitting.[12] It is interesting to note that in the primary references alluded to above (Eph 2 and

---

[11]Saucy, 35.

[12]Cf. Edward G. Selwyn, *The First Epistle of St. Peter*, 158.

1Pe 2), the verbs which describe the building of the temple are usually in the present tense, conveying a sense of ongoing action. Perhaps it could be said that Christians are not "completed projects," but rather are still "under construction." As Paul suggests, they "are being built together to become a dwelling in which God lives by his Spirit" (Eph 2:22).

It was previously noted that the Church is indwelt by the Spirit, both individually and collectively. The apostle Paul questioned the Corinthian believers, "Don't you know that you yourselves are God's temple and that God's Spirit lives in you? . . . God's temple is sacred, and you are that temple" (1Co 3:16-17). It is interesting to observe that in this passage, Paul is writing to the church corporately (the term "you" is plural in the Greek), but in 1Co 6:19, Paul writes to individuals ("you" is singular): "Do you not know that your body is a temple of the Holy Spirit, who is in you, whom you have received from God?" In both texts, as well as in a similar passage in 2Co 6:16ff, the term for temple is *naos*, from the verb *naio*, "to dwell, or inhabit." While there is another Greek term which is used for the larger temple as a whole, the word *naos* is used to refer to the inner sanctuary, the holy place which symbolized the dwelling place of the Lord. How awesome to realize that the Church, personally and corporately, is the habitation of God!

## Church Government

An area that probably sounds the least "spiritual" to many readers of this chapter is that of church government. It should be noted, however, that this is an area addressed in Scripture, and can often cause confusion and dissension due largely to a lack of correctly understanding and applying the biblical principles of ecclesiastical organization. There are some who go to the extreme of believing that the Church is spiritual in nature and therefore the Bible does not offer any guidelines for order and structure, and others who go to the opposite extreme of asserting that the Bible lays out carefully detailed prescriptions for church government (which, ironically, often resemble their own!). Probably the most accurate view is that the Bible does give principles for organization, and even some examples of how those principles are applied, but it does not mandate any certain form or model for all circumstances. It should be remembered that while in many respects the first century church offers patterns and examples worthy of emulation, one should not seek to replicate the exact patterns of the New Testament Church in every category (nor would one even be able to do so, due to different cultural and geographical circumstances, etc.). Indeed, the New Testament gospel message is eternal, but it also needs to be made contemporary in order for it to be effective.

Throughout Christian history, there has been a variety of forms of church government, with varying degrees of authority being granted to the clergy or to the laity. When analyzed, however, these many types can usually be seen to primarily conform to one of three major models of church government: episcopal, presbyterian, and congregational.

The episcopal form of government is usually considered to be the oldest form of polity in church history. The term episcopal comes from *episkopos*, meaning one who oversees, and is often translated in the New Testament as "bishop." While in biblical times the bishop served in much the same capacity as the modern pastor (cf. 1Ti 3:1-7), early in the history of the ancient church the bishop's position was exalted above other church offices. To oversimplify a more complex subject, this was due largely to two reasons: the external persecution of the church, and the internal rise of heresies in the Christian community. The bishop was perceived as one who could be a pillar of strength and who could provide an authoritative voice on matters of the faith (especially important in the days before the New Testament canon was formulated). Through the years, those who have favored the episcopal system of church organization have tended to have a strong, centralized form of polity, under the direction of the bishop or overseer.

The presbyterian system of church government also can make biblical claims for its origin, as the New Testament does refer to those who fulfill the office and function of a *presbuteros*, or "elder." This becomes a bit confusing, however, in passages such as Titus 1:5, which gives instructions for ordaining a "presbyter" (*presbuteros*), but later in 1:7 refers to this person as a "bishop" (*episkopos*). A key concept which undergirds the presbyterian form of government is "representational leadership." For example, many supporters look to the example of the first church council meeting in Jerusalem (Ac 15), in which the church of Antioch voluntarily decided to send representatives to the

Jerusalem-based apostles to discuss a doctrinal dispute. There is no evidence that the apostles "mandated" their coming, nor that the Antioch delegation was received as "inferiors," but rather as equals who were seeking a mutually agreeable resolution. Thus, the idea of representational leadership and mutual cooperation among church bodies is central to the presbyterian system of church organization.

The congregational form of government, as the name suggests, views every local church congregation as essentially autonomous, and that there is no person or organizational structure above the local church, with the exception of the Lordship of Christ. A key concept in this form of polity is democracy, in which all members of the local congregation see themselves as equals who share the authority and responsibility for the local assembly. The minister is typically ordained by the local church (as opposed to the regional or national denomination) in recognition of the minister's call of God to full-time service. While there is much more freedom from ecclesiastical oversight in this structure, this does not suggest that all congregational churches are "radically" independent; rather, there is often a genuine spirit of voluntary cooperation and agreement in matters of doctrine and practice.

As noted above, historically there has been a variety of governmental systems employed by the Church at large, and many modifications and even combinations of the above three types. No one system is inherently "right" or "wrong," and each of them has positive and negative aspects. Whichever system of polity one chooses to follow, one should observe that the Bible presents two primary principles which must underlie any church organization. First, Christ is the absolute head of the Church. Christians must always recognize His sovereignty and be sensitive to His direction through the indwelling presence of the Holy Spirit. Cf. W. D. Davies, "The ultimate New Testament criterion of any Church order . . . is that it does not usurp the Crown Rights of the Redeemer within His Church."[13] Second, there should be recognition of the basic unity of the Church. While there are diversities of denominations, geographical

---

[13]Quoted in Saucy, 119.

areas, cultures, etc., the Church is still a "oneness in multiplicity,"[14] and nothing should hinder the fellowship of true believers in Christ.

## Ordinances of the Church

One of the most disputed theological areas in the history of the Christian church has been over what are usually called sacraments or ordinances. Few would debate that there are two observances, instituted by Christ himself, which have been regularly practiced throughout Christian history—water baptism and the Lord's Supper. During the long course of its history, however, the Roman Catholic Church has added five more practices (confirmation, ordination, marriage, penance, and extreme unction) so that by the time of the Protestant Reformation, the Catholics held firmly to seven "sacraments" to which their followers must adhere. Without exception, the major Reformers of the sixteenth century reduced this tradition of the Catholic church and reaffirmed that water baptism and the Lord's Supper were the only two rites which Christ ordained for His people to observe. Since that time, the vast majority of the Protestant Church has followed this belief. There has, however, been some degree of controversy among these Protestant groups concerning how to properly interpret the theological significance of these events. Since the days of Augustine both of these have been deemed "an outward and visible sign of an inward and spiritual grace." The problem, however, is what exactly does that imply? Should these rites be understood as sacraments, or as ordinances?

The term sacrament (from the Latin *sacramentum*) is probably the older, and certainly the most widely used of these two options. The usage of this term has an interesting background. A *sacramentum* was originally a sum of money deposited by two parties in litigation with one another. After the court's decision, the winner's money was returned, and the loser's was forfeited and was called a "sacrament" because it was considered sacred and was offered to the gods. In a similar way, the term was also applied to the oath of allegiance taken by new enlistees into the Roman army. Eventually early Christians picked up this idea and related it to their pledge of obedience and consecration to the Lord. In his translation of the Latin Vulgate, the

---

[14]Saucy, 119.

church father Jerome (ca. A.D. 400) chose to use *sacramentum* for the Greek term *musterion* ("mystery"). This added a rather secretive, mysterious significance to what the church already regarded as their "sacraments." Many "sacramentalists" through the years have, to varying degrees, believed that the sacraments themselves can serve as a means of conveying saving grace to an individual.

Largely because of the mystical connotation that accompanies the word sacrament, many Evangelicals and Pentecostals prefer to speak of the Lord's Supper and water baptism as "ordinances" of the church. This term is also derived from the Latin language (from *ordo*, "a row, an order"), and simply conveys the idea that these sacred rites were instituted by the command of Christ. He has ordained that these be observed in the church, not because of any magical or salvific (saving) powers which are attached to them, but rather because they symbolize the greater significance of what Christ has already done in the believer's life.[15] It should be noted that some who would not regard themselves as "sacramentalists" still use the term "sacrament" interchangeably with "ordinance" without making any distinction in meaning. Thus, one should not only determine what is meant by the actual term used, but also by the implications and significance attached to the ceremony itself by the participant.

The ordinance of water baptism has been practiced by the Christian community from its beginning. In fact, other similar baptismal ceremonies predate Christianity, including that of John the Baptist, Jewish proselyte baptism, and even baptismal rituals among ancient pagan religions. The meaning of Christian baptism, however, supersedes all of these. Most importantly, Christian baptism identifies the believer with Christ. Christians are baptized "into" (*eis*) the name of Christ (cf. Ac 8:16), suggesting that one has entered into the realm of Christ's lordship and sovereignty. It is a sign that one has died to the old way of life and has entered newness of life through the redemptive work of Christ. Water baptism for the Christian also signifies identification with the body of Christ, the Church. In many religions, the ceremony of baptism was understood as an initiation into the community. The Christian who has undergone baptism is

---

[15]Cf. H. Orton Wiley, *Christian Theology*, Vol. 3, 155-156. Cf. also Saucy, 191-192.

giving public testimony to the world that the believer now identifies with the people of God. One of the reasons why water baptism was usually practiced so quickly following conversion in the New Testament was for the new convert to immediately be involved in the full life of the Christian community.

Historically there have been three modes or methods of baptism: immersion, affusion (pouring) and sprinkling. These modes also have been the cause of dissension among some Christian groups, to the point that some have been severely persecuted over this issue. This is due more to traditional and cultural differences than to biblical understanding. Most scholars would agree that the basic meaning of the verb *baptizo* is to immerse or submerge. It is possible that one might be compelled on occasion to use another mode (for example, when baptizing an elderly or disabled person). The mode of baptism should never become more important than the spiritual truth which baptism symbolizes.

The Lord's Supper or Holy Communion has also been an integral part of Christian worship since the earthly days of Christ, when He instituted this on the night of His betrayal at the Passover meal. Jesus instructed His disciples to participate in this meal "in remembrance" of Him. This term (from the Greek *anamnesis*) means almost the opposite of today's understanding; rather than looking back to the past, it suggests a dynamic recalling of the past into the present, so that there is a genuine sense of participation in the experience being "remembered." There is a three-fold sense of this remembrance—past, present, and future. When the Church gathers to partake of elements which represent Christ's sacrifice (His body and blood), they are recalling the past event of the Cross when He gave himself "once for all." There is also a present sense of "remembrance" at the Lord's table, in that the Church is proclaiming not only the memory of a dead hero, but of an alive and spiritually present Savior. Further, there is a future sense of "remembrance," anticipating the Lord's return when the Church shall be reunited with Christ for all eternity.

Not only does the Lord's Supper suggest a sense of participation with the risen Lord, but it indicates that the Christian is having true fellowship with other believers. The vertical fellowship is complemented by a horizontal fellowship; the love of God is vitally linked with loving one's neighbor. True fellowship with Christ necessitates the conquering of all barriers that would hinder true *koinonia* (fellowship) among the members of His body (cf. 1Co 10:16-17). It is for this reason that most in the Evangelical and Pentecostal tradition practice "open communion," which means that all true believers, regardless of their other differences, are invited to join in the fellowship with the Lord at His table.

## The Mission of the Church

Why does the Church exist? Does it have a specific purpose, or mission, to perform? Certainly, Christ did not call the Church into being and empower it with the gift of the Holy Spirit for it simply to exist as an end in itself. There are several important aspects of the mission of the Church which, if fulfilled in a balanced manner, would help believers, individually and collectively, to fulfill the calling of God and to glorify His name.

One of these aspects is evangelization. In some of Jesus' final words before His ascension, He instructed His followers to evangelize the world and to make new disciples (cf. Mt 28:19; Ac 1:8). While this was a command and not an option or a suggestion, Christ did not expect His followers to accomplish this seemingly overwhelming task without His assistance. They were commissioned to go under His authority (Mt 28:18) and in the power of the Holy Spirit (Ac 1:8). The task of evangelism is one without restrictions, whether geographical, racial, or social. Whether one is witnessing Christ to one's local neighbor, or sharing Christ with someone in a distant land, one is still being faithful to the essence of Christ's command. As Millard Erickson declares, ". . . local evangelism, church extension or church planting, and world missions are all the same thing. The only difference lies in the length of the radius."[16] In considering the task of evangelization, one should not lose sight of the fact that while believers may be the means of sharing the good news, it is still the Lord of the harvest who "brings forth the increase." Christians will not be judged by their "success" (according to this world's standards), but by their faithfulness in service.

A second important facet of the mission of the Church is worship. From an old English word which means "worth-ship," this term

---

[16]Erickson, 1054.

denotes the worthiness of one who receives special honor which accords with that worth.[17] In true worship, one's attention is focused upon the Lord, and not on oneself or one's needs. This does not mean, however, that worship does not have any personal benefits. As one concentrates attention upon the Lord, one invariably will be blessed and spiritually strengthened. Worship should characterize every aspect of one's life as a believer. The apostle Paul stated, "So whether you eat or drink or whatever you do, do it all for the glory of God" (1Co 10:31).

A third important component of the Church's mission is edification, or building up the body of Christ (cf. Eph 4:12-16). In practical terms, edification is accomplished in a variety of ways. For example, the task of teaching and instructing others in the ways of God is a vital means of enriching the household of faith. Also, having true Christian fellowship and social interaction is important if one is to have a balanced Christian walk. Paul wrote of sharing with those who have need (2Co 9), suffering or being honored with members of the Christian community (1Co 12:26), admonishing and correcting those in need of spiritual discipline (1Co 5; Eph 4:15), and bearing one another's burdens (Gal 6:2). All of these are significant ways in which edification may be achieved.

A fourth aspect of the biblical mission of the Church is social concern. Too often among modern Evangelicals and Pentecostals, the first three aspects of the Church's mission are taken very seriously, but this last aspect is sadly neglected or minimized. By contrast, however, Scripture is replete with admonitions for the Church to fulfill this God-given duty, along with the other important aspects of the Church's total mission. Jesus' earthly ministry and teaching was characterized by a loving concern for the suffering and deprived of this world (cf. Lk 10:25-37; Mt 25:31-46). The same concern is evidenced in the epistles of His followers (cf. Jas 1:27, 2:1-11; 1Jn 3:17-18). Those who have been favored with the gracious blessings of God have a responsibility to share in meeting the needs of those who desperately need a tangible witness of the love of Christ.

---

[17]E. F. Harrison, "Worship," in *Evangelical Dictionary of Theology*, 1192.

To conclude, the Church needs to maintain a balanced perspective as it attempts to fulfill these essential aspects of its mission. Each component is vitally important; however, an overemphasis on one to the neglect of the others can be very detrimental to the full life of the Church. For example, too much stress on evangelism may indeed bring many new converts into the local church, but what will they receive when they arrive if there is no emphasis on worship or edification? An accent on worship and/or on edification will strengthen the church and bless the saints, but if not balanced with the other aspects of the Church's mission the Church can become self-centered and its outreach ministries may suffer. Too strong a focus on social concern can lead to a neglect of eternal concerns for the sake of temporal relief if the Church loses sight of its spiritual priorities. In seeking to maintain and fulfill a balanced approach to accomplishing its mission in the world, the Church must be adaptable and versatile, but never compromising its essential purpose and goal—to be faithful in the service of Christ, and to do all for His glory.

## For Reflection and Discussion

1.  Discuss the similarities and the differences between the local, visible church and the universal, invisible church. When talking about the church, why is it important to distinguish the term "universal" from related terms such as "ecumenical" and "catholic?"

2.  In what ways is the church similar to, and different from, the kingdom of God?

3.  The biblical image of the church as the body of Christ suggests that the church is a unity in diversity. What does this mean? Give some modern examples of how this can be evidenced in your own church.

4.  Briefly describe the major facets of the three basic types of church government, noting at least one positive and one negative aspect of each type. Which form of government do you prefer, and why?

5.  Discuss the difference in meaning of the terms sacrament and ordinance. Do most Evangelicals and Pentecostals prefer to describe water baptism and the Lord's Supper as a sacrament or an ordinance? Why?

6.  From your own understanding of theology, do you think it is acceptable for infants and very young children to be baptized in water? Should local church leadership withhold the elements of the Lord's Supper from those who are not saved? Discuss your reasoning for both issues.

7.  This chapter referred to four primary aspects of the mission of the church. From your own experience, do you believe that your local church adequately involves itself in these four aspects? Are there other aspects of the mission of the church that should be added to those highlighted in this chapter? What are some of the dangers of not having a properly balanced emphasis in regard to the church's mission?

# One Body With Many Members
## 1 Corinthians 12:12

THE TASK OF THE STUDY OF MINISTRY is the task of locating and integrating practical theology within the context of theology as a whole. Ministry cannot be understood as mere practical application of a set of principles nor as a sophisticated methodology for building the church and reaching the world. Karl Barth warns of the danger of practical theology becoming no more than "the theory of a trade, which is oriented by every conceivable practical consideration but not by Scripture, history, and dogma, and which is therefore theologically empty."[1] For a Pentecostal understanding of ministry, surely the danger declared by Barth is echoed. It is not enough for ministry to be defined only by purely practical tasks nor only in theoretical propositions. Ministry must be defined as informed by Scripture,

---

[1]Karl Barth, *Church Dogmatics*, IV/3, 88.

history, and doctrine. Ministry is the work of God incarnated through persons empowered by the Holy Spirit to bring the world into reconciliation with God through Jesus Christ.

This study of ministry will begin with a look at the nature and foundation of ministry and proceed to examine the practice of ministry by the Church.

## The Nature and Foundation of Ministry

The proper place to begin the study of ministry is to examine the scriptural record which provides both the theological basis and the practical mandate for the Church. It is an underlying assumption of the discussion in this chapter that ministry precedes a theology of ministry. Therefore the theology of ministry developed in this chapter is informed by ministry. It is the ministry of God which informs and defines a theology of ministry for the Church. This is "God's own ministry of revelation and reconciliation in the world, beginning with Israel and culminating in Jesus Christ and the Church."[2]

It was Jesus Christ who came to do the ministry of the Father and it is the Holy Spirit who empowers the Church to carry out the ministry of Jesus Christ. This concept is consistent with the paradigm for theology found in chapter 1 of this text. Matthew 11:27 displays the necessity of placing the interrelationship of the trinitarian God at the center of the development of all theology. For a theology of ministry it is no less important to maintain the trinitarian structure of God than it is for the development of a theology of scripture, salvation, or any of the other theological issues. As well, it is the Act of God in Jesus Christ which gives meaning to a theology of ministry for the Church.

Clearly, Jesus Christ was calling the Church to ministry when he offered the Great Commission as instruction for the church to take the gospel into the far reaches of the world.

> Therefore go and maké disciples of all nations, baptizing them in the name of the Father, and of the Son, and of the Holy Spirit, and teaching them to obey everything I have commanded you. And surely I will be with you always, to the very end of the age" (Mt. 28:19-20).

---

[2]Ray S. Anderson, "A Theology for Ministry," in *Theological Foundations for Ministry*, 7.

Jacob Firet proclaims this message as the Church's reason for existence and an imperative through which the Church is surely defined with a redemptive-historical necessity.[3]

The importance of this imperative to our study on ministry is multifaceted. The message communicated by Christ to the disciples is an apostolic message which determines that the ministry of the Church is not a new message but is in one sense a continuation of the message of Christ (Jn 17:6-19). The message is both historical and redemptive. The message carried by the Church is to bring others into the discipleship of Christ. The Church does not usurp the position of Christ but carries the message of Christ. It is only through the empowerment of the Holy Spirit that the Church is able to complete its commission. This is a central focus of Pentecostal theology and ministry. While certain evidences of empowerment by the Holy Spirit often receive priority, the attention is more properly directed toward the One who empowers the believer and the message for which the believer and the Church are empowered.

It is the ministry of the Holy Spirit to unite the ministry of the believer with the ministry of Jesus Christ. Anderson states that this action by the Holy Spirit "establishes a reciprocity between dogma and experience which continually discloses and disciplines."[4] This brings one to the diversification of ministries within the Church. All ministries are a form of Christ's ministry in that it is the Holy Spirit who empowers the believer to carry forth the commission to minister. The diversification of ministries is a concretization and specification of the ministry of Christ, who himself is an incarnation of the Father for the purpose of ministry to the world. Therefore ministry is both incarnational and evangelical. Incarnational in that the ministry of the Church is only the ministry of Christ who Himself is the Incarnate One. Evangelical for the ministry of the church is to and for the world.

Alan E. Lewis accurately portrays the incarnational and evangelical center of ministry in his essay "Unmasking Idolatries: Vocation in the *Ecclessia Crucis.*" Lewis contends that God's call and

---

[3]Jacob Firet, *Dynamics in Pastoring*, 62.

[4]Anderson, 8.

Christ's cross are synonymous.[5] It is God who calls humanity but the call is only through the crucified and risen Son. Thus the Great Commission (Mt 28:19-20) is the call to the Church to carry the message of the cross to a world alienated from God, a world which God is pursuing out of love.

The ministry of the Church is determined by the ministry of Christ. Ministry is not only "that to which people respond" (pragmatism) nor a response to human needs (utilitarianism). Primarily ministry is an intentional act of God by which the mission of Jesus Christ continues through the empowerment of the Holy Spirit calling the Church into the cross of Christ in order to bring to the world the message of Christ.

The commission to ministry and the possibility for ministry by the Church are rooted in the actuality of ministry by Jesus Christ (Ac 1:1-4). It is this relationship that prevents ministry from being defined solely as human effort.

In the cross, God in Christ has identified with the godless and at the same time has become a servant to the godless. Jesus Christ becomes the one rejected in order that the rejected ones can be reconciled to God. Ministry springs from this relationship and in the cross the possibility for the reconciled to bear the message and carry out the ministry of Christ becomes actuality. Paul writes the following to the church in Corinth, "for the message of the cross is foolishness to those who are perishing, but to us who are being saved it is the power of God."[6] Ministry as possibility for the Church is integrally related to the actuality of the cross. It is because God in Jesus Christ has chosen the Church and the Church has chosen to respond to God's call to ministry that it is enabled to minister. It is through the Holy Spirit that the Church is empowered and enabled for this ministry.

Ministry is also a commission of love. As the Father loved the world and demonstrated this love by choosing Jesus, as Jesus expressed His love for the world by choosing to give His life a

---

[5]A. E. Lewis, "Unmasking Idolatries: Vocation in the Ecclesia Crucis," in *Incarnational Ministry: The Presence of Christ in Church, Society, and Family*, 113.

[6]1 Corinthians 1:18. It is the word of the cross which authenticates ministry.

sacrifice for the world, so the church must love the world by giving itself for the sake of the world. This can only be accomplished through the power of the Holy Spirit. The power of the Spirit is the power of weakness—weakness as prefigured in the cross. Weakness in one's self-sufficiency becomes power in God's all-sufficiency and the Church is enabled to enact love for the world through its bearing of the message of the crucified and risen Christ. It is granted that this schema for understanding the nature and foundation for ministry is neither exclusive nor comprehensive but it is helpful in understanding the nature and foundation of ministry. It maintains the absolute linkage of theology and ministry, it gives priority to the ministry of God, and it acknowledges the necessity of a trinitarian foundation and hence an authentication of Spirit-empowered ministry by the Church.

Ministry by the Church includes ministry which is both to the Body and ministry which is to those outside of the Church. This activity is wholly consistent with the ministry of God— first within the trinitarian structure itself and then to those alienated from God. This concept is found in both the Old Testament and in the New Testament.[7] To be called to ministry is to be involved in the mission of God in the world. It is to be a bearer of the message of the gospel.

A final comment on the distinctiveness of Pentecostal ministry is in order. The implications of the move from the mission and ministry of Christ to the mission and ministry of the Church are profound. It is clear from the prologue to the Acts of the Apostles that Luke believes that the ministry and mission of Jesus Christ is communicated to and continued through the Church. Stronstad declares that it is through the "transfer of the Spirit" that the disciples are empowered to continue to do and teach those things which Jesus began to do and teach (Ac 1:1). It is then Jesus, who was the bearer of the Holy Spirit, that at Pentecost becomes the giver of the Holy Spirit.[8]

---

[7]In the Old Testament, Isaiah 49:6 states that "it is too small a thing for you to be my servant to restore the tribes of Jacob and bring back those of Israel I have kept. I will also make you a light for the Gentiles, that you may bring my salvation to the ends of the earth." In the New Testament it is recorded in the Epistle of 1 Peter 2:9, "but you are a chosen people, a royal priesthood, a holy nation, a people belonging to God, that you may declare the praises of him who called you out of darkness into his wonderful light."

[8]Roger Stronstad, *The Charismatic Theology of St. Luke*, 49.

Murray Dempster cultivates this thought in relation to the mission of the church.[9] The implications are equally as important for the development of a biblical understanding of ministry. The concept of the empowerment of the Spirit for ministry has both eschatological and ethical considerations. Ministry is eschatological for it is a continuation of the ministry of Christ in the world through the power of the Spirit and it is ethical for it brings through the act of ministry a glimpse of what "life is like" when God reigns.

The concept of Pentecost/kingdom as a means of uniting the Lukan formulation of ministry within the Acts of the Apostles with the formulation of ministry as presented in the gospels is further developed by Macchia.[10] What does this mean for an understanding of Pentecostal ministry? This means that the message preached and the ministry of enacting the message is the same message in the gospels as it is in the Acts. The message of the Pentecostal church is the message of the kingdom which Jesus preached. This provides historical/redemptive continuity and signifies the necessary incarnational and evangelical criteria. Having considered the nature and foundation of ministry it is now appropriate to examine the practice of ministry within and through the Church.

## Ministry as a Call to Ordination

It is true that there is a divinely called and scripturally ordained ministry provided for the purpose of leading the Church. Here it is vitally important that we understand ministry and leadership as it exists in the Church and not as it exists in the world.

As has been previously established the ministry of the Church is a continuation of the ministry of Christ. Therefore the ministry of leadership in the Church must maintain this same orientation. Ordination is not a form of law which places some members of the Church in direct control of other members of the community. Rather it is servant leadership which proclaims and exemplifies righteousness, love, justice, and mercy and thus enables the Church to be free from the world (Mk 10:43-45).

---

[9]Murray Dempster, *Called and Empowered: Global Mission in Pentecostal Perspective*, 24.

[10]F. D. Macchia, "Spirituality and Social Liberation; The Message of the Blumhardts in the Light of Würtemberg Pietism, with Implications for Pentecostal Theology," 296-304.

Ordination is that gift to the Church which facilitates the Church in the edification of its life. Therefore ordination can only be understood within the context of the Church itself. This does not mean that the Church ordains one to ministry, for it is only Christ himself who executes the ordination, but always within the Church. Torrance has clearly stated this fundamental assertion regarding ordination, "It is the risen and ascended Lord who acts directly through His Spirit ordaining His servant to the ministry, but He does that in and through the Church. . . ."[11] The practice of ordination is present in both the Old and New Testaments (Dt 34:9; Ex 28:41; Ac 6:3-6; 1Ti 4:14). Though the practice of ordination is evident it is not to be understood as a precondition of the call to ministry but rather as ratification of the call.[12] This defines ordination not as a calling exercised by the Church but as a calling by Christ recognized by the Church.

Continuing with this idea it is also to be understood that the ministry to which one is ordained is more important than the one who is ordained. This establishes the message as more important than the messenger. The earthen vessel is chosen to carry the divine Word but not to displace the divine Word. At every point the ordained individual is totally dependent upon the historical/redemptive message of Christ and upon Christ himself.

The ordained ministry is clearly the "reign of grace." The ones who fulfill this ordained ministry are those who have received this call from Jesus Christ. Otto Weber describes this transaction within the context of Ephesians 4:7ff: "Jesus Christ has led a host of captives . . . and he gave some apostles, some prophets, some evangelists, some pastors and teachers." The call to ordained ministry is not a call to the "reign of glory" but a call to the "reign of grace."[13] Those who are called unto ordained ministry are first called unto Christ. Again, it is evident that the call to ordination must be within the context of the Church. Therefore those called to ordination must come under the reign and rule of Jesus Christ. They do not function according to the

---

[11]T. F. Torrance, "Conflict and Agreement in the Church," in *Theological Foundations for Ministry*, 397.

[12]Donald Bloesch, *Essentials of Evangelical Theology*, Vol. 2, 119.

[13]Otto Weber, *Foundations of Dogmatics* Vol. 2, 567.

norms of the world order but according to the norms of the Kingdom of God.

A look at those ministries which are generally considered as "ordained ministry" is in order.

*Apostles:* Apostles (*apostoloi*) most simply defined, are those who are sent by God to perform a specific task. P. C. Nelson asserts that "there is no one definition of the word apostle which clearly distinguishes such an individual from other ministers of the gospel."[14] It would seem the concept of apostle is applied within the Church first to the "Twelve." It was the Twelve who following the work of Christ became the "founding fathers" of the Church. The gift given to the apostle is one of leading the Church community in a particular fashion. Weber comments that the common position of the Church regarding the time for persons bearing this office is that "it is now past." He also notes that this was the position of Calvin and other Reformers.[15] Hammond holds that apostles were called to the task of leading the infant Church following Pentecost.[16]

The background for *apostolos* is the Hebrew word *shaliach* (from *shālah*, to send). The emphasis is on the sender rather than on the one being sent. The one sent is an extension of the sender. It is here one sees the significance of the ministry (Mk 3:13-19). The apostles are called into Jesus' own "sending" and therefore become the primary witnesses to Him. As with other ordained ministry it is the message which takes precedent over the messenger. Apostolic succession refers not to the messengers but to the message received by the earliest Christian communities directly from the apostles. This message is still received in the tradition of the "Twelve." It was the message rather than the title by which Paul described his own apostleship (Gal 1, 2).

*Prophets:* The word prophet is taken from the Greek word *prophetes* which means "one who speaks for someone else." A prophet is a person who speaks for God in the sense of conveying God's message.[17] As with the case of the apostle the prophet is not one set

---

[14]P. C. Nelson, *Bible Doctrines*, 90.

[15]Weber, 580.

[16]T. C. Hammond, *In Understanding Be Men: A Handbook of Christian Doctrine*, 162.

[17]Nelson, 90.

in the Church to "lord over" others but to serve others. With the apostles the prophets laid the foundation of the infant Church.[18] The prophet like others in ordained ministry has no special relationship to Christ which is withheld from the "ordinary church member." The ministry of the prophet is a service and a function within the Church.

*Evangelists:* According to Nelson the evangelist is "one who proclaims the gospel."[19] The word is derived from the Greek *euangelion* meaning "good news." The particular ministry of the evangelist is to spread the good news of the Gospel—the possibility of forgiveness and reconciliation with God. This ministry is prefigured in the ministry of Christ (2Co 5:19). It is important that the evangelist "develop paradigms adequate to the realities of most of the world's people."[20] This mandate places the evangelist with a primary responsibility to proclaim the gospel to those who have not been reconciled to God. The proclamation must be announced in a manner which retains the integrity of the message (the Gospel) and confronts the hearer in a way which is comprehensible and to which the hearer may respond.

*Pastor-Teachers:* This group of persons is called to provide the Church with instruction in living the Christian life. This is included in the image of feeding the flock (Jn 21:15-17; Ac 20:28). In the New Testament pastor-teachers are found to serve along with the previously discussed ministries. According to Schillebeeckx it was not until the post-apostolic period that pastor was used as a general term to refer to all church leaders.[21] Nelson distinguishes between the two groups. He contends that it is the specific duty of teacher to "expound the Word of God." Pastors are particularly charged with providing for the spiritual needs of the congregation.[22]

---

[18]Ephesians 2:19-20 "… members of God's household, built on the foundation of the apostles and prophets, with Jesus Christ himself the chief cornerstone."

[19]Nelson, 91.

[20]William E. Pannell, "Evangelism: Solidarity and Reconciliation," in *Incarnational Ministry: The Presence of Christ in Church, Society, and Family*, 199.

[21]E. Schillebeeckx, *Ministry: Leadership in the Community of Jesus Christ*, 145, n.10.

[22]Nelson, 91-92.

## Ministry as a Call to the Laity

The call of ministry to the laity is best recognized in the Great Commission (Mt 28:19-20). The term "laity" is rooted in the Greek word *laos*. This refers to those belonging to the people of God, the *laos* (2Co 6:16; 1Pe 2:9-10). Hendrik Kraemer acknowledges this by stating that "in this light all members of the Church are *laikoi*, and only on this basis can they get other, more specific qualifications."[23]

Though in this chapter the ordained ministry is considered prior to consideration of lay ministry it is true that only on the basis of the call to lay ministry can one be called to ordained ministry. The laity in the Church are not inferior to those who are called to ordained ministry. It is those laity who see themselves as active and integral members of the Body of Christ who are empowered to fulfill the responsibility for the Church's mission.[24]

Kraemer notes that as early as the late first century the terms *laikos* and *laos* were having their meaning changed from the meaning as used in the early Church.[25] Today the evolution of meaning has conferred upon the term laity the idea of ignorance. This places the lay membership of the Church over against the professional clergy of the Church and serves to hinder the Church as it fulfills its call to mission and ministry. This more recent definition and usage is not in keeping with the theology of laity as developed in the Scripture.

All members of the Church are ministers. These ministers serve the Church with a variety of functions, each function providing necessary ministry and service. Kraemer asserts that "in the primitive Church every activity or function which contributed to the upbuilding of the Christian community was brought under the category of *diakonia*."[26] Since *diakonia* is rendered service this means that all Christians are servants and ministers.

---

[23]Hendrik Kraemer, *A Theology of the Laity*, 49.

[24]Kenneth W. Van Wyk, *Laity Training Resource Kit*, 25.

[25]Ibid., 50ff. The terms originally referred to all members of the church. This signifies a change from understanding the whole church as a royal priesthood. As a result of this change the laity are reduced to mere object, with no understanding of calling in its own right.

[26]Kraemer, 139.

There are some members who serve the Church in the special capacity of deacons and deaconesses (Ac 18:26, 21:9; Ro 16:1, 3-4, 12). As with those called to ordained ministry the emphasis is on the message rather than on the messenger. Deacons and deaconesses are placed as representatives of the servant ministry of the Church. The Church is essentially ."ministerial" in nature. That the English equivalent of *diakonoi* (servants) consists of both males and females is apparent in the aforementioned passages. Kraemer insightfully and critically comments on the later development of excluding women from the group of ministers when he writes,

> the later, exclusively male development of the functioning of the Church, interspersed with interesting timid endeavors to reserve some place for certain categories of women in the Church's official service, represents an estrangement from the dominant thought of the New Testament that the *whole* Church, regardless of sex, is diakonia Ministry.[27]

Paul defines this new "people of God" in Galatians 3:26-29.

> You are all sons of God through faith in Christ Jesus, for all of you who were baptized into Christ have been clothed with Christ. There is neither Jew nor Greek, slave nor free, male nor female, for you are all one in Christ Jesus. If you belong to Christ, then you are Abraham's seed, and heirs according to the promise.

If the Church is to recognize ministries as authentic and as called by God then it must do so in light of the criteria by which Paul defined the people of God. It is the resurrected Christ who for Paul, serves as a hermeneutical criterion. None is to be excluded based on race, gender, social status or ethnicity for it is by the grace of God that each one is called to service. All believers are ministers and each believer has a gift of ministry (Ro 12:4-6, 1Co 12:4-7, 14:12). The resurrected Christ through the present ministry of the Holy Spirit enables the Church to fulfill its call to ministry and its commission to re-present Jesus Christ to the world.

## Ministry as a Call to the Church

The previous sections of this chapter have dealt with the nature and foundation for ministry and the functions of individuals in

---

[27]Ibid., 142.

ministry. The final section of the chapter will consider the Church as a ministering community. The ministries previously considered are to be seen as committed by Christ to the Church as a whole and not to special individuals. The "whole church is itself the true officebearer commissioned for ministry."[28] It is in this sense that the Church is and becomes a re-presentation of Christ.

First, the Church is an apostolic community.[29] The apostolic ministry of the Church is fulfilled as the Church lives out the historical-redemptive message and thus provides continuity with the message proclaimed by Christ. The possibility of this mission hinges on the Pentecost bestowal of the Holy Spirit. The Church is turned outward into the world (Jn 17:18). Barth contends that true apostolic succession is not to be determined by historical criticism which may provide an understanding of the office of the apostle, but true apostolic succession is the existence of the Church in following the apostles in their testimony to Christ.[30]

How is the Church an apostolic community? The Church is an apostolic community as it continues to hear and obey the Word of the Lord. It is the ministry of the Holy Spirit at work in the ministering Church who empowers the Church to live out the Word of God. By living out the Word the Church submits to the authority of Scripture and therefore is determined by Scripture. The Church is apostolic in that it stands for the true Word over against a false word. As the Church fulfills the apostolic mandate to witness to the Living Christ the Church itself continues the apostolic tradition.

Second, the Church is a ministering community. Kraemer states "the Church is ministry." This does not detract from the ministry or ministries of the Church but declares that the Church itself is ministry. This is not to say that the Church does not have ministries but that the Church *as* ministry underlies the ministries of the Church.[31] The basis

---

[28]Helmut Thielicke, *The Evangelical Faith*, Vol. 3, 230.

[29]It must be noted that the author of this chapter is indebted to Ray S. Anderson for his development of the Church as the re-presentation of Christ. This includes viewing the ministry of the Church as an apostolic community and as a ministering community.

[30]Karl Barth, *Church Dogmatics*, IV/1, 719.

[31]Kraemer, 136-137.

for this thought is the fact that it was Jesus Christ who was the *diakonos par excellence* (Mk 10:45) and it is the Church which is commissioned to serve the world in the way Christ himself served the world, therefore providing continuity to the message of the gospel. The act of service is directed to God (2Co 6:4), to man (Lk 22:27), to the gospel (Col 1:23), and to the Church (Mk 9:35).

Barth contends that the Church exists for the world and it is the ministry of the Church to expend itself for the world.[32] Surely this is true if it is acknowledged that the Church exists to provide continuity to the historical-redemptive message of Jesus Christ and therefore have its life determined by the life of Christ (Mt 5:13-14, Jn 17:18). This is a critical juncture in the development of a theology of ministry. The Church must respond to God's summons to be called out of the world in order to be sent back into the world. Why this summons and commission? The answer is again that it is the Church who is called to continue the ministry of Christ and this ministry can only occur within the world.

Following the response to the summons is the fulfillment of ministry. Bonhoeffer contends that the question which demands response at this point is "what is the will of God?."[33] The will of God for humanity is both that one *is* good and that one *does* good. The two are inseparably linked together. This linkage mandates ministry and prohibits the idea that Christianity is only a set of religious beliefs. To be Christian is to be reconciled to the Living God, thereby thinking and acting out that relationship.

The incarnational life of the Church is preserved as it ministers to the needy, binds the broken, feeds the hungry, and heals the sick. The evangelical center of the Church is preserved as it proclaims the gospel—a message of reconciliation. For the Church to be the Church it must be incarnational with an evangelical center, it must both be and act Christian. Ministry is integral to the definition of the Church.

Just as the world needs the Church so the Church needs the world in order to minister as Christ ministered. It is the Church as ministry which gives form to the presence of Christ. The Church as

---

[32]Barth, IV/3, 762.

[33]Deitrich Bonhoeffer, *Ethics*, 55-72.

ministry, as a ministering community empowered by the Pentecost sending of the Holy Spirit, embodies the message of the gospel.

*For God so loved the world that He gave His one and only Son, that whoever believes in him shall not perish but have eternal life. John 3:16*

## For Reflection and Discussion

1.  Explain the idea "ministry must be defined as informed by Scripture, history, and doctrine." How does this address the tension between a theological understanding of ministry and practical ministry?

2.  How is the message of the Great Commission both historical and redemptive? What is the importance of the Holy Spirit in fulfilling the Great Commission?

3.  Discuss the three-fold schema for understanding the nature and foundation for ministry.

4.  Discuss "ministry as a call to ordination" in the context of both the historical and the contemporary Church.

5.  Explain the biblical concept of lay ministry. What does it mean to the life of the Church that all believers are ministers?

6.  In the chapter it was stated that "the Church exists for the world." What does the mean for the contemporary Church?

7.  Write a one page *credo* on "Ministry is. . . ."

# 11

## I Am the Lord Who Heals You
### Exodus 15:26

BIBLICAL TERMS FOR HEALING
REASONS FOR HEALING
HEALING AND THE ATONEMENT
THE GIFTS OF HEALINGS
THE CHURCH AS HEALING COMMUNITY

O NE OF THE MOST SIGNIFICANT CONVICTIONS which has characterized Pentecostal doctrine and practice in the twentieth century is the belief in divine healing. In an era of increasing skepticism concerning anything deemed supernatural or rationally questionable, Pentecostals have been at the forefront of growing numbers of Christian believers who are rediscovering the biblical concept of healing, and are becoming cognizant that divine healing is a blessing of God available for every generation. Such a firm tenet of faith, however, can often be more convincing in theory than in practice. Many who sincerely believe that God *can* heal still wonder if He *will* heal. Some who are prayed for are wonderfully healed; others apparently are not. Are such persons out of God's will? Do they lack faith? If one asks the Lord in prayer, "if it be your will" to heal, is that a sign of humility or of doubt? These issues and others will be addressed as this chapter will attempt to explore the biblical and theological foundations of this marvelous gift of God known as healing.

## Biblical Terms for Healing

There are numerous words used in Scripture to describe God's healing activity. The most frequently used Old Testament term in this regard is *rapha*. Various forms of *rapha* are used 66 times in the Hebrew Scriptures, referring either to literal or figurative healings. Examples of *rapha* being used in regard to a literal, physical healing would include the story of Abraham's encounter with Abimelech in Genesis 20, when God forgave and "healed" Abimelech and his family so that their progeny could continue (v. 17). In Numbers 12:13, Moses prayed for God to heal Miriam from her leprosy (an affliction which resulted from her rebellion, and from which she was healed after experiencing a time of separation from the people). In another instance King Hezekiah asked for, and received, a sign from the Lord that he would be healed of his illness (2Ki 20:8). In this same context, however, the miraculous healing of the king (v. 5) was accompanied by an ancient medicinal treatment (cf. v. 7, "a poultice of figs" was applied to Hezekiah's boil, and he recovered). While the Hebrew mindset understood God to be the ultimate source of all physical healing, the Jewish people recognized that this did not prevent them from using other tangible means to assist in the healing process.[1] In a like manner, they understood that healings may be progressive rather than instantaneous, and may involve a natural period of recuperation (cf. Ex 21:18-19; Lev 13:18, 14:3; Pr 3:7-8).

Many of the uses of *rapha* in the Old Testament are in connection with a figurative or metaphorical sense of healing. Such very meaningful usages of this concept would include being "healed" from sin (cf. Isa 6:10, 19:22, 57:18-19; Jer 3:22). Such symbolic healing also pertains to the restoration of natural elements (cf. 2Ki 2:21-22; 2Ch 7:13-14; Eze 47:7-8), the healing of the emotionally and spiritually downtrodden (cf. Ps 147:3; Jer 17:14) and the revitalization of the nation of Israel (cf. Ps 60:1-2, 107:20; Hos 6:1, 14:4). Relating to this broader, holistic view of healing, Kirby asserts that

---

[1] One will note a similar attitude in the New Testament, when Paul encourages Timothy to use a natural remedy to counter his frequent stomach ailments (1Ti 5:23).

In the Hebrew covenant community, all healing, whether by the instantaneous intervention of a man of God, a homespun remedy, or nature's own time, was understood as the work of God. In the Hebraic mind, *salvation and healing were synonymous concepts*, parallel modes of divine activity.[2]

Soon after Israel's deliverance from Egyptian bondage, God made Himself known to Israel as Yahweh-Rapha (or more specifically, Yahweh-Ropheka, "the LORD, the one healing you," Ex 15:26). It was in this context, soon after the Exodus, that Israel encountered the bitter waters of Marah which were "healed" by a divine miracle of God through the hand of Moses. The literal and the figurative nature of healing were combined here as God announced to Israel that in return for their obedience, He would not allow them to experience the plagues which were brought upon Egypt, for Yahweh was indeed Israel's Healer. There is no doubt, then, that healing is depicted as one of the major features of God's saving activity in the Old Testament. Kirby likens this to a divinely initiated process of growth for Israel, leading to "wholeness *and* holiness within the wholesome community."[3]

The most frequently used New Testament terms for healing are *iaomai* ("to heal, to cure") and *therapeuo* ("to serve, to take care of, to heal"). These words occur most often in the Gospels, and are typically used in connection with Jesus' ministry of healing.[4] In contrast to the Old Testament, where most of the usages of *rapha* refer to spiritual or metaphorical healings, the New Testament terms *iaomai* and *therapeuo* most frequently are related to healings of physical diseases or afflictions.[5] There are, however, some instances in which these Greek

---

[2]Jeff Kirby, "The Recovery of Healing Gifts." In *Those Controversial Gifts*, George Mallone, ed, 104.

[3]Ibid., p. 106.

[4]*Iaomai* is used twenty times in the gospels, five times in Acts, and only three times in the rest of the New Testament (Heb 12:13; Jas 5:16; 1Pe 2:24). *Therapeuo* is found thirty-seven times in the gospels, five times in Acts, and only has two more occurrences in Revelation (13:3, 12).

[5]For several examples of *iaomai* used in connection to physical healing, cf. Mt 8:8, 13; 15:28; Lk 6:18-19; Ac 9:34. Examples of *therapeuo* in this regard include Mt 4:23-24; Mk 3:2, 10; Jn 5:10.

terms are also used as metaphors for spiritual healing (e.g. Mt 13:15; Heb 12:12-13). Additionally, the Greek verb *sozo*, which is normally translated "to save" and is used in reference to being saved from sin, is also employed in the New Testament to convey the idea of healing from sickness or affliction. For example, on behalf of his young daughter Jairus requested Jesus to "come and put your hands on her so that she will be healed [*sothe*] and live" (Mk 5:23). After witnessing Jesus' deliverance of the demon-possessed man named Legion, the crowds began to testify how the man "had been cured [*esothe*]" (Lk 8:36). A related term, *diasozo* ("to save thoroughly"), is also used several times in relation to Jesus' healings (cf. Mt 14:36; Lk 7:3).

From this brief inductive study of the biblical terms, it may be readily observed that healings are multifaceted in character. Scripture often refers to healings of the physical body, but there are also many references to healings that are emotional or spiritual in nature. Some healings are perceived to be instantaneous and directly from the hand of God, while others are understood to be more gradual and to involve some type of human activity or natural process. The application of verbs such as *sozo* to situations in which one is physically healed or spiritually delivered may indicate that for the New Testament mindset, as well as the Old, salvation extends to the whole person (and not simply the "spiritual" aspects). Perhaps some of the older Bible translations may be helpful here, as frequently they would indicate that the one who was healed had in fact been "made whole" by the power of God.[6] This is in keeping with the Hebrew concept of *shalom* ("peace, wholeness, or well-being"), a term often used in the Old Testament to convey the idea of the "healthiness" that God desired to characterize every aspect of the lives of His people. At times the Greek language of the New Testament also makes this explicit. Such is the case in John 7:23 where Jesus healed "the whole man" (*holon anthropon*) on the Sabbath.

---

[6]Cf. the KJV descriptions of healing in Mt 15:28 and Ac 9:34. This is not to suggest that the more modern versions are inaccurate by translating such terms as "healed" or "made well," but simply that in most cases more is involved than only a physical healing.

## Reasons for Healing

At first glance, the reasons or purposes for healing seem obvious—one is sick or afflicted, and needs to be restored to health! However, there are other items to be considered beyond that which is most conspicuous.

Few theologians would disagree that the ultimate reason for sickness and death entering into the world can be attributed to the Fall of humanity into sin (cf. Ge 3:3; Ro 5:12). Sickness and death are often biblically depicted as part of the curse which extends to nature itself (Ro 8:19-22). This curse and all of its consequences will someday be forever removed (Rev 22:3); however, until then humanity will continue to be subject to the conditions of a world not yet redeemed. Believers are redeemed from the curse of the law through the saving work of Christ (Gal 3:13); this, however, refers to spiritual deliverance from sin. Physically, believers are still mortals who live in a fallen world, and this includes the prospect of having to contend with various sicknesses and afflictions, some of which may have their culmination in physical death. Thus, while sickness and death were introduced into the world as a result of the Fall, this by no means indicates that every specific instance of sickness or death is a direct consequence of personal sin. Jesus clearly taught against such a notion in John 9:1-3 (cf. also Lk 13:1-5).

Another important reason for healing is that through such an event God is glorified and the gospel is proclaimed. God is both a God of love and a God of power—through acts of healing, both of these characteristics are vividly displayed to humanity. This does not mean that God desires to draw attention to himself for the sake of sensationalism or vanity, but rather to focus the attention of humankind upon the truth of the gospel, that they might be saved. Healings provide one means of attesting to that truth, namely that God so loved sinful humanity that He sent Christ, who victoriously conquered sin through His own shed blood, and who is able to restore wholeness to that which was broken. Healings announce to a skeptical world that God loves and cares about it, and that He is willing to intervene in human affairs. Referring to Jesus' earthly ministry of healing, Kirby states that His

> . . . healing miracles were evidence that the kingdom of God, the tangible reign of God, had begun to invade history . . . miracles of

healing served the dual purpose of authenticating the divine source of the gospel and the genuineness of its messengers.[7]

Just as healings helped to authenticate the messianic mission of Jesus (cf. Lk 5:23-24), so they likewise rendered credence to the ministry of His followers (Mt 10:7-8; Ac 3). Yet healings were not the focal point of their ministry, nor should they be of ministry today. In the Christian era, healings have always served as a concrete manifestation and demonstration of the gospel message—but the essence of that message is not relief from temporal affliction, but eternal salvation through the suffering and death of Christ. Harper correctly notes that

> Our concentration on the healings of Jesus will be an abortive exercise if we do not see the cross as the centrepiece of it all . . . It is the cross, not miracles, which is the heart of the Christian faith. It is the greatest miracle, the most sensational healing.[8]

## Healing and the Atonement

Since the late nineteenth century, the connection of healing with the atonement of Christ has been a prevalent teaching within the Holiness and especially Pentecostal traditions. Two early prominent advocates that healing is a part of the atonement were A. J. Gordon and A. B. Simpson.[9] Such persons taught that when sin entered the human race through the Fall, the curse upon humanity included sickness. Since illnesses and afflictions were therefore not an intended part of God's created order, but resulted from the Fall, they must be dealt with like all the rest of the effects of the Fall, not by natural but through spiritual means. Christ's atoning death, then, provided not only the remedy for human sin but also for human sickness. Simpson clearly affirmed this concept by stating, "If sickness be the result of the Fall, it must be included in the Atonement of Christ."[10] Early

---

[7]Kirby, 111.

[8]Michael Harper, *The Healings of Jesus*, 177-178.

[9]Gordon was the Baptist founder of Gordon College and Seminary. Simpson, a former Presbyterian, founded the Christian and Missionary Alliance Church. Both men were highly respected and influential Holiness leaders in the late 19th and early 20th centuries.

[10]A. B. Simpson, *The Gospel of Healing*, revised edition, 34.

Pentecostal leader Charles F. Parham took this idea even further, stating in 1902 that

> The healing of the sick is as much a part of the gospel as telling them of Heaven . . . This is the great salvation ... that heals the body as well as the soul . . . Healing is as certainly purchased in the atonement of Jesus Christ as salvation.[11]

These essential concepts concerning healing were adopted by most of the Pentecostal movements of the early twentieth century. A. B. Simpson's "Fourfold Gospel," which exalted Christ as Savior, Sanctifier, Healer, and Coming King, was borrowed by several Pentecostal groups. While Pentecostals also emphasized the need for sanctification, they typically substituted "Baptizer" (in the Holy Spirit) in place of Sanctifier in their typical fourfold arrangement.[12] The emphasis that healing was a part of the atonement of Christ was likewise embraced by most of the early Pentecostal fellowships (now sometimes referred to as "Classical Pentecostals" to distinguish them from the newer "Charismatic" groups). For example, the Assemblies of God "Statement of Fundamental Truths" teaches that "Divine healing is an integral part of the gospel. Deliverance from sickness is provided for in the atonement, and is the privilege of all believers (Isa 53:4-5; Mt 8:16-17; Jas 5:14-16)." Similarly, the "Declaration of Faith" of the Church of God (Cleveland, Tennessee), states, "Divine healing is provided for all in the atonement."

A key passage for this discussion is Isaiah 53, which many Evangelicals and Pentecostals feel to be a prophetic precursor of the sufferings of the Messiah. Regarding the relation of healing to Christ's atonement, verses 4-5 are often cited as support:

> [4] Surely he took up our infirmities and carried our sorrows, yet we considered him stricken by God, smitten by him, and afflicted. [5] But he was pierced for our transgressions, he was crushed for our iniquities; the punishment that brought us peace was upon him, and by his wounds we are healed.

---

[11]Charles F. Parham *The Sermons of Charles F. Parham*, 46-48.

[12]Groups that either officially or unofficially advocate these four essential truths include the International Church of the Foursquare Gospel (which derives its name from this "foursquare" message), and the Assemblies of God (which commonly refers to these four concepts as its cardinal doctrines).

The term used in verse 4 for "infirmities" is *chali*, which in the Hebrew usually means physical sicknesses (although there are places in which it is also used metaphorically, e.g., Isa 1:5 and Hos 5:13).[13] The noun for "sorrows" is *ma'kov*, a term having to do with pain which appears fifteen times in the Old Testament. In at least three of those references (Ex 3:7; 2Ch 6:29; Job 33:19) *ma'kov* refers to physical pains; Brown, Driver, and Briggs suggest that the other usages (including Isa 53:4) refer to mental pain or distress.[14] Erickson concurs that Isaiah 53:4 conveys the idea of mental anguish or sorrow, perhaps as a result of the Suffering Servant's physical infirmities.[15] Since the overall context of Isaiah 53 is soteriological in nature, some scholars such as those mentioned above believe that verse 4 is speaking of spiritual sickness and pain. In response it should be noted (as mentioned earlier in this chapter) that Scripture frequently describes spiritual *and* physical healing in close proximity. In many of the Old Testament passages which some interpret as exclusively speaking of spiritual infirmities or pains, the case could be equally made to support a more literal interpretation of physical sicknesses and/or pains along with the figurative meaning (cf. Dt 7:15, 28:61, both of which use *chali*; Job 33:19 and Jer 51:8, which both use *ma'kov*). This "both/and" arrangement seems to be the proper way of interpreting Isaiah 53:4 as well. Concerning the Isaiah passage, Fee admits that it is "ambiguous," stating "it is clearly a metaphor for salvation," while "in the prophetic tradition such salvation also included the healing of the people's wounds incurred in their judgment."[16]

The verbs used in this passage are also integral to this debate. The first verb, *nasa*, ("took up" our infirmities) appears often in the Old Testament, and has the basic meaning of "to lift up" or "to bear, carry." Sometimes *nasa* refers to a vicarious bearing of guilt, as it

---

[13]Francis Brown, S. R. Driver, and Charles A. Briggs, *The New Brown-Driver-Briggs-Gesenius Hebrew and English Lexicon*, 318.

[14]Ibid., p. 456.

[15]Millard J. Erickson, *Christian Theology*, 839.

[16]Gordon D. Fee, *The First Epistle to the Corinthians*, The New International Commentary on the New Testament, 594, n. 62.

clearly does in Isaiah 53:12 ("he 'bore' the sin of many").[17] The second verb, *saval*, is used only nine times in the Old Testament, usually in reference to carrying a heavy load. While this most often means to carry something in a literal sense, it is also used at least twice in connection with vicarious bearing: Lamentations 5:7, and Isaiah 53:11 ("he 'will bear' their iniquities").[18] It is significant that the same two verbs used in Isaiah 53:4 for "took up [*nasa*] our infirmities" and "carried [*saval*] our sorrows" are used later in that same chapter to speak of what Christ would vicariously bear ("their iniquities," v. 11; "the sin of many," v. 12). The point is that just as Christ atoned for the sins of humanity, He also could be portrayed in Isaiah 53:4 as the One who representatively bore their sicknesses and pains.

An important New Testament passage which seems to connect healing with Christ's atonement is Matthew 8:16-17. In this context, Jesus miraculously heals Peter's mother-in-law of a fever, and later heals many others from that community who were brought to Him. Matthew indicates that

> This was to fulfill what was spoken through the prophet Isaiah: 'He took up our infirmities and carried our diseases.'

Here Matthew quotes from Isaiah 53:4, directly applying that prophecy to an instance of physical healing. As was true with the study of the original text in Isaiah, there is some controversy over the proper application of the verbs used by Matthew for "took up" (*lambano*) and "carried" (*bastazo*). Some suggest that Matthew was attempting to portray Christ as the One who sympathetically bore these physical weaknesses, and that it was not his intent to link this with Christ's vicarious bearing of sin on the Cross.[19] Fee correctly observes that Matthew does not refer specifically to the Cross in this context, but rather sees this event as something being prophetically fulfilled during Jesus' earthly ministry.[20] Others, however, do see a

---

[17]Brown, Driver, and Briggs, 669-671.

[18]Ibid., 687.

[19]For a representative of this opinion, cf. Erickson, 840. Note a similar usage of "sympathetic bearing" of burdens in Gal 6:2.

[20]Gordon D. Fee, *The Disease of the Health and Wealth Gospels*, 15.

connection between the vicarious or substitutionary bearing of sickness as well as sin, and feel that Matthew is faithfully interpreting Isaiah in this regard. For example, Delitzsch indicates that in this passage

> . . . it is not the sins, but 'our diseases' . . . and 'our pains' that are the object, [and] this mediatorial sense remains essentially the same. The meaning is not merely that the Servant of God entered into the fellowship of our sufferings, but that He took upon Himself the sufferings which we had to bear and deserved to bear, and therefore not only took them away . . . but bore them in His own person, that He might deliver us from them. But when one person takes upon himself suffering which another would have had to bear, and therefore not only endures it with him, but in his stead, this is called *substitution*. . . .[21]

Young concurs with this position, stating that

> The reference in Matthew 8:17 is appropriate, for although the figure of sickness here used refers to sin itself, the verse also includes the thought of the removal of the consequences of sin. Disease is the inseparable companion of sin.[22]

Young emphasizes that it is the consequences of sin and not sin itself that Matthew mentions. Referring to the fact that Christ vicariously bore the sicknesses of humanity, Young declared that "what is meant is not that he became a fellow sufferer with us, but that he bore the sin that is the cause of evil consequences, and thus became our substitute."[23] This is in agreement with the "position paper" adopted by the Assemblies of God in 1974:

> . . . atonement provides for the consequences of sin. Even where sickness is not the direct result of sin, it is still in the world because of sin. Therefore it is among the works of the devil Jesus came to destroy (1Jn 3:8) and is thus included in the atonement. . . . Christ in His atonement was concerned about providing for sickness as well as sin. Matthew 8:16,17 not only confirms this, but shows that the

---

[21]F. Delitzsch, *Isaiah*, in Commentary on the Old Testament, Vol. VII, 316.

[22]Edward J. Young, *The Book of Isaiah*, Vol. 3, 345.

[23]Ibid., 346.

atonement includes divine healing as a means of meeting the needs of those who come to Jesus.[24]

First Peter 2 is another New Testament passage which alludes frequently to Isaiah 53. In connection with the issue of healing and the atonement, many cite as support Peter's remark in verse 24, "by his wounds you have been healed" (cf. Isa 53:5). It is especially popular in some charismatic circles to emphasize the switch from the present tense in Isaiah ("we *are* healed") to the past tense in 1 Peter ("you *have been* healed") as an indication that healing has already been guaranteed for those who simply claim it by faith.[25] A careful study of 1 Peter 2, however, will reveal that the apostle is not here referring to physical healing, but rather to being restored to wholeness from the spiritual sickness of sin.[26] The point that Peter is making throughout this soteriological passage is that Christ took the punishment of humanity as their substitute —they were suffering from the illness of sin, but through Christ's atoning work, they have been restored to spiritual well being.[27] To interpret 1 Peter 2:24 in this way does not in the least diminish the Scriptural teaching on physical healing, but rather emphasizes the "both/and" nature of healing. In discussing the New Testament understanding of Isaiah 53, Fee points out that Jesus, the apostles, and the Early Church clearly expected that God would heal, and accepted the Isaian passage "both as a metaphor for salvation (1Pe 2:24) and as a promise of physical healing (Mt 8:17)."[28]

To conclude this section, perhaps it is best to say that healing is provided through the atonement of Christ, in the sense that all of the blessings of God to His children are in some fashion connected to the reason for the Incarnation—the Eternal Word "became flesh" in order

---

[24]"Divine Healing: An Integral Part of the Gospel." (Adopted by the Assemblies of God General Presbytery, August 20, 1974), pp. 8-9.

[25]The term used in 1 Peter 2:24, *iathete*, is the second person plural, first aorist passive indicative of *iaomai*. Both the KJV and NASB accurately translate it as "you were healed."

[26]Cf. Fee (*Health and Wealth*, p. 15), who in reference to Peter's quotation from Isaiah, says "The usage here is metaphorical, pure and simple."

[27]For a more thorough exegetical treatment of this passage, see Wayne Grudem, *1 Peter* Tyndale New Testament Commentaries, 131-134, and I. Howard Marshall. *1 Peter* The IVP New Testament Commentary Series, 94-96.

[28]Fee, *First Corinthians*, 594, n. 62.

to give His life for the sins of the world. The New Testament writers clearly saw the Cross as the heart of God's redemptive activity. Fee states, "In this sense, and in the sense that sickness is ultimately a result of the Fall, one may perhaps argue that healing also finds its focal point in the atonement."[29] Turner agrees, noting that historic Pentecostalism "put healing back into the spiritual agenda, and located it firmly in the atonement . . . where it rightly belongs—indeed what benefit of salvation does not derive from the atonement?"[30]

Prior to the Cross Jesus often healed the sick, and the argument has therefore been made that healing could not be a part of His atonement. As Wright aptly submits, however, any problem here would pose a further problem with the forgiveness of sins, since Jesus also forgave sins before Calvary. Wright declares that "In the mind of God, Calvary was an accomplished fact before the foundation of the world (1Pe 1:20; Rev 13:8). God was able, therefore, to dispense the blessings of the Cross before the actual crucifixion."[31]

Another difficulty which arises in regard to this issue is that all who come unto Christ by faith are forgiven of sins, yet not all believers are healed of sickness. How then can healing be a part of the atonement? One should remember that the primary reason for the Incarnation was for Christ to vicariously bear the sins of the world. Sickness, while ultimately a result of sin, should not be equated with sin. Sickness may produce suffering and physical pain, but it is not connected with moral guilt or legal penalty. Thus, it is sin alone, and not sickness, which requires atonement.

From another perspective, it should be noted that there is an "already/not yet" aspect to the benefits of the atonement. While on the one hand all of the effects of the Fall are canceled by the atonement (cf. 1Jn 3:8), it is apparent that some of these benefits are not yet realized (cf. Ro 8:19-25). Even one's salvation, made possible by the "once for all" atoning sacrifice of Christ, is in a sense not yet completed (i.e., one "has been" saved, or justified; one "is being" saved, or sanctified; and one "shall be" saved, or glorified). In a

---

[29]Fee, *Health and Wealth*, 16.

[30]Max M. B. Turner, "Spiritual Gifts, Then and Now," *Vox Evangelica* 15 (1985):48.

[31]Gordon Wright, *In Quest of Healing*, 57-58.

similar manner healing is provided for through the atonement. While some may receive their healing in this life, others must persevere as they eagerly await the "redemption of our bodies" (Ro 8:23). Victory over death was secured through the atonement of Christ (Heb 2:14-15; Rev 1:18), and yet believers still die and will not experience total victory over death until the resurrection (1Co 15:53-57). This "already/not yet" understanding of the atonement is reflected in the Assemblies of God position paper on healing:

> We receive the forgiveness of sins now in connection with the redemption of our souls. We shall receive the redemption of our bodies when we are caught up to meet the Lord and are changed into His likeness. . . . Divine healing is a foretaste of this, and like all the blessings of the gospel, flows from the atonement.[32]

## The Gifts of Healings

Chapter 7 of this volume deals with the gifts of the Holy Spirit. In the present context, however, it is important to briefly examine one of the spiritual gifts listed by Paul in 1 Corinthians 12. Three times in that chapter (vv. 9, 28, 30) the apostle refers to *charismata iamaton*, or "gifts of healings." These are the only explicit mentions of this gift in the New Testament, although the gift is obviously exercised frequently in the ministry of the Church. It is also interesting that this is the only spiritual gift mentioned in 1 Corinthians 12 which is specifically identified by the plural term *charismata* for "gifts" (as opposed to the singular *charisma*, "gift"). The word "healings" (*iamaton*) is also in the plural. There are various opinions on what this signifies. For instance, Alford suggests that it might "indicate different kinds of diseases, requiring different sorts of healing."[33] Kirby feels that the double plural indicates the great variety in those equipped with healing gifts and in the various effects rendered by them.[34]

It should be noted that the gifts of healings, like all the other spiritual gifts, depends solely on God's grace (*charis*). Such gifts are not deserved or "possessed" by the one through whom they are transmitted nor by the one who is their recipient; rather they are

---

[32]"Divine Healing," 9.

[33]Cited in Wright, 65.

[34]Kirby, 102.

manifestations of the Holy Spirit, given as He determines for the building up of the body of Christ (cf. 1Co 12:7-11). Bittlinger agrees with this assessment, stating that "Every healing is a special gift. In this way the spiritually gifted individual stands always in new dependence upon the divine Giver."[35]

It seems significant that Paul's first mention of this gift (1Co 12:9) is in relation to the spiritual gifts of faith and miracles. While these three have their own identity, it is apparent from the biblical record that they frequently operate in connection with one another. Divine healings are evidences of the miraculous power of God, and are often given by Him in response to the believer's faith. Williams agrees that the gifts of faith and healings are closely correlated. He sees faith as the background and energizing force for the gifts which follow, in particular for healings.[36] In a similar respect, Martin believes that the gifts of healings are intentionally associated with the next gift, "miraculous powers" (or literally, "workings of powers," *energemata dunameon*, another double plural; v. 10), in order to "evoke the sense of abundance and variety in the gifts that spring from faith."[37] While these spiritual gifts are in some ways interrelated, it should be accentuated that they are still separate gifts and should not be merged. For example, one may be apportioned a gift of faith for some other reason besides the effecting of healings or miracles. One may be greatly used by the Lord to function in one particular gift, but may not be so used in the operation of the other gifts. Regarding the operation of the gifts of healings along with all of the other gifts of the Holy Spirit, one should always be reminded of the admonition of the apostle Paul: "All these are the work of one and the same Spirit, and he gives them to each man, just as he determines" (1Co 12:11).

## The Church as a Healing Community

Just as healing characterized the earthly ministry of Jesus, so He intended it to be a part of the ministry of His followers (e.g., Mt 10:1, 7-8; Lk 10:1, 9). Healings were a vital element of the ministry of the

---

[35]Cited in Fee, *First Corinthians*, 594, n. 66.

[36]J. Rodman Williams, *Renewal Theology*, Vol. 2, 369.

[37]Francis Martin, "Gift of Healing," in *Dictionary of Pentecostal and Charismatic Movements*, 352.

Early Church, often serving to authenticate the validity of the gospel message (cf. Ac 3:1-10, 5:12-16, 19:11-12). Healings continued to be evidenced in the following centuries of Christian history, being attested in the writings of such early leaders as Justin Martyr and Irenaeus, and later prominent figures such as Basil of Caesarea, Gregory of Nazianzus, and Augustine. In his major work written near the end of the second century, *Against Heresies*, Irenaeus spoke of many true disciples of Christ who had "received grace from him [and] use it in his name for the benefit of the rest of men." This included some who would "cure the sick by the laying on of hands and make them whole."[38] The great theologian of the ancient Western Church, Augustine (354-430) at first taught that Christians in his generation should no longer expect the continuance of healings. However, near the end of his life he admitted that he was mistaken. In his classic work, *The City of God*, Augustine makes reference to "nearly seventy attested miracles," including miracles of healing, which had occurred in the previous two years in his city of Hippo. Three years before his death, Augustine wrote in *Retractions* that the sick who were prayed for were not always healed; however, he further stated

> But what I said should not be taken as understanding that no miracles are believed to happen today in the name of Christ. For at the very time I wrote this book . . . a blind man in [Milan] was given back his sight; and so many other things of this kind have happened. . . .[39]

As time transpired, the ministry of healing and the operations of spiritual gifts in general increasingly declined in the history of the church (although there have always been notable exceptions). Prayer for the sick as described in Scripture became reinterpreted by the medieval Catholic Church as "last rites" for the dying. This ceremony was accepted as one of their seven sacraments ("Extreme Unction"). An interesting change in Roman Catholic doctrine has developed since Vatican II (1962-1965), in which extreme unction was broadened in its meaning and even the terminology was changed to "Anointing the Sick." Many religious movements, both Catholic and Protestant, have

---

[38]Cited in Ronald Kydd, *Charismatic Gifts in the Early Church*, 44.

[39]Cited in Morton T. Kelsey, *Healing and Christianity*, 184-185.

begun to take a renewed interest in their spiritual heritage, and are realizing that genuine healings, while often minimized, have always had a place in the practice of their tradition.[40]

The Epistle of James sets forth a principle for healing in the context of the local church community. James 5:14-16 states

Is any one of you sick? He should call the elders of the church to pray over him and anoint him with oil in the name of the Lord. And the prayer offered in faith will make the sick person well; the Lord will raise him up. If he has sinned, he will be forgiven. Therefore confess your sins to each other and pray for each other so that you may be healed. The prayer of a righteous man is powerful and effective.

Several brief observations may be made concerning this passage. James teaches that the sick person should call for the church elders (*presbuteros*) to pray. There is certainly nothing wrong with summoning the church leadership, but it is doubtful here that James is implying that *only* those in such a capacity are able to effectively pray for healing. The point seems to be that one is to request those of one's own spiritual fellowship to intercede on one's behalf. It is not necessary to make a pilgrimage to a great shrine or to visit some famous healer in order to receive healing from the Lord. In a similar fashion, it is unwarranted to demand that on every occasion the sick must be anointed with oil before healing will come.[41] Oil had a variety of usages in biblical times, including as a medicinal agent (cf. the action of the "good Samaritan," Lk 10:34), and as a symbol of being set apart and blessed by God (e.g. the anointing of Old Testament kings and prophets). It is doubtful in this context that

---

[40]For a good study of the history and practice of healing in church history, see Paul G. Chappell, "Healing Movements," in Burgess and McGee, eds. *Dictionary of Pentecostal and Charismatic Movements*. Also see David E. Harrell, Jr. *All Things Are Possible*.

[41]Anointing with oil was used on other occasions in Scripture as part of prayer for the sick (e.g., Mk 6:13). In other instances, however, it was not evidenced. Instead, a variety of actions accompanied such prayer (e.g., laying on of hands, Mt 9:29, Ac 28:8; Jesus placed mud on the eyes of a blind man, Jn 9:6-7; a hemorrhaging woman touched Jesus' garment, Mk 5:27-29; Peter's shadow, Ac 5:15, and Paul's handkerchiefs, Ac 19:12, were instrumental in healing). On other occasions, there are no such actions mentioned as necessary for healing (cf. Mt 4:24, 12:22; Ac 8:7).

James is prescribing a combination of prayer and medicine,[42] but rather that he is viewing the act of anointing as symbolizing the touch of the Holy Spirit upon the sick individual. In verse 14, "pray" (*proseuxasthosan*) is the primary verb, while "anoint" (*aleipsantes*) is a participle, denoting an important but secondary action.

Critical to the healing mentioned in James 5 are the words of verse 15: "the prayer offered in faith will make the sick person well." The Greek wording here is literally, "the prayer of faith will save the sick." This phrase has been the cause of some ambiguity —is James referring to the faith of the one who does the praying (as suggested by the NIV interpretation), or to the sick person's faith, or to none of the above? Tasker notes that the "prayer of faith" does not differ from other kinds of prayer, because there is no true Christian prayer which does not involve faith. Nor does James imply that only if there is a sufficient degree of faith will the prayer be answered.[43] Tasker suggests that James' point is that there is no circumstance in life in which faith is impossible, and therefore there is no situation in which a Christian cannot resort to prayer. In this particular case, Tasker believes that it was the combined prayers and faith of the sick person and the elders of the church which were expressed to a sovereign, omnipotent God who always hears and responds to the cries of His people.[44]

James further teaches in verse 15 that such a prayer of faith "will save [*sosei*] the sick." As noted earlier in this chapter, the Greek verb *sozo* ("to save") is used in the New Testament both in reference to salvation from sin and, as in this passage, to restoration of health or wholeness (hence the NIV translation, "will make the sick person well"). Such healing is indeed closely associated with "the prayer of

---

[42]Such a position is favored by Donald W. Burdick in "James," *The Expositor's Bible Commentary* Vol. 12, 204.

[43]This is in agreement with the Assemblies of God statement on divine healing. "Jesus did not turn away from those who had little faith or weak faith. Those who are sick often find it is not easy to express faith, and Jesus did a variety of things to help them ... The faith, however, had to be in the Lord, not in the means used to help them express their faith. This seems to be the reason for the great variety of means used, lest people get their eyes on the means rather than on God" (pp. 11-12).

[44]R. V. G. Tasker, *The General Epistle of James*, 132.

faith," but James' final clause in this verse should be emphasized: "the Lord will raise him up." This passage should not be understood as an all-inclusive promise to heal every person in every circumstance in which a "prayer of faith" is offered. It is God's desire for Christians to pray in faith for healing, but He alone decides when and in what manner to heal.

In modern times, many Christians continue to receive marvelous healings from the hand of God. Some are healed of physical sicknesses and afflictions; others receive emotional or spiritual wholeness through the gracious provision of the Lord. As in biblical days, some are healed instantly while others receive their healing in a progressive manner (cf. Mk 8:22-25; Jn 9:6-7). There are still other believers, however, who are not healed in this lifetime. Such persons often have great faith in the Lord and live a consistent and committed Christian life, yet their continued infirmity prompts some modern-day "Job's comforters" to search for a "lack of faith" or "hidden sins" on the part of the sick individual. Such imprudent and insensitive actions by some sincere but misguided persons have been the source of much confusion and needless heartache placed upon those who already are suffering. How, then, is the modern believer to understand who, when, and if it is God's will to heal or not to heal?

Long ago, the Lord inspired the prophet Isaiah to proclaim

'For my thoughts are not your thoughts, neither are your ways my ways,' declares the LORD. 'As the heavens are higher than the earth, so are my ways higher than your ways and my thoughts than your thoughts.' (Isa 55:8-9)

In a similar fashion, the apostle Paul explicated

Oh, the depth of the riches of the wisdom and knowledge of God! How unsearchable his judgments, and his paths beyond tracing out! Who has known the mind of the Lord? Or who has been his counselor? Who has ever given to God, that God should repay him? For from him and through him and to him are all things. To him be the glory forever! (Ro 11:33-36)

From these Scriptures and countless others, it is obvious that no person, regardless of one's depth of spiritual insight or maturity, fully knows the mind or will of God for every circumstance. To do so would cause one to exchange places with God! There are few other situations in which this is seen to be more true than in the case of healing.

While the Bible is replete with instances of miraculous healings by the power of God, there are also some examples of those who did not receive healing. The prophet Elisha was used mightily by God to perform miracles, including healings, and yet the time came when "Elisha was suffering from the illness from which he died" (2Ki 13:14). Scripture gives no hint that Elisha was in any respect out of God's will; in fact, God used him to prophesy one last time before his death (cf. 2Ki 13:15-20). Similarly, in the New Testament, Paul was greatly used by the Lord in a healing ministry, but the apostle himself suffered physically (cf. 2Co 4:10-12, 16-17, 12:7-9; Gal 4:13-15). Paul's associate Trophimus was too sick to continue on the missionary journey, but there is no allusion to any sin or lack of faith on his part (2Ti 4:20). Paul's friend Timothy suffered stomach problems, for which the apostle advised a medicinal remedy rather than exhorting him to pray more or to exercise more faith for healing (1Ti 5:23). Epaphroditus became gravely ill and was healed, not because of any special action or spiritual attainment, but because "God had mercy on him" (Php 2:26).

Such biblical examples are by no means intended to convey the impression that God is spasmodic or whimsical in dispensing His gifts of healings. Rather, they are evidences that in biblical times as well as today, God is the one in charge and that He will heal or not heal according to His divine purposes. David Lim aptly articulates this:

> It is God's will to heal, unless God has a higher will for the immediate situation. That is to say, God always desires the best for us that we might glorify Him most effectively. He is not simply the head of the department of welfare to give us what we need. His gifts are purposeful, that we may build up the Church and touch lost humanity for Him. If He works through seeming tragedy, that is His prerogative. We must keep looking to Him, not the circumstances. We evaluate what is best on a temporal basis. God knows what is best on an eternal basis.[45]

God desires for His people to have faith. God ministers in many instances when faith is not greatly evidenced. God wants His children

---

[45]David Lim, *Spiritual Gifts: A Fresh Look*, 294.

to pray and to expect answers to prayer. Sometimes answers are not immediately given, and some specific prayers are not answered in the affirmative. All of these statements, while seemingly paradoxical, are true, simply because God is a sovereign God. Rather than causing one to feel as though exercising faith for healing is a futile effort, the recognition that God is totally free to be God is liberating and refreshing. Such a grasp of reality enables one to abandon self-reliance and to place one's total trust in a gracious God! Such a one will know that God is not under obligation to the human request, but one will still be confident of the divine promise that "if we ask anything *according to his will*, he hears us. And if we know that he hears us—whatever we ask—we know that we have what we asked of him" (1Jn 5:14-15, emphasis added). Referring to this both/and emphasis of having faith in God for healing and yet trusting in the wisdom of a sovereign and gracious Lord for His will to be done, Fee states

> The mystery of faith is that there is a wonderful correlation between our asking and trusting, and what goes on about us. God doesn't have to answer prayer, but He does. God doesn't have to heal, but He graciously does. Healing, therefore, is not a divine obligation; it is a divine gift. And precisely because it is a gift, we can make no demands. But we can *trust* Him to do all things well![46]

---

[46]Fee, *Health and Wealth*, 22.

## *For Reflection and Discussion*

Ps 197 & 198

1.  What are some of the various ways in which the primary Hebrew and Greek words for healing are used in Scripture? Does the modern church seem to fully understand the biblical concept of healing?

2.  Is it theologically correct to say that Satan causes illness in the life of a Christian believer? Give biblically-based reasons to support your response.

3.  What is meant by the statement that healing is a part of the atonement? How have some persons taken this idea to extremes and misconstrued its biblical meaning?

4.  Is it always God's will to heal the sick? Discuss the problems posed by both sides of this issue. What is your personal response, and why?

5.  Discuss the possible implications of the phrase "gifts of healings" being in the plural. Do some individuals possess the gifts of healings? Why are some more greatly used in a healing ministry than others?

6.  Read and discuss James 5:14-16. What are the important aspects of this passage? What are its implications for the modern church?

7.  Have you ever been healed (physically, emotionally, or spiritually)? Has the Lord ever directly used you to pray for and to witness the healing of someone else? Share with a friend your experiences of healing.

# 12

# The Hope of Glory
## Colossians 1:27

## Foundations of A Pentecostal Eschatology

Perhaps there is no topic which brings more intrigue to a discussion of Christian theology than the topic of eschatology. Whether it is a discussion of death and the afterlife, a dialogue about the time of the rapture, or an engaging conversation about the future existence of a literal one thousand year millennium the verbal exchange is likely to be lively and animated.

Eschatology is that section of theology which considers the teaching of the Church regarding the consummation of history within the purpose of God in Jesus Christ. The term itself is a compound construction of two Greek words: *eschatos*, meaning "last" and *logos*, meaning "subject or word." It is important to note that eschatology refers primarily to time rather than to space. It is the consummation of history at the end of time. It is *when* God in Christ will consummate his rule over creation. It is not primarily *where* this consummation will occur. The term itself has been in use only since the nineteenth century and though the concept of the future and final destiny of creation is integral to the Scripture and biblical theology it is a recent designation in systematic theology.

Pentecostal eschatology has been thoroughly couched in the expectation of the future events of God. Cecil M. Robeck, Jr., documents the significance of the place the promise of the return of Christ has played in the complex set of movements with "eschatological overtones" which came together to form the Pentecostal Movement.[1]

It is this anticipation of the future and the relationship of the future to the past and present which characterizes Pentecostal eschatology. The hope in Jesus Christ is realized when He puts the final enemy (death) under his dominion, sin and evil are overcome, and God will become " all in all" (1Co 15:28). It is hope in Jesus Christ which is the central focus of Pentecostal eschatology; He is the "hope of glory" (Col 1:27). Paul Jewett, though himself not a Pentecostal, writes,

it is hardly possible to overestimate the importance of eschatology to Christian faith, for it is the nail on which everything hangs. Life without faith is empty, and faith without hope is impossible.[2]

Pentecostal eschatology clearly proclaims the imminent return of Jesus Christ. It is a return which is both certain and impending. Because it is imminent it is not possible to set the scene of completed events necessarily preceding the return of Christ. No one can establish the date for the consummation of this hope. In fact it is reported in the Gospel of Matthew that "no one knows about that day and hour, not even the angels in heaven, nor the Son, but only the Father."[3] It is Christ himself who without knowing the completeness of the future preaches an eschatological message of the certainty of the future and

---

[1]Cecil M. Robeck, Jr., "Faith, Hope, Love, and the Eschaton," *PNEUMA: The Journal of the Society for Pentecostal Studies* 14, no. 1 (1992): 1.

[2]Paul K. Jewett, "The Doctrine of Last Things", 1.

[3]See specifically Matthew 24:36. However the entire section encompassing Matthew 24-25 is pertinent to this discussion.

exhorts humanity to be steadfast in hope, attentive, and watchful for the return is imminent.

Robeck contends that because the return is imminent it is not dateable, it is premillennial, and it is pretribulational. He states

> it is, after all, a blessed hope that not only will Christ gather all believers before things go bad for a period of tribulation, but it is a blessed hope that Christians will not have to suffer such a devastation.[4]

It is hope—hope in Jesus Christ—which characterizes the message of Pentecostal eschatology and consequently it is this same hope expressed through the eschatological message which mobilizes Pentecostals to action in the world. It is not hope in a fantasy world somewhere in the future but it is a recognition of the presence of the future in one's current world and of the consummation of history inaugurated by the return of Jesus Christ.

The question which must be answered is, "what is the eschaton, what is the 'last thing' which is the proper object of the hope of the believer?" F.F. Bruce suggests that the term *eschaton* (last thing) really should be replaced with *eschatos* (last one) for it is not the absolute end of time which is the hope but it is the person of Jesus Christ. He is the fulfillment of the hope of the people of God.[5] This understanding allows one to remain faithful to the Hebrew concept of eschatological dualism, the "already" (the present age) and the "not yet" (the age to come). In the first advent of Jesus Christ the Kingdom of God is come in Him and in the second advent the Kingdom will be fulfilled.

This eschatological dualism denies the singular perspective, proposed by some, which suggests that the death of Jesus proved him to be wrong regarding the Kingdom. This position proposes that the Sermon on the Mount was an interim ethic based on Jesus' own conviction and understanding that the Kingdom was at hand.[6] The use of the Hebrew eschatological dualism also opposes the suggestion that the Kingdom came wholly in the events of the life, death, and

---

[4]Robeck, 3.

[5]F.F. Bruce, "Eschatology," *Dictionary of Theology*, 190.

[6]Albert Schweitzer, *The Quest of the Historical Jesus*.

resurrection of Jesus Christ. In this position the Kingdom is entirely "now" with no mention of a future aspect.[7]

Pentecostal eschatology must affirm, against the singular perspectives just mentioned, the Hebrew concept of eschatological dualism. It is at the heart of Pentecostal theology that through the presence and power of the Holy Spirit the Kingdom is present in the world (the already) and that this presence is a guarantee and first fruits of the future (the not yet). Because of the abiding presence of the Spirit and the contemporaneity of Jesus Christ and because of the impending fulfillment of this age as it is met by the age to come the Pentecostal believer lives a life bound up in an eschatological hope—the hope is Jesus Christ.

## Old Testament Eschatological Themes

In the Old Testament the most prominent eschatological theme is the hope of the People of God. The hope, as possibility, is expressed even prior to the creation. God, who is the Creator, existed prior to and outside of creation. In the creation of humanity God created the possibility of covenant and relationship. God who, in grace, provides the possibility and actuality for the redemption of humanity, brings hope to humanity. Therefore, humanity is not bound by an end (*telos*) determined by evolutionary principle or by chance. Humanity is bound to an end that is determined from outside of creation itself. It is God who eschatologically determines the final state of humanity. It is God who as the hope of humanity has decided to stand with humanity in the struggle against evil. This theme is portrayed throughout the Old Testament.

The faith of Israel was directed toward the hope of a future. There was a better time ahead, the nation would one day be victorious. The promise to Abram, "... and all peoples on earth will be blessed through you" (Ge 12:3), will be fulfilled.

In the Old Testament the People of God existed parallel with but also incongruous with the surrounding nations. In the midst of the present the expectation is of a better future. The mythical religions on the one hand call Israel to a denial of her present and future while Yahweh calls Israel to a confessional life acknowledging the presence

---

[7]C. H. Dodd, *Parables of the Kingdom.*

of God. Hence, one sees God visiting His people. It is not the appearance of Yahweh merely for the sake of appearance. "The sense and purposes of his appearances lies not in themselves, but in the promise and its future."[8]

It is only the coming of Yahweh which can bring realization of the covenant promises. Humanity cannot by its own efforts succeed in bringing history to its eschatological fulfillment. It is this expectant hope in the future (the hope in Yahweh) which makes the People of God distinctive. The realization of this hope is lodged in the covenant between Yahweh and his people. He is the God who brings into existence that which does not exist and who "calls things that are not as though they were" (Ro 4:17). Times may be difficult and circumstances adverse but the hope of the People of God is that what they now experience is not "God's final act" but that in that "final act" the people will realize the fulfillment of the promise of God.[9]

The message of the prophets was often a message about the future. At a time when the People of God were burdened by miseries and the lure and influence of the false hopes of the nations the prophetic voice called the People to denounce the false hopes and remember the covenant Yahweh has made with them. This covenant is the message of true hope and deliverance; it is Yahweh himself who is the hope. Amos clearly expresses this in his announcement of impending disaster and the only source of hope:

> *This is what the Lord says to the house of Israel:*
> *Seek me and live; do not seek Bethel,*
>     *do not go to Gilgal, do not journey to Beersheeba.*
> *For Gilgal will surely go into exile,*
>     *and Bethel will be reduced to nothing.*
> *Seek the Lord and live, or he will sweep through the house of Joseph*
>     *like a fire; it will devour, and Bethel will have no one to quench*
>     *it.*[10]

In conjunction with this announcement of disaster and hope is the introduction of the term, Day of the Lord. The Day of the Lord is an

---

[8]Jurgen Moltmann, *Theology of Hope*, 100.

[9]Stephen Travis, *I Believe in the Second Coming of Jesus*, 14.

[10]Amos 5:5-6. This theme may be seen in the writings of other prophets. These include Isaiah, Jeremiah, Hosea, Ezekiel, Micah, Zephaniah, and Zechariah.

eschatological formula referring to the time when the Lord will intercede for his people to save them from their enemies.

> Woe to you who long
>    for the day of the Lord!
> Why do you long for the day of the Lord?
>    That day will be darkness, not light.
> It will be as though a man fled from a lion
>    only to meet a bear,
> as though he entered his house
>    and rested his hand on the wall only to have a snake bite him.
> Will not the day of the Lord be darkness, not light—pitch-dark,
>    without a ray of brightness?
>                (Amos 5:18-20)

The day of the Lord is seen both as a time of salvation and a time of judgment (Isaiah; Ezekiel; Hos 2:16ff). The prophet Joel announces this two-fold understanding of the day of the Lord:

> And afterward, I will pour out my Spirit on all people. Your sons and daughters will prophesy, your old men will dream dreams, your young men will see visions. Even on my servants, both men and women, I will pour out my Spirit in those days. I will show wonders in the heavens and on the earth, blood and fire and billows of smoke. The sun will be turned to darkness and the moon to blood before the coming of the great and dreadful day of the Lord. And everyone who calls on the name of the Lord will be saved; for on Mount Zion and in Jerusalem there will be deliverance, as the Lord has said, among the survivors whom the Lord calls. (Joel 2:28-32)

The theme is also detected in Old Testament apocalyptic literature. Daniel's compatriots when commanded to worship an image made by King Nebuchadnezzar replied:

> O Nebuchadnezzar, we do not need to defend ourselves before you in this matter. If we are thrown into the blazing furnace, the God we serve is able to save us from it, and he will rescue us from your hand, O king. But even if he does not, we want you to know, O king, that we will not serve your gods or worship the image of gold you have set up.[11]

The focus in this text is upon the assurance that God will fulfill His promises and the hope of the people which the assurance brings. The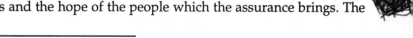

---

[11]Daniel 3:16-18.

focus is not the preservation from misery and suffering but in the fact that "even if he does not" deliver from the immediate danger He will be triumphant.

The Old Testament is eschatologically significant for its patterns of covenant. The Mosaic covenant encouraged Israel to remember the grace of God. He had saved her and made her his people. The covenant with Abraham assured Israel that her future ultimately rested not in her self-sufficiency but in the purposes of God.[12] If there is any hope in the present and for the future it is in the God who in His grace has covenanted with his people and thereby bound himself to them.

## New Testament Eschatological Themes

New Testament eschatology is consistent with and grows out of the eschatology of the Old Testament. In Jesus Christ the salvation announced in the Old Testament becomes reality. However the historic work of Christ is not complete fulfillment of that which is to come but rather is only a partial realization of the final state. The historic work of Christ must be seen as a necessary part of the move of history for it is on this work that the hope of the future rests. The Apostle Paul declares this position when he writes:

> For no matter how many promises God has made, they are "Yes" in Christ. And so through him the "Amen" is spoken by us to the glory of God. Now it is God who makes both us and you stand firm in Christ. He anointed us, set his seal of ownership on us, and put his Spirit in our hearts as a deposit, guaranteeing what is to come.[13]

Clearly the Old Testament eschatological structure of the "already" and the "not yet" are evident in the writing of Paul. Already the People of God have a partial eschatological realization in the historic person and work of Jesus Christ and the continuing presence of the Holy Spirit. That the fulfillment of this hope is in the future is also apparent in the preceding text. The dialectical relationship between eternal life which is a present reality and eternal life which is a future hope is sustained. It is the Holy Spirit who is both an abiding presence

---

[12]John Bright, *Covenant and Promise: The Prophetic Understanding of the Future in Pre-Exilic Israel*, 196.

[13]Second Corinthians 1:20-21.

and a guarantee of the future which is characteristic of Pentecostal eschatology. It is not only a kingdom ethic or the historic event of Jesus Christ that is eschatologically significant. It also is the Spirit of God, sent by Christ, at work in the present age as a partial realization of the age to come which is at the heart of Pentecost and Pentecostal eschatology.

Central to the teaching of Jesus was the message of the Kingdom of God. George Ladd chronicles the significance of this message in the teaching of Jesus.[14] Even the many scholars who hold vastly different positions about the meaning of the kingdom assert the centrality of the message of the kingdom in the teaching of Jesus.

It is important to understand the meaning of the kingdom, for one's understanding will influence and determine one's perspective on culture, society, and ministry. If one views the kingdom to be completely a future event there may be the tendency to forsake the necessary mission of rescuing the poor and oppressed from the world. If one sees the kingdom as entirely a present reality there may be the tendency to overlook the importance of spiritual deliverance. The teaching of Jesus addressed both the present and the future aspects of the kingdom. Luke records Jesus' reply to the Pharisees when asked when the kingdom of God would come:

> Jesus replied, 'The kingdom of God does not come visibly, nor will people say, "Here it is," or "There it is," because the kingdom of God is within you' (Lk 17:20-21)

Louis Berkhof is convinced of the future nature of the kingdom and writes:

> Though the Lord refers to the Kingdom as a present reality, He more often speaks of it as a future state of consummate happiness, in which the whole life of man and of society will be in perfect harmony with the will of God . . . clearly the Kingdom of God is an eschatological concept.[15]

Jesus provides an example of the future reality of the kingdom when in His preaching He proclaims, "repent, for the kingdom of heaven is near" (Mt 4:17). The New Testament message of looking back to the

---

[14]George E. Ladd, *Crucial Questions about the Kingdom of God*, 63-98.

[15]Louis Berkhof, *The Kingdom of God*, 18.

historical Christ is complemented with a message of looking forward to the coming Christ. Weber says this point is "the unique thing about Christian eschatology— it makes statements about the expectation of something which is already here." The People of God live with Christ in their midst and in conflict with the present world order but also as those who hope for the return of the Resurrected One.[16]

The book of Acts and the Gospel of John, sustain the eschatological dualism found in the Old Testament and in the Synoptics. In John 3:3, 5 the message of Jesus is recorded as portraying both the present and future realities of the kingdom. The present reality is evident in verse three, "unless a man is born again, he cannot see the kingdom of God." In verse five it is evident that it is entrance into the reality of the present kingdom that is necessary if one is to enter the Kingdom of God in the future. The eschatological message proclaimed by the primitive church unquestionably contains the same dualism of the "already" and the "not yet."[17]

## Perspectives on the Rapture and Tribulation

The preceding section develops the structure for understanding eschatology. In the sense that theology is dependent on Jesus Christ all theology has an eschatological dimension. The remainder of this chapter will concern itself with prominent eschatological themes.

A central theme of eschatology is the "blessed hope." It is the return of Jesus Christ and the fulfillment of the ages for which the Christian expectantly looks. Jesus Christ is bringing the kingdom to fulfillment; it will occur soon (Rev 1:1). The Assemblies of God doctrinal statement regarding this position is representative of the normative Pentecostal position:

> The resurrection of those who have fallen asleep in Christ and their translation together with those who are alive and remain unto the coming of the Lord is the imminent and blessed hope of the church.[18]

---

[16]Otto Weber, *Foundations of Dogmatics*, Vol. 2, 679.

[17]Acts 1:3, 2:16, 23, 33-36, 38-39, 3:18-24.

[18]The General Council of the Assemblies of God, *Statement of Fundamental Truths*, Article V — Constitution, Revised 1983 General Council, (Springfield, MO: Gospel Publishing House), Statement 13.

The expectation of the *parousia* lives based in the Resurrection of Jesus Christ and the gift of the Spirit.[19] The soon coming of Christ will parallel the coming of Christ in the Incarnation. There is a direct link between the two. Here is a focus of Pentecostal eschatology. The direct link is the presence of the Spirit. The One who was historically present is now eschatologically present through the Spirit and He is also the One for whom the church expectantly awaits (Tit 2:13).

The imminence of the return means that the return is not dateable and therefore could happen at any time. Jesus instructed His disciples to be prepared for His coming (Mt 24:3, 42-51, 25:1-13; Mk 13:37; Lk 12:37; Jn 14:2-3). Because the return is not dateable there are no additional events which must occur prior to the return and no additional prophecies must be fulfilled. The believer is encouraged to look for the Lord's return rather than for other cataclysmic eschatological events. This assumes it is the return of Christ which is to mark the beginning of the fulfillment of this age.

So do not throw away your confidence; it will be richly rewarded. You need to persevere so that when you have done the will of God, you will receive what He has promised. For in just a very little while, He who is coming will come and will not delay. (Heb 10:35-37)

After that, we who are still alive and are left will be caught up with them in the clouds to meet the Lord in the air. And so we will be with the Lord forever. Therefore encourage each other with these words. (1Th 4:17-18)

It was this state of expectancy which characterized the believers of the first century Church and which is to characterize believers of the present age. The blessed hope (the Rapture of the Church) includes the idea that Christians will not have to suffer the extreme devastation and misery accompanying the Great Tribulation which is to cover the earth. This Great Tribulation is distinct from tribulation which all persons experience throughout the course of life. It is in fact the Great Tribulation which includes the reign of the Antichrist and the pouring out of God's wrath upon the wicked (Da 12:1-2, 10-13;

---

[19]*Parousia* means "presence" or "coming." The term refers to the soon coming of the Lord, a coming that is just about to happen. The emphasis is not on the coming again but on the soon coming.

Mt 24:15-31; 2Th 2:1-12). Pentecostal eschatology considers Christ's coming to be imminent and therefore, most often Pentecostals ascribe to a pretribulational position. The Assemblies of God position paper on the "Rapture of the Church" states:

> Since Scripture does not contradict itself, it seems reasonable to conclude that the passages describing Christ's coming *for* the saints and *with* the saints indicate two phases of His coming.[20]

It is in conjunction with the rapture, Christ coming for the saints, that believers are judged to determine rewards for service (Mt 24:15-31; Rev 22:12).[21]

In summary, the pretribulation rapture position holds to three basic convictions: 1) the rapture of the church is a taking out of the world, prior to the Great Tribulation, the believers who are living and those believers who have died (1Th 4:15-17), 2) the period of Great Tribulation is a distinct seven-year period in the history of the earth (Da 9); and 3) the return of the Lord is imminent (Mt 24; Jas 5:8; 1Th 4:16-18-5:1). It is these convictions which contribute to a sense of expectancy for the Christian. This sense of expectancy brings with it the motivation to fulfill the mission of the Church to take the gospel to the "ends of the earth."

While the pretribulation rapture of the Church is the position most commonly held in Pentecostal theology, brief statements about two alternative positions are in order. The two positions are 1) the posttribulation rapture and 2) the midtribulation rapture.

The primary difference between the pretribulation rapture position and the posttribulation position is that the posttribulation position holds that the church will be present during the period of Great Tribulation. The difference between the Great Tribulation and tribulation in general is one of degree. Because the church has suffered persecution at various times throughout history there is no reason to assume this will not be the case in the future. The church while experiencing Great Tribulation will not experience the wrath of God.

---

[20]*Rapture of the Church*, Report of the Committee to study the rapture of the Church, (Springfield, MO: GPH), 7

[21]P.C. Nelson, *Bible Doctrines*, 105 and Myer Pearlman, *Knowing the Doctrines of the Bible*, 389.

The wrath of God is directed only toward the wicked.[22] The posttribulational position denies the removal of believers from tribulation at the rapture. The meeting of the saints and the Lord is to join with the Lord in celebrating and inaugurating his rule on the earth (Mt 25:6; Ac 28:15-16; 1Th 4:17).

Midtribulationism shares some beliefs with both pretribulationism and posttribulationism. The characteristics of the midtribulation position are its contentions that the Church will be present during the tribulation but removed prior to and preserved from the wrath and that the "elect" of Matthew 24 is the Church. Variations of midtribulationism exist and therefore one is likely to find great diversity among those who espouse this position.[23]

## Perspectives on the Millennium

A second major eschatological theme is the millennium. The view is sometimes referred to as "chiliasm" (from the Greek word *chilia* meaning thousand). This position refers to the one thousand year reign of Christ on the earth. In relationship to the millennium there are three major positions which are espoused: these are: 1) premillennialism, 2) postmillennialism, and 3) amillennialism. A variation of the premillennial position is dispensationalism. Pentecostal eschatology has been characterized by the premillennial position although through the influence of sources such as the Scofield Reference Bible many have interpreted eschatology and the millennium with a dispensational hermeneutic.

According to the Premillennial position the millennial reign of Christ is one aspect of the second coming of the Lord. The Premillennial position contends that the rapture will be followed by the visible return of Christ with his saints to reign on the earth for one thousand years. The key passage for premillennialism is Revelation 20:1-6.

And I saw an angel coming down out of heaven, having the key to the abyss and holding in his hand a great chain. He seized the

---

[22]For an examination of the scriptural evidence presented to substantiate this position see the following references: Jn 3:36; Ro 1:18; 1Th 1:10, 5:9; 2Th 1:8; Rev 6:16-17, 14:10, 16:19, 19:15.

[23]For additional discussion of this position and the positions of the Partial-Rapture view and the Imminent Posttribulational position see Millard J. Erickson, *Contemporary Options in Eschatology*, 163-181.

dragon, that ancient servant, who is the devil, or Satan, and bound him for a thousand years. He threw him into the Abyss, and locked and sealed it over him, to keep him from deceiving the nations any more until the thousand years were ended. After that, he must be set free for a short time.

I saw thrones on which were seated those who had been given authority to judge. And I saw the souls of those who had been beheaded because of their testimony for Jesus and because of the word of God. They had not worshiped the beast nor his image and had not received his mark on their foreheads or their hands. They came to life and reigned with Christ a thousand years. (The rest of the dead did not come to life until the thousand years were ended.) This is the first resurrection. Blessed and holy are those who have part in the first resurrection. The second death has no power over them, but they will be priests of God and of Christ and will reign with him for a thousand years.

The major tenets of premillennialism are found in this passage. These tenets are: 1) the millennial reign will be preceded by widespread deterioration of the world and the period of Great Tribulation, 2) the cataclysmic nature of the inauguration of the millennial reign, 3) the millennium is inaugurated by the second coming of the Lord, 4) there are two bodily resurrections, (a resurrection of believers and a resurrection of nonbelievers), and 5) the millennial reign of Christ will be an earthly reign of universal peace with Christ bodily present and exercising absolute control.

Crucial to the discussion regarding the premillennial position are two points. First, it is important to note the exegetical evidence for two bodily resurrections. In Revelation 20:4-5 it is apparent there are two resurrections.

> . . . They came to life and reigned with Christ a thousand years. (The rest of the dead did not come to life until the thousand years were ended.) This is the first resurrection.

For those who deny that the second resurrection as well as the first resurrection is a bodily resurrection lies the burden of proving that the same word, *ezesan* (come back to life), can hold two different meanings within the same passage. Ladd has stated that, unlike in passages such as Luke 9:24, Luke 9:60, and John 3:18, 36,

> in Revelation 20:4-6 there is no such contextual clue for a similar interpretation of scripture. The language of the passage is quite clear

and unambiguous. There is no need to interpret either word spiritually in order to introduce meaning to the passage. At the beginning of the millennial period, part of the dead come to life; at its conclusion, the rest of the dead come to life.[24]

Second it is critical to premillennialism that the reign of Christ be an earthly reign. It is often objected that the millennial reign as presented by premillennialists is temporal and therefore unnecessary. However, it is not the functional necessity of the reign which must be addressed but rather, the scriptural indication and theological significance of such a reign. The concept of temporality is not foreign to Pentecostals. It is the reign of Christ through the Spirit which is characteristic of the church age and is itself a temporal concept. The idea of "already" and "not yet" as contemporaneous realities carries through both Old and New Testaments. That the reign is temporal does not detract from its significance. There is a direct link between the present reign of the veiled Christ and the sovereign and future reign.[25] For the premillennialists the millennial reign commences with and sustains the full authority and rule of Jesus Christ. It is not a reign progressively entered into but one which is initiated by the cataclysmic event of the second coming of the Lord.

Postmillennialism holds that the kingdom of God and the millennial reign of Christ are present realities. This view treats the kingdom as the rule of God within the hearts of humankind. The rule of God will gradually transform society and eventually God's rule will govern all persons in all places (1Co 15).

The postmillennial position emphasizes both the preaching of the gospel and involvement in society. This present earthly reality, when fulfilled, will usher in the coming of the Lord. The current millennial period is not to be interpreted as a literal one thousand year reign but as a reign which when complete will be acknowledged with the return of Jesus Christ. It is a positive aspect of postmillennialism that its adherents have often been involved in the cause of Christ in advocating for the oppressed, feeding the hungry, and ministering to the needy. It is the present reality of the kingdom which enables this

---

[24]Ladd, 141-150.

[25]Ro 14:7; 1 Co 15:27 ff; Col 1:13; Php 2:9; Heb 1:3, 10:12-13.

involvement. The consummation of the millennium is signaled by the bodily return of Christ.

While this position is not normative for Pentecostal eschatology it is a position held by some theologically conservative groups. The argument against postmillennialism must be made on exegetical grounds rather than from experience. It is not sufficient to disregard the view because of what one sees in the world. For a list of scripture references used by postmillennialists to support the position see the footnote[26] and the treatment of the topic by Erickson in *Contemporary Options in Eschatology.*[27]

Amillennialism asserts that there will be no literal earthly reign of Christ in the future. The kingdom of God is completely a spiritual reign. Erickson describes the tenets of amillennialism as: 1) belief in two resurrections, 2) a millennium which is not a literal one thousand years, and 3) a belief that there is no literal fulfillment of prophecy at a future time.[28] While there is a consistent belief in two resurrections it is most often considered that the first resurrection is spiritual and the second resurrection is bodily. Some amillennialists do hold to two spiritual resurrections.

Though it is being considered within the context of the discussion on millennial interpretations, the dispensational position is more than either a perspective on the millennium or a view of the rapture. Dispensationalism is a hermeneutic which greatly influences one's interpretation of Scripture.

Dispensationalism is a particular type of pretribulational premillennialism which originated in the early 1800's with J. N. Darby and the Plymouth Brethren Movement and was later popularized by the Scofield Reference Bible. Central to dispensationalism is the belief that the Bible is always to be interpreted in a literal sense. Other tenets of dispensationalism which are crucial to eschatology include: 1) the distinction between Israel and the Church, 2) the distinction between the kingdom of God and the kingdom of heaven, and 3) the purpose of the millennium as a time for the restoration of national Israel. Major

---

[26]Psalms 47, 72, 100; Isaiah 45:22-25; Hosea 2:23; Matthew 13, Matthew 24:14, 28:18-20.

[27]Erickson, 55-72.

[28]Ibid, 76-84.

difficulties occur in the theory for it is difficult to sustain distinct differences between Israel and the Church and between the kingdom of God and the kingdom of heaven. A final difficulty with this position is its seeming loss of exegetical coherence as it attempts to interpret prophecy literally and historical narrative allegorically.

## Hope and Judgment as Eschatological Themes

God's justice and righteousness are eschatological themes prominent in the Word of God. Fallen humanity is subject to the judgment of God. It is the hope of humanity, reconciliation with God through Jesus Christ, which makes possible deliverance from this judgment. The possibility of deliverance authenticates the possibility of judgment. Noah and his family are saved from destruction by the God who judges the wicked of the earth, the God who delivers the nation of Israel also scatters the nation. George Ladd writes,

> There are theologians today who insist that the love of God demands that hell be evacuated of every human being, that God cannot be a righteous and just God if a single soul finally perishes. The very idea of eternal punishment is repugnant to the modern mind. There is indeed a need to vindicate the judgment of God as well as to display his unlimited love. The 'sterner aspects of God's love' cannot be diluted into sentimentality that does not take sin seriously.[29]

Certainly the declaration recorded in the Gospel of John 3:18 explicates this truth: "Whoever believes in him is not condemned, but whoever does not believe stands condemned already because he has not believed in the name of God's one and only Son."

The final judgment will be one in which the wicked dead will be raised and judged according to their works. Whosoever is not found written in the Book of Life, together with the devil and his angels, the beast and the false prophet, will be consigned to everlasting punishment in the lake which burns with fire and brimstone, which is the second death.[30]

---

[29]George E. Ladd, *A Theology of the New Testament*, 631.

[30]The General Council of the Assemblies of God, *The Statement of Fundamental Truths*, Article V—Constitution, Revised 1983 General Council, (Springfield: Gospel Publishing House), Statement 15.

It is essential that one recognize the significance of the choices which one makes. An essential characteristic of being human is the responsibility which is endowed in the relationship between God and humanity. Human beings are not like the animals who are bound to an existence which is only physical. Human beings are those who "bear God's image in our nature, [who] have to live eternally with the implications of who we are and what we have done."[31]

The Apocalyptist records vivid scenes of the final judgment. At one point the scene is the rider whose name is "Faithful and True" judging and making war. At another point it is the Judge seated on a throne judging individuals on the criterion of whether or not their names are written in the Book of Life. It is a judgment which is both final and eternal.[32]

## A Glimpse at Personal Eschatology

In addition to the cosmic and cataclysmic eschatological events presented in Scripture there are some events which are of eschatological significance to the individual. The distinction is in the nature of the occurrence of the event and not in the breadth of application. For the purposes of this discussion topics of individual eschatology to be considered include: 1) death, 2) the intermediate state, and 3) hell.

Prior to the consideration of the nature and meaning of death one must consider the nature and meaning of human life. The discussion of theological anthropology is taken up in a prior chapter. Therefore this discussion assumes some familiarity with life as determined and defined by the intent of God and by the life and death of Jesus Christ. Where is one to find a response to the question of death? Eberhard Jungel states that "death is mute and renders us speechless."[33] It is inevitable that every individual must die (Heb 9:27). Both death and the dead are unable to speak concerning the nature and meaning of death. For the Christian the response to death comes from beyond death itself. It is the response of Jesus Christ which informs the

---

[31]David Allan Hubbard, *The Second Coming: What Will Happen When Jesus Returns?*, 96.

[32]Isaiah 33:14, 66:24; Matthew 24-25; Mark 9:43-48; Romans 6:23; Revelation 19:11-21, 20:11-15, 21:8.

[33]Eberhard Jungel, *Death: The Riddle and the Mystery*, preface.

Christian community about death. For the Christian it is life which sheds light on the meaning and nature of death.

From Scripture it is evident that there is a physical aspect to death and it is also evident that the cessation of physical life is not the end of existence but a limitation of earthly existence (Ecc 12:7; Mt 10:28; Lk 12:4-5; Jn 13:37-38). There are the two streams—physical death and spiritual death. There are also references in Scripture to spiritual and eternal death (Eph 2:1-2; Ro 6:23; Rev 20:6, 21:8).

Paul the Apostle states that death is not a friend to humanity but an enemy (1Co 15:26). This implies that death is not the original purpose of God for humanity but is an attempt to frustrate the purpose of God. It is interesting that in the creation narrative death is only mentioned in respect to humans (Ge 2:17). Anderson contends the issue at stake is one of relationship to God and to others. The theological consideration of this passage is not biological death, which is pertinent to both animals and humans, but death as separation from God which is specifically a human issue.[34] It is the resurrection which presents a resounding "No!" to death. In the Second Adam, Jesus Christ, death has no hold or determinative power. Biological death is to be understood in light of the divine promise of continuing life to those who are reconciled to God. Those who are reconciled may experience biological death but spiritual and eternal death are not the inheritance of the believer.[35]

A second theme related to individual eschatology is the intermediate state. The intermediate state refers to the condition of Christians during the period between their death and the resurrection. The New Testament distinguishes between *Hades*, the intermediate state, and *Gehenna*, Hell.[36] The Hebrew term *Sheol* is roughly equivalent to the Greek term *Hades*.

The state of the righteous dead is presence before God. In the Pauline corpus the key passage dealing with the intermediate state is 2 Corinthians 5:1-10. In this passage Paul contends that to be away

---

[34]Ray S. Anderson, *Theology, Death and Dying*, 46-48.

[35]For a more complete discussion of the topic see Millard Erickson's *Christian Theology*, 1167-1184.

[36]Joachim Jeremias, *Theological Dictionary of the New Testament*, Vol. 1, 657-658.

from the body is to be present with the Lord. This position confirms Old Testament thought as well as the words spoken by Jesus to the dying thief (Lk 23:39-43). The majority of texts dealing with the intermediate state concern the state of the righteous rather than the state of the wicked.

*Gehenna*, Hell, is the New Testament term for the place of final punishment. The writers of the Synoptic Gospels depict Hell as a place of fiery torment (Mk 9:43, 48) and as a place of darkness (Mt 8:12, 22:13). Both of these metaphors are used to represent the state of those who spend eternity separated from God. Paul asserts that the final state of the wicked will be punishment with everlasting destruction and exclusion from the presence of the Lord (2Th 1:9).

While many questions remain unanswered it is apparent that there is both an intermediate state and a final state for both the righteous and the wicked. The eschatological hope of the righteous is found throughout the teaching of both the Old and New Testaments. Always it is the grace of God which encourages this hope and always this hope finds its expression in the death, resurrection, and ascension of Jesus Christ.

The final act of history, occurring at the termination of the millennial reign, is the consummation of the kingdom of God. The new heavens and the new earth where there is no sickness, oppression, or misery but where righteousness, peace, and justice rule (2Pe 3:13; Rev 21-22) becomes the realized goal for humanity. The Crucified One who is the Resurrected One brings us to the end of our history. The goal whose pursuit has encouraged believers of all ages is come. The One who has given present significance to human life will sustain this significance in the age to come. This is the eschatological reality which is integral to Pentecostal theology. The *Eschatos* is contemporary with humanity through the Holy Spirit. The temporal life at the same time is moving toward and participating in its eternal destiny.

Jesus Christ the Alpha and the Omega, Jesus Christ the one who was, the one who now is, and the one who is coming brings together the ends of the ages. The completion of the present age meets the single end of the coming age and reconciled humanity lives forever in the presence of God.

## For Reflection and Discussion

1. Jesus Christ is the blessed hope to which the Church looks. How does hope in Christ influence the mission and life of the contemporary Church?

2. How does the concept of Hebrew dualism influence Pentecostal eschatology? What is the significance of "the already" and "the not yet?"

3. Discuss the various views on the rapture and the tribulation. Make a case for the position to which you hold.

4. Discuss the three major views of the millennium. How does the millennial view to which you ascribe influence your practical Christian living?

5. Write a one page essay distinguishing between *Gehenna* and *Hades*.

6. Write a two page *credo* on "The Hope of Christ and the Life of the Church."

# Bibliography

Anderson, Ray S. *Historical Transcendence and the Reality of God*. Grand Rapids: Eerdmans, 1975.
———. "A Theology for Ministry." In *Theological Foundations for Ministry*, ed. Ray S. Anderson. Grand Rapids: Eerdmans, 1979.
———. "Living in the Spirit." In *Theological Foundations for Ministry*. Grand Rapids: Eerdmans, 1979.
———. *Theology, Death and Dying*. Oxford: Blackwell, 1986.
Assemblies of God General Presbytery. "Divine Healing: An Integral Part of the Gospel." August 20, 1974.

Bancroft, Emery. *Christian Theology*, second revised edition. Grand Rapids: Zondervan, 1976.
Barrett, C.K. *The Epistle to the Romans*. New York: Harper & Row, 1957.
Barth, Karl. *Church Dogmatics*, 13 vols. trans. G. W. Bromiley and T. F. Torrance. Edinburgh: T. & T. Clark, 1983.
Berkhof, Louis. *The Kingdom of God*. Grand Rapids: Eerdmans, 1951.
———. *Systematic Theology*. Edinburgh: The Banner of Truth Trust, 1981.
Bloesch, Donald. *Essentials of Evangelical Theology*, 2 vols. New York: Harper & Row, 1978.
Boice, James Montgomery. *The Sovereign God*. Downers Grove, Ill.: InterVarsity, 1978
Bonhoeffer, Deitrich. *Ethics*. New York: MacMillan and SCM Press, 1955.
———. *The Cost of Discipleship*, second edition. New York: Macmillan, 1959.
Bright, John. *Covenant and Promise: The Prophetic Understanding of the Future in Pre-Exilic Israel*. Philadelphia: Westminster Press, 1976.
Bromiley, Geoffrey W. *Historical Theology: An Introduction*. Grand Rapids: Wm. B. Eerdmans Publishing Company, 1978.
Brown, Francis, Driver, S. R. and Briggs, Charles A. *The New Brown-Driver-Briggs-Gesenius Hebrew and English Lexicon*. N.p.: Christian Copyrights, Inc., 1983.
Bruce, F.F. *Commentary on the Book of Acts*. Grand Rapids: Eerdmans, 1954.
———. "Eschatology," *Dictionary of Theology*. Grand Rapids: Baker, 1960.
———. "Tradition and the Canon of Scripture." *The Authoritative Word*, ed., Donald K. McKim. Grand Rapids: Eerdmans, 1983.
Brumback, Carl. *What Meaneth This?* Springfield: Gospel Publishing House, 1947.
Bruner, Frederick Dale. *A Theology of the Holy Spirit*. Grand Rapids: William B. Eerdmans, 1970.
Burdick, Donald W. "James," *The Expositor's Bible Commentary*, 12 vols. Grand Rapids: Zondervan, 1981.
Buswell, J. Oliver. *A Systematic Theology of the Christian Religion*. Grand Rapids: Zondervan Publishing House, 1962.

Cairns, David. *The Image of God in Man*. New York: Philosophical Library, 1953.
Calvin, John. *Institutes of the Christian Religion*, 2 vols. ed., John T. McNeill, Philadelphia: The Westminster Press, 1960.
Carter, Howard. "The Pentecostal Movement." *The Pentecostal Evangel* (May 18, 1946) 3:7-8.
Chappell, Paul G. "Healing Movements." In *Dictionary of Pentecostal and Charismatic Movements*, eds. Stanley M. Burgess and Gary B. McGee. Grand Rapids: Zondervan, 1988.

Conn, Charles W. "Glossolalia and the Scriptures," *The Glossolalia Phenomenon*, ed., Wade H. Horton. Cleveland: Pathway Press, 1966.

Constitution of the General Council of the Assemblies of God, revised 1969. "Statement of Fundamental Truths," Article V, Section 8.

Costas, Orlando. *The Integrity of Mission: The Inner Life and Outreach of the Church*. San Francisco: Harper & Row, 1979.

Cousar, Charles B. *Galatians*, eds. James L. Mays, Patrick D. Miller, and Paul Achtemeier, Atlanta: John Knox Press, 1982.

Dana, H.E. and Mantey, Julius R. *A Manual Grammar of the Greek New Testament*. New York: The Macmillan Company, 1927.

Darwin, Charles. *The Origin of Species*. N.p.:1959

Delitzsch, Franz *Commentaries on the Old Testament*. Grand Rapids: Wm. B. Eerdmans Publishing Company, n.d.

———. *Isaiah*, eds. Keil and Delitzsch, Grand Rapids: Eerdmans, 1969.

Demarest, Bruce A. "Process Trinitarianism." In *Perspectives on Evangelical Theology*, eds. Kenneth Kantzer and Stanley Gundry. Grand Rapids: Baker Book House, 1979.

———. *General Revelation*. Grand Rapids: Zondervan, n.d.

Dempster, Murray. *Called and Empowered: Global Mission in Pentecostal Perspective*. Peabody: Hendrickson, 1991.

Dodd, C. H. *Parables of the Kingdom*. London: Nisbet, 1935.

Erickson, Millard J. *Contemporary Options in Eschatology*. Grand Rapids: Baker Book House, 1977.

———. *Christian Theology*. Grand Rapids: Baker Book House, 1985.

———. *Does It Matter What I Believe*. Grand Rapids: Baker, 1992.

Ervin, Howard. *These Are Not Drunken As Ye Suppose*. Plainfield, New Jersey: Logos International, 1968.

Fee, Gordon D. *The Disease of the Health and Wealth Gospels*. Costa Mesa, Calif.: The Word For Today, 1979.

———. *The First Epistle to the Corinthians*. The New International Commentary on the New Testament. Grand Rapids: Eerdmans, 1987.

Feinberg, Paul D. "The Meaning of Inerrancy." *Inerrancy*, ed., Norman L. Geisler. Grand Rapids: Zondervan, 1979.

Ferguson, Sinclair B. "The Reformed View," in *Christian Spirituality: Five Views of Sanctification*, ed. Donald L. Alexander, Downers Grove, Ill.: InterVarsity Press, 1988.

Firet, Jacob. *Dynamics in Pastoring*. Grand Rapids: Eerdmans 1986.

Fung, Ronald Y. K. *The Epistle to the Galatians* The New International Commentary on the New Testament. Grand Rapids: Eerdmans, 1988.

*The Person and Work of the Holy Spirit*. A study paper presented to the General Assembly of the Presbyterian Church in the United States, 1971.

Green, Michael. *I Believe in the Holy Spirit*. Grand Rapids: Eerdmans, 1983.

Gromacki, Robert G. *The Virgin Birth*. Grand Rapids: Baker Book House, 1981.

Groome, Thomas H. *Christian Religious Education: Sharing Our Story and Vision*. San Francisco: Harper & Row Publishers, 1980.

Grudem, Wayne. *1 Peter*. Grand Rapids: Eerdmans, 1988.

Guthrie, Shirley C., Jr. *Christian Doctrine.* Atlanta: John Knox Press, 1968.

Hammond, T. C. *In Understanding Be Men: A Handbook of Christian Doctrine.* Leicester, England: Inter-Varsity Press, 1968.

Harper, Michael. *The Healings of Jesus.* Downers Grove, Ill.: InterVarsity, 1986.

Harrell, David E., Jr. *All Things Are Possible.* Bloomington: Indiana University Press, 1975.

Harris, R. Laird. *Inspiration and Canonicity of the Bible.* Grand Rapids: Zondervan, 1984.

Harrison, E. F. "Worship." in *Evangelical Dictionary of Theology,* ed. Walter A. Elwell. Grand Rapids: Baker, 1984.

Henry, Carl F.H. *God, Revelation, and Authority,* 6 vols. Waco: Word Books, 1976-1983.

Hodge, Charles. *Systematic Theology.* Grand Rapids: Eerdmans, 1982 reprint.

Holdcroft, L. Thomas. *The Holy Spirit.* Gospel Publishing House: Springfield, 1979.

Horton, Stanley M. *What the Bible Says About the Holy Spirit.* Springfield: Gospel Publishing House, 1976.

Hubbard, David Allan. *The Second Coming: What Will Happen When Jesus Returns?* Downer's Grove: InterVarsity Press, 1984.

Jeremias, Joachim. *Gehenna. Theological Dictionary of the New Testament,* eds. Gerhard Kittel and Gerhard Friedrich, trans. Geoffrey Bromiley, Grand Rapids: Eerdmans, 1964-1976

Jewett, Paul K. "The Doctrine of Last Things". Unpublished document, Fuller Theological Seminary.

Jungel, Eberhard. *Death: The Riddle and the Mystery.* Philadelphia: Westminster, 1974.

Kaiser, Walter C. "*Min* (Kind)." In *Theological Wordbook of the Old Testament.* R. Laird Harris, et al., eds. Chicago: Moody Press, 1980.

Kelsey, Morton T. *Healing and Christianity.* New York: Harper, 1973.

Kirby, Jeff. "The Recovery of Healing Gifts." In *Those Controversial Gifts,* ed. George Mallone, Downers Grove, Ill.: InterVarsity Press, 1983.

Kraemer, Hendrik. *A Theology of the Laity.* Philadelphia: The Westminster Press, 1958.

Kuiper, R. B. *The Glorious Body of Christ.* Grand Rapids: Eerdmans, n.d.

Kydd, Ronald. *Charismatic Gifts in the Early Church.* Peabody, Mass.: Hendrickson, 1984.

Ladd, George E. *Crucial Questions about the Kingdom of God.* Grand Rapids: Eerdmans, 1952.

———. *A Theology of the New Testament.* Grand Rapids: Eerdmans, 1974.

Leith, John H., ed., *Creeds of the Church,* revised edition. Atlanta: John Knox Press, 1973.

Lewis, A. E. "Unmasking Idolatries: Vocation in the Ecclesia Crucis," in *Incarnational Ministry: The Presence of Christ in Church, Society, and Family,* eds. Christian Kettler and Todd H. Speidell, Colorado Springs, CO: Helmers & Howard, 1991.

Lim, David. *Spiritual Gifts: A Fresh Look.* Springfield: Gospel Publishing House, 1991.

Longenecker, Richard C. *Galatians.* Dallas: Word Book Publisher, 1990.

Macchia, F. D. "Spirituality and Social Liberation; The Message of the Blumhardts in the Light of Würtemberg Pietism, with Implications for Pentecostal Theology," Doctoral dissertion, University of Basel, Switzerland, 1989.

Marshall, I. Howard. *1 Peter.* Downers Grove, Ill.: InterVarsity, 1991.

Martin, Francis. "Gift of Healing," in *Dictionary of Pentecostal and Charismatic Movements,* eds. Stanley M. Burgess and Gary B. McGee. Grand Rapids: Zondervan, 1988.

Menzies, William W. *Understanding Our Doctrine.* Springfield, Mo.: Gospel Publishing House, 1971.
Minear, Paul S. *Images of the Church in the New Testament.* Philadelphia: Westminster, 1960.
Moltmann, Jurgen. *Theology of Hope.* London: SCM Press Ltd, 1967.

Nelson, P. C. *Bible Doctrines.* Springfield: Gospel Publishing House, 1981.

Outler, Albert C. *Theology in the Wesleyan Spirit.* Nashville: Discipleship Resources-Tidings, 1975.

Pannell, William E. "Evangelism: Solidarity and Reconciliation," in *Incarnational Ministry: The Presence of Christ in Church, Society, and Family,* eds. Christian Kettler and Todd H. Speidell, Colorado Springs: Helmers and Howard, 1990.
Parham, Charles F. *The Sermons of Charles F. Parham.* New York: Garland, 1985 reprint.
Pinnock, Clark H. "The View of the Bible Held by the Church: The Early Church Through Luther," *Inerrancy,* ed., Norman L. Geisler. Grand Rapids: Zondervan, 1979.
———. *Biblical Revelation.* Chicago: Moody, 1971.
Pruitt, Raymond M. *Fundamentals of the Faith.* Cleveland, Tenn.: White Wing Publishing House and Press, 1981.
Pun, Pattle P. T. "Evolution." In *Evangelical Dictionary of Theology,* ed. Walter A. Elwell. Grand Rapids: Baker, 1984.

Robeck, Cecil M., Jr., "Faith, Hope, Love, and the Eschaton," *PNEUMA: The Journal of the Society for Pentecostal Studies* 14, no. 1 (1992):1.
Robertson, A.T. *Word Pictures in the New Testament.* New York: Harper and Brothers Publishing Company, 1950.
Rogers, Jack B. "The Church Doctrine of Biblical Authority," *The Authoritative Word,* ed. Donald K. McKim. Grand Rapids: Eerdmans, 1983.

Saucy, Robert L. *The Church in God's Program.* Chicago: Moody Press, 1972.
Sauer, Erich. *The King of the Earth.* Palm Springs, Calif.: Ronald Haynes Publishing, 1981.
Schillebeeckx, E. *Ministry: Leadership in the Community of Jesus Christ.* New York: Crossroad Publishing Company, 1981.
Schweitzer, Albert. *The Quest of the Historical Jesus.* London: Black, 1911.
Selwyn, Edward G. *The First Epistle of St. Peter.* London: Macmillan, 1961.
Shank, Robert. *Life in the Son,* second edition. Springfield, Mo: Westcott Publishers, 1961.
Simpson, A. B. *The Gospel of Healing,* revised edition. Harrisburg, Pa.: Christian Publications, 1915.
Strong, Augustus H. *Systematic Theology.* London: Pickering & Inglis, 1907./Old Tappan, N.J.: Revell, 1907.
Stronstad, Roger. *The Charismatic Theology of St. Luke.* Peabody, Mass: Hendrickson Publishers, Inc., 1991.

Tasker, R. V. G. *The General Epistle of James.* Grand Rapids: Eerdmans, 1976.
Thayer, Joseph Henry. *Greek-English Lexicon of the New Testament.* Grant Rapids: Zondervan Publishing House, 1962.
Thielicke, Helmut. *The Evangelical Faith,* 3 vols. Grand Rapids: Eerdmans Publishing Co., 1982.

Thiessen, Henry C. *Lectures in Systematic Theology*, revised edition. Grand Rapids: Eerdmans, 1979.
Tillich, Paul. *Systematic Theology*, 3 vols. Chicago: University of Chicago Press, 1957-1963.
Torrance, T. F. "Conflict and Agreement in the Church," in *Theological Foundations for Ministry*, ed. Ray S. Anderson Grand Rapids: Eerdmans, 1979.
——. *Reality and Evangelical Theology*. Philadelphia: The Westminster Press, 1982.
Travis, Stephen. *I Believe in the Second Coming of Jesus*. Grand Rapids: Eerdmans, 1982.
Turner, Max M. B. "Spiritual Gifts, Then and Now," *Vox Evangelica* 15 (1985):48.

Unger, Merrill F. *Unger's Commentary on the Old Testament*. Chicago: Moody Press.

Van Wyk, Kenneth W. *Laity Training Resource Kit*. Orange, California, 1984.

Warfield, Benjamin B. *Biblical and Theological Studies*. Philadelphia: The Presbyterian and Reformed Publishing Company, 1968.
Weber, Otto. *Foundations of Dogmatics*, 2 vols. Grand Rapids: Eerdmans, 1983.
Wesley, John. *A Plain Account of Christian Perfection (1767)*. London: The Epworth Press, 1952 reprint.
Wesley, John. "The Scripture Way of Salvation" (1765), in *Creeds of the Churches*, ed. John H. Leith Atlanta: John Knox Press, 1973.
Wiley, H. Orton. *Christian Theology*. Kansas City, Mo: Beacon Hill Press, 1952.
Williams, J. Rodman. *Renewal Theology*, 3 vols. Grand Rapids: Zondervan, 1988-1992.
Wright, Gordon. *In Quest of Healing*. Springfield, Mo: Gospel Publishing House, 1984.

Young, Edward J. *The Book of Isaiah*, 3 vols. Grand Rapids: Eerdmans, 1972.

# Index of Scripture References

## John

## *1 Corinthians*

# Index